W9-CXK-070

THE
WRONG
HORSE

ALSO BY WILLIAM MURRAY

The Americano
Best Seller
The Dream Girls
The Fugitive Romans
The Getaway Blues
The Hard Knocker's Luck
Horse Fever
Italy: The Fatal Gift
I'm Getting Killed Right Here
The Killing Touch
The King of the Nightcap
The Last Italian
Malibu
The Mouth of the Wolf
Previews of Coming Attractions
The Self-Starting Wheel
The Sweet Ride
Tip on a Dead Crab
When the Fat Man Sings

THE
WRONG
HORSE

*An Odyssey Through
the American Racing Scene*

WILLIAM MURRAY

Little, Brown and Company

Boston New York Toronto London

Copyright © 1992 by William Murray

All rights reserved. No part of this book may be reproduced in any form or by
any electronic or mechanical means, including information storage and retrieval
systems, without permission in writing from the publisher, except by a reviewer
who may quote brief passages in a review.

First Paperback Edition

This edition is reprinted by arrangement with Simon and Schuster.

The chapter "The Easy Way" appeared originally in *The New Yorker* in somewhat
different form.

Library of Congress Cataloging-in-Publication Data
Murray, William.
    The wrong horse : an odyssey through the American racing
scene / William Murray.
        p.   cm.
Originally published: New York : Simon & Schuster, c 1992.
ISBN 0-316-59131-9
1. Horse racing — United States.   I. Title.
[SF335.U5M87   1994]
    798.4'00973 — dc20   94-5206

10 9 8 7 6 5 4 3 2 1

RRD-VA

Published simultaneously in Canada by Little, Brown & Company (Canada)
Limited

Printed in the United States of America

This one is for Alice, who cares.

"The gift that God gave me is racehorses."
—DIANE CRUMP, horse trainer

CONTENTS

1

THERE'S ALWAYS FRESH

"You don't need a lot of money at the track, you need winners."
—GERRY OKUNEFF, professional handicapper

THE BACKSIDE, or stable area, of any racetrack is dust and hay and manure and mud, horses and riders, the soft music of hooves striking the racing surface in the early-morning mist and, in California, the wonderful, improvised phrases of Spanglish, the state's own racing lingo, in the air: "That *caballo*? *Esta* fuckin' beautiful, man. She work *como el viento*, that's no shit." And the backside is also flies and greasy cafeteria food and forty-four-cent coffee in plastic cups, laughter and good talk, the rumble of the horse vans coming and going, the electricity of renewed hope in the air, and above all, it is the animals themselves, the protagonists of the drama, incorruptible in their innocence and beauty.

On a warm, sunny, smog-free California day, Santa Anita Park, which bills itself as "one of the world's foremost racing facilities," can be a delight to the casual visitor. The sun beats down over the green, flower-strewn infield and bathes in orange the steep slopes of Old Baldy and the Sierra Madre in the background, while the jockeys and their mounts warm up on the dark-brown oval of the main track for the first race on the opening day of the winter meet,

December 26, 1990. Filing out past the stands, then breaking into a gallop as they head for the starting gate seven-eighths of a mile away, the horses strain against the bit, heads bowed against the tug of the reins, their riders either standing in their stirrups or sitting quietly in the saddle next to the outriders on their escort ponies. The twelve Thoroughbreds are about to compete for a total purse of fourteen thousand dollars. It is a contest of no lasting significance, but it is being heavily bet. The fine card and matching weather have attracted a crowd of over forty-five thousand fans, each alive with the hope of picking a winner in the nine races to be run before sunset.

Just inside the main entrance to the track, a costumed mariachi band has been serenading the public. Young couples are spreading blankets and picnic lunches about the emerald-green turf of the infield, and kids gambol about Anita Chiquita, the children's playground, while their parents prepare to do battle at the betting windows. Arriving patrons equip themselves with official programs that set forth all the information about the day's racing (the number of each horse, its jockey and owner and trainer, the opening odds, etc.) and a fairly detailed explanation of how to interpret it. The more sophisticated bettors also equip themselves with racing forms and/or so-called tout sheets that carry selections made by professional handicappers. By 12:30 P.M., just before post time for the first race, the dark-green Santa Anita grandstand looks like an ocean liner stranded in a sea of cars parked bumper-to-bumper in the surrounding lots.

Inside the starting gate, the horses strain to be let loose, their riders hunching down low in the saddles, ready for the explosion of power and grace that will mark the beginning of the race. Above the gate, alone on his metal tower, the official starter, a middle-aged ex-cowboy named Tucker Slender, stares down, waiting for that precise moment when all the horses are in line, heads pointed forward, ready to run. Only then will he push the button that will cause the stall gates to spring open and release the animals. When he does so, the full field of twelve contestants will burst into the clear, their hooves pounding the dirt, the thunder all but drowned out by the great roar of the crowd as it begins to root its favorites home. The event, coming as it does less than a week before New Year's Day, when all Thoroughbreds officially become one year older, marks the start of another racing season.

A five-to-two shot named Moon Madness pops into the clear from the outside post, settles into stride as the horses turn into the stretch and finishes first in fast time as the lights on the tote board—the official track scoreboard—blink the final odds and the order of finish. A pretty teen-age girl, who happens to be holding a winning five-dollar ticket, hugs her boyfriend and jumps up and down, squealing with excitement when, after a few minutes, the tote flashes the official payoff, $7.40 for every two dollars wagered on Moon Madness's nose.

"Oh, that's great, just great," grumbles a fat, angry-looking man who has watched the whole race in close-up on a TV monitor inside the grandstand area. "A favorite yet and I must have bet this bum five times and he don't win for me and suddenly he's a fuckin' champ. You believe this?" His outburst falls on unsympathetic ears, because it turns out that most of the people around him are holding winning tickets or are alive in the daily double. "Hey, man, watch your mouth," a husky-looking citizen admonishes the complainer. "I'm here with my wife."

The grumbler departs to seek the comfort of his friends, the hard-core bettors who never miss a day at the track or who consider themselves professional horseplayers. It takes one of the latter to straighten the grumbler out. "Come on, Marty," he tells him, "the numbers on this horse told you he was a major contender, right? Only you don't play favorites. You could have used him in the double, or you could have passed the race. Wise up."

Marty curses his luck again and shuffles away. His friend, a large, heavyset bald man with a mustache who is known at the track as Sour Sam, watches him go without a trace of sympathy. "There goes a loser," he says to no one in particular. "Favorites win one of three races and he don't play 'em. If you could pick one race out of three every day at the right price, you'd be rich. Most of the time in this game you're gonna be on the wrong horse."

Although racetracks all over the country are bent on luring more and more new customers and put on special promotions—

rock concerts, senior-citizens' days, giveaways—to wheedle them onto the premises, the backbone of support is made up of hard knockers like Sam. A native New Yorker whose father was a bookie, he has been going to the races since the age of fourteen and has never held a legitimate job in his life. Some years ago he moved permanently to California, mainly because he felt that New York racing had gone sadly downhill since the creation of the state-run off-track betting parlors and also because "them New York winters was killing me." Every working day at Santa Anita he can be observed between races standing around a bar in the grandstand, not far from his favorite TV monitor.

Sam usually makes no more than three or four bets a day, mostly of several hundred dollars each and always in the show hole, which means that his horses have to run third or better for Sam to collect. He claims to have made a good living this way for years, but it has to be noted that he drives an ancient Pontiac that sounds as if a reggae combo is tuning up under the hood, lives in a one-room walk-up in downtown Hollywood, owns two thread-bare pairs of gray slacks and only one sports jacket, and has never been seen to smile.

Sour Sam has no official existence. He has never paid income taxes, does not possess a Social Security card, has no medical insurance or retirement plan, has never voted, does not own a credit card, keeps his operating money in a shoebox under his bed, and deposits what savings he has with a brother who tends bar in Las Vegas. In the modern sense, Sam is a nonperson, which helps to explain his habitual look of restrained despair. He remembers vividly the day he realized he was hooked on the races. "I borrowed twenty bucks off my mom one day when I was tapped," he said. "I hit a twelve-to-one shot on the nose and made a nice score, but I never told her I'd won. I stiffed my own mother."

The irony of Sam's status is that he and his fellow plungers form a nucleus without which no track could operate successfully. Although he himself has become over the years a shrewd, tight-fisted bettor, most of his cronies are not. Guys like the Desperado, Fat Eddie, and Tap-Out will each of them run more money through the parimutuel machines in one race than a whole busload of tourists from Azusa in a week, but the hard knockers get no credit for it from the racing establishment. They are, in fact, regarded as slightly unclean—social lepers who ought to be compelled to wear warning bells around their necks. This is another source of sadness to Sam, who feels that instead of opprobrium, he and his friends should receive praise and special recognition in the form of lifetime passes and free reserved seats over the finish line, perhaps even a medal for valor in the face of insurmountable odds. Not only is it expensive to play the races (you have to pay a brutal commission of at least fifteen cents out of every dollar, what gamblers call the vigorish, just for the privilege of risking your money), but too often they are won by horses going off at odds too low to justify a wager. In the immortal words of Gerry Okuneff, one of the best professional handicappers I know, "There is a Dummy God at the track who watches over the fortunes of the dummies who bet on obvious favorites. When the Dummy God is on his throne, there's nothing to do but wrap up."

To an inexperienced bettor, the wisdom of a hard knocker like Sam is worth a fortune. His basic advice to neophytes has always been never to bet more than you can afford to lose, bet only on horses you feel strongly about, for whatever reason, and never listen to tips. Most important, you should not expect to win consistently unless you are ready to make the sacrifice of learning how to read the *Daily Racing Form*, the horseplayers' bible, which contains all the information necessary to estimate a horse's chances in a race—its record of wins and also-rans, its last performance, its latest workout—but to the uninitiated looks about as easy to decipher as the Rosetta Stone. "You want to have a good time and no worries, bet two dollars a race on horses with cute names or the longest tails," Sam once said. "Or bet on some cute jockey. But don't take it serious. Serious is my racket."

On this particular day, Sam seems less depressed than usual. "This one horse here in the second with the funny name is a cinch to be in the money and ought to pay good on account of most people don't bet in the show hole in these long turf races," he says. "Then I got a real good number on a first-time starter named Personable Joe in the fourth and also on another maiden named

Dinard in the sixth. Both of them should pay good. Girl of France is a cinch to be in the money in the seventh, but it's a short field with an obvious favorite in there, so it don't figure to pay enough and I'll pass that one. Then, in the ninth, I gotta like Comedian and the race is wide open, so he should pay good. If I'm winning, I'll play him, otherwise I'll pass. So that's four good numbers today. I ought to make some money."

The trouble is that Sam doesn't really believe that any card can produce four really good bets in any one day, so he mumbles something about maybe having to pass the maiden races to wait for the ninth. "Maidens you don't really know enough about," he explains, "no matter what the numbers say. I'll probably pass 'em, depending on what this one horse does in here. We'll see."

Meanwhile, in the paddock out behind the grandstand, about fifteen minutes before the second race, a groom leads Sam's "one horse," a four-year-old chestnut gelding named Treat Tobeatya-feet, around the walking ring with the seven horses he'll compete against. The owners and their friends and relatives stand on the grassy patch inside the ring and watch their animals circle as the public crowds about the outside fence to catch the action. Sam never goes to the paddock. "I ain't no beader," he says. "What do I need to see them animals for? I seen about two million horses in my time and I never met one that told me anything."

Horses talk only to the people who spend most of their time around them—their trainers, riders, grooms and other stablehands. They've all been up since well before dawn, taking care of the more than two thousand animals stabled on the premises. In that dim, early-morning light the big, beautiful creatures seem to move like ghosts between the long, low, green barns, the soft sound of their hooves beating a muted drumbeat in the brown earth. Each day the horses are taken out of their stalls, walked or galloped for several miles, washed, fed, and generally tended as if worth a million dollars, which, of course, some of them are. Every five or six days, if sound and in active training, a horse will be asked to run in a workout, at distances ranging usually from three furlongs (three-eighths of a mile) to a mile, depending on what sort of race the animal is prepping for. By ten o'clock in the morning, when the last of the horses are being tucked away in their stalls again and a hush, broken only by distant traffic noises and the soft stamping and snorting of the animals themselves, has fallen over the backstage world of the track, the men and women whose livelihoods depend on racing have put in a full working day, and the race itself becomes a form of unpaid overtime. In the paddock, most of them look tired, especially those whose charges have little chance of winning.

The jockeys now appear. Little people dressed in boots, white breeches, caps and brightly colored silks, they fan out toward their mounts. Corey Nakatani, a smart young rider on his way up, joins the group around Tony Chavez, the trainer of Treat Tobeatyafeet. In his red and white silks, Nakatani nods briskly at Chavez's brief instructions; he's ridden the horse before, knows him well and clearly expects to win. The paddock judge now calls out, "Riders up!" and Chavez gives his jockey a leg up into the saddle. Treat Tobeatyafeet has drawn the number one post position and leads the line of eight horses as they file out toward the gap leading to the main track. The tote board blinks the odds, establishing Nakatani's mount as the favorite, at odds of nine to five. "Hey, Corey, don't fall off!" someone in the crowd calls out as the horses pass by.

Having bet five hundred dollars to show on his selection, Sam arrives at his post under the TV monitor just in time to see the gate spring open and the animals explode into the clear. As expected, Treat Tobeatyafeet easily grabs the lead, then holds it for most of the way around the mile and a quarter distance on the turf course to win comfortably. He pays $3.40 to show, which means that Sam has just won a total of three hundred and fifty dollars on his investment. "I wish it was always this easy," he says. "The problem is sometimes they don't run like they figure to or I'd be a rich man. *You* go figure it."

Santa Anita Park was built in 1934 by Dr. Charles Henry Strub, a dentist who'd plunged heavily in the stock market, went broke in 1929 and had been living on credit ever since. He understood, however, that in a time of depression, with two out of every seven Americans unemployed, horse racing could supply a much needed diversion while at the same time catering to the gambling instincts frustrated by the collapse of Wall Street. In an era when any display of luxury was regarded as extreme bad taste, Doc Strub determined to lavish on his establishment every amenity he could think of. He also decided to charge for everything, on the sensible theory that no one appreciates what he can get for nothing.

His most important backer turned out to be movie producer Hal Roach, who had the necessary real estate—about two hundred acres of what had once been an old Spanish land grant, the Rancho Santa Anita, on the outskirts of Pasadena and about fifteen miles from downtown Los Angeles. The site had been acquired from the estate of Elias J. Baldwin, better known as Lucky, who had bred and raced horses and in 1907 built his own track on the property. He was a memorable eccentric and much survives today at Santa Anita to remind visitors of his presence: the old Reid Adobe where he lived, his Queen Anne cottage, his horse-and-buggy barn, the lake he dredged—all preserved on the grounds of the Arboretum Park next to the track. Also still roaming the grounds are the descendants of the hundreds of peacocks Baldwin originally imported from China. One old trainer remembers the surroundings that first year of racing as "just a big prairie with hundreds of these peacocks all over the place. You could hear the Red Car, the old trolley, leaving for L.A., all the way from Pasadena."

Doc Strub was not only a gambler but a man of discernment. He chose for his emporium a Spanish-American architectural motif that harmonized perfectly with the track's spectacular ambience, and it has been adhered to through all the enlargements and improvements over the years. It cost a million dollars to build the original Santa Anita and every dollar was well spent. A racing writer named David Alexander recalls being overwhelmed at his first glimpse of the place in 1936. "The total effect was breathtaking," he wrote. "And a painless dentist, whose motive, they said, was money, had brought it into being." Doc Strub, who died in 1958, could have asked for no finer epitaph.

The money has always been an important consideration. Santa

Anita is one of the biggest and most successful racetracks in the country. It holds two meetings a year, fall and winter, with an average daily attendance of about twenty-three thousand and an on-site betting handle of well over five million dollars a day. (The total attendance, including all the off-track betting facilities in and out of state, comes to about thirty thousand, betting about seven and a quarter million dollars a day.) Forty-three states now license betting on various forms of horse racing—including pacers, trotters, Appaloosas, Arabians and quarter horses, as well as Thoroughbreds—and thirty-two put on live meets at over a hundred tracks for a total yearly attendance of over fifty-six million. All these ventures pour money into state coffers, an average of seventeen cents out of every dollar wagered, a figure that tends to keep the politicians in line.

The sport as an industry currently faces some severe problems, mainly in the form of much more competition for the gambling dollar, while the increased amount of racing all over has tended to a decline in quality. About forty thousand Thoroughbreds are now foaled every year in this country, but many will never make it to the track. Horses are fragile creatures, prone to all sorts of ailments that can put them out of competition for months at a time or incapacitate them permanently. This has led to a growing emphasis on sophisticated medication to keep injured or chronically sore animals in competition, and the temptation to cheat by administering illegal drugs has increased as well.

The paranoia factor concerning the honesty of horse racing is very high, but there's actually very little cheating going on. The general rule is that the bigger the track and the richer the purse, the less likely is there to be any hanky-panky. Visitors to Santa Anita can generally count on getting a fair run for their money, though every now and then a jockey will ride an odd-looking race or a mount will display a startling reversal of form. "The problem ain't the horses," Sam observes. "The problem is with the larcenous human heart. To ensure absolute honesty, you'd have to have all the horses ridden by monkeys and trained by gorillas. But then you got a problem—who tells the gorillas what to do?"

. . .

Sam likes the feel of the new folding green in his pocket, so he now decides to pass the two maiden races. This is a costly decision, because both Personable Joe and Dinard win, paying $3.60 and $5.20 to show. Sam is still ahead, of course, but he could have been up over a thousand dollars if he'd stuck to his original game plan. "I never lost a race by passing it," he likes to say, but the fact is that he's committed a major betting blunder—wrapping up to protect his winnings rather than betting to make a real killing. His temper is being strained by the fact that a small blonde who bets according to the numbers she has dreamed about has parlayed an opening ten-dollar wager into a pot of about two hundred, all of which she now plans to invest on a longshot named Bedevilled, number two in the eighth and feature race, the Malibu Stakes. Sam stares at her glumly as she chirps away to her boyfriend at the bar.

Much more is at stake for the owners and trainers of the animals in the eighth. They are competing for a pot of over a hundred thousand dollars, about fifty-five percent of which will go to the winner. In the private Turf Club and in the grandstand boxes over the finish line, the owners of these expensive three-year-old colts and geldings regard the proceedings with far more sangfroid than the small blonde or the punters risking their welfare checks on somebody's nose. Owning a racehorse is much like owning a yacht; if you have to worry about how to pay for one, you shouldn't be in the game at all.

It is primarily in the Turf Club, in its atmosphere of rooted money and chic, that the timeworn phrase "sport of kings" seems most applicable. Organized horse racing dates back to seventeenth-century England, when Charles II and some of his cronies first imported the Arab stallions from which the modern Thoroughbred is descended. These animals were bred to native stock, and three of them were so terrific that their progeny founded the Thoroughbred line. They were called the Darley Arabian, the Byerly Turk and the Godolphin Barb. All Thoroughbreds descend from one of these three, but most great racehorses can trace their ancestry back to the Darley Arabian's great-great-grandson,

Eclipse, who was foaled in 1764; he was the best of the best. The term "Thoroughbred" first appeared in the *English Stud Book* published in 1808, and immediately caught on with the racing public.

Breeding is still paramount in the sport today, and the object of every rich owner and big stable is ostensibly the mating of one expensive champion to another to produce the best-pedigreed animal possible. This takes money, lots of it. Every year the best horses, once their racing careers are over, are retired, often syndicated for millions of dollars and bred, with stud fees sometimes running as high as a hundred thousand dollars and more. The top mares are also worth millions, and being a successful breeder is nice work, if you can get it.

None of this is of the slightest concern to Sour Sam, the other hard knockers or the public at large. They're there for the racing and that's it. When the eleven entries in the Malibu Stakes break from the gate, the little blonde who dreams numbers begins to scream. She has wagered most of her winnings on Bedevilled across the board, and now she has the pleasure of watching him come in second, at odds of twelve to one. He pays $8.60 to place and $5.20 to show, which means that she has more than doubled her money and stands to collect over four hundred dollars. Not a bad way to build on a ten-dollar stake.

Rattled by her success and afraid to come away with nothing, Sam decides to pass Comedian in the ninth. Comedian runs second and pays $4.20 to show, which means that Sam could have doubled his money. He takes little pleasure in his winning day, because he has to live with the fact that he could have won a lot more and has allowed a devotee of the Dummy God to unsettle him. "I tell myself I got stone ears," he says, as he shuffles glumly away. "I allowed this dumb little broad to get to me. I ought to be shot."

The worst time at any track comes at the end of the day, when the public is filing out, leaving in its wake the tons of debris that the clean-up crews will take hours to haul away. Five favorites have won, two more than average, and the spectacle of the racing itself has been exhilarating, for there are few things more beautiful in life than a competitive Thoroughbred in action, a thousand pounds of magnificently proportioned bone and muscle in rhythmic concert. Still, the underside of the sport is at its most visible now, especially in the sour, disappointed look of the bettors who have lost their grocery money and leave convinced that somehow they've been cheated out of it. It's too difficult for most losers to face the truth, which is that betting horses is a tough racket and requires more than luck to make a consistent winner.

Now, as the sun begins to set and shadows lengthen over the trash-strewn infield and emptying parking lots, the last image is that of a stooper, a little old lady in a skirt down to her ankles who leans over to scoop up discarded tickets by the handful. Every day bettors throw away winning tickets, some of which the stoopers will salvage and cash in, but it's a tough way to survive at the track, not unlike working as a geek in a carnival.

Up in the second-floor money room, meanwhile, the day's handle is being counted, the bills in various denominations being stacked and tucked away in a vault until the following morning. This is where all the daily dreams fade and finish, banished by the grim reality of who winds up with most of the loot.

On the backside, however, the dreams never die. The horses and their keepers sleep through the night, awaiting the early dawn of a new day with its quota of hope, of promise, of providing for every hard knocker in the world a possible pot at the end of a glorious rainbow.

I once asked Sam how he had managed to survive the disastrous losing streaks that periodically afflict even the smartest horseplayers. "There's always fresh," he said.

2

THE EASY WAY

"The best thing in the world is to win at the racetrack. The second best thing is to lose at the racetrack."

—Old racetrack aphorism

THE CHASE began when I was sixteen years old and home from prep school on vacation. I was spending a weekend at my father's apartment in New York, and that Friday night my beautiful cousin Isolde and her husband, Harry, came to dinner. I had never met Harry. All I knew about him was that he had money, that they lived in Washington, D.C., and traveled a good deal. However, I liked him right away. He was a tall, ingratiating man in his early forties with bright, deep-set eyes, curly hair and an amiable smile. He was considerably older than Isolde, who was still in her twenties, but he seemed much younger than his years, perhaps because he didn't make the mistake of talking down to me. In the soft, upper-class drawl of his native Virginia, he regaled me with cheerful anecdotes about great sporting events, and it soon became evident that he'd attended every major boxing match since the Dempsey-Firpo fight. When I discovered that he also possessed an encyclopedic knowledge of baseball, I was completely won over.

After dinner, on our way out of the dining room, Harry put his arm affectionately around my shoulders. "I'm certainly glad we had a chance to talk at last," he said. "We obviously share many of the same interests."

I asked him how long he and Isolde would be in town.

"Oh, just a few days," he said. "The card looked so good this week it gave us an excuse to get to New York."

"The card?" I asked, puzzled.

"Harry goes to the horse races," my father said, with obvious sarcasm.

"The sport of kings," Harry said.

"Do you go, too?" I asked Isolde.

"Oh, no," she said, laughing. "I come to New York to shop."

The rest of the evening Harry talked about horses. He'd been enthusiastic about most sports, but I soon gathered that horse racing was his life. He had attended meets at every major track all over the world, and he could apparently remember the name of every horse in every race he'd ever seen. He was full of long, detailed stories about the great races in which he'd won huge sums of money, usually by the length of a nose or an outstretched lip. And he relived each tense moment, often bounding to his feet at the climax of a story to give an exact imitation of the way a jockey whipped his tiring steed down the stretch or to recreate the eccentric running motion of some favorite front-runner. His ecstatic involvement was contagious and I listened, absorbed.

"You must have won a lot of money over the years," I said after a while.

"Harry doesn't talk much about the races he loses," my father observed drily.

Harry laughed. "Your father's right," he said. "It's not much fun when you lose."

"I've never seen a horse race," I said.

"I'm going out there tomorrow," Harry said. "Why don't you come along?"

I could immediately sense my father's disapproval, but I decided to ignore it and I told Harry I'd be delighted. My father wasn't exactly a spoilsport, but he used to write me letters full of good advice. "So far as business is concerned," he said in one of them, "we know that only hard work will ever produce results," and occasionally he'd remind me that at twenty-one I'd be entirely on my own, and I'd better begin to think about a profession.

The trouble was that I had this secret conviction that the making of money was basically a frivolity, like butterfly collecting and croquet, one of those harmless pastimes that no grown-up could take seriously. The way Harry talked, you could make thousands betting on horses, and it fit in with how I felt about money in general. I didn't underrate its importance, but I wasn't about to devote my life to it. Here was my father, a classical scholar and musician, wasting his time as a talent agent. That wasn't for me and I had already told him so, which had inevitably led to a certain amount of friction between us. I now told him that I could see nothing wrong with betting on horses, which struck me as reasonably sane compared with such other gambling propositions as the stock market, and I intended to look into it.

Harry chuckled, but my father only looked at him grimly. "If you have one of your usual days," he said, "it will be a good lesson for him."

At noon the next day, Harry and I met in a bar on the Long Island level of Penn Station. He was more sportily dressed than the night before, in a plaid sports jacket, gray slacks and an ascot, but his entire demeanor had changed. Though he greeted me cordially enough and ordered me a tomato juice, he was too engrossed in his newspaper to pay any further attention to me. From time to time he'd stop peering intently at the page he was reading just long enough to scribble some hasty notations on the margin. I maintained a discreet silence and sipped my tomato juice. Finally, after about twenty minutes of this, Harry suddenly glanced at the wall clock and stood up. "Come on, boy," he said tersely. "I don't care about the first race, but I've got to get something down on Velvet Glove in the second." He tucked the paper under his arm, picked up a black doctor's satchel from under the table and swept us out at a gallop into the station. We bounded down a flight of stairs and entered a waiting railroad car just as the doors started to close.

The car, an antiquated Long Island model with parallel rows of cracked-leather seats, seemed to be full of small, round men smoking cigars and also reading newspapers. All the seats were taken and standees were packed in a dense, sweating mass up the aisle. We remained standing, and as the train began to move slowly out of the station, Harry put the satchel down between his feet and resumed his intense scrutiny of the newspaper. It wasn't until we were well out of the tunnel and curving down past Jamaica that Harry again took notice of me. With a deep, contented sigh he folded up the paper, stuffed it into his side pocket and lit a cigarette. "That gives me a pretty good start," he said and glanced out the window. "Well, I see we're almost there."

"What kind of paper was that you were reading?" I asked.

"Oh, I should have told you," he said. "That's a racing form. It has all the past and present data on the horses running in each race at all the tracks. You can't really handicap a race without it."

"Could I see it?"

"Certainly," he said and handed me the paper.

There were a couple of short columns of news stories and brief accounts of other sporting events, but most of the paper consisted entirely of the names of horses, each one appearing over a large block of complex, indecipherable information consisting mostly of numbers and abbreviated names, words, and phrases. None of it made any sense to me, but finally, in a section devoted to the doings that afternoon, I came across the name Velvet Glove. "Is this the one you're betting on?" I asked.

Harry nodded and glanced nervously around at the other passengers. "Yes," he said in a low voice. "He hasn't done much and he ought to go off at six to one or better."

"If he hasn't done much, what makes you think he can win?"

Harry jabbed a forefinger at the meaningless block of information. "Look here," he said. "See that? He breaks fast. In every race he's ever run he gets out in front."

"I gather he doesn't stay there," I said.

"That's just it," Harry said. "Those races were all at a mile or more and he was carrying a lot of weight. Today he's in with cheap horses at only six furlongs, and he's not giving weight away to anyone. If he breaks on top, he could do it. And the price will be lovely."

"How do you know all that about him?" I asked. "Is it all in here?"

"Let me show you something," Harry said and held the paper out between us. "See these lines here?"

"Yes. What about them?"

"That's what the horse has done in all of his most recent races."

"You mean all you have to do to figure out the winner is learn how to interpret this gibberish?" I asked.

Harry smiled. "Well, not quite," he said calmly, with what I now realize was incredible patience. "There are unknown factors."

"Like what?"

"Sometimes a horse simply won't run," he explained, "no matter what the figures say."

I peered more closely at the exotic hieroglyphics on the page before me and I'd have asked more questions, but the train slowed down and the passengers began to mass toward the doors. Harry thrust the newspaper back into his pocket and picked up his black satchel. I noticed that he was sweating slightly and that his eyes had a strange abstracted look. As the train came to a halt, he put a hand on my shoulder and pushed me toward the exit. "We only have a few minutes before post time," he said tersely. "If we get separated, we'll meet at the bar on the main floor of the grandstand, near the finish line."

The rest of that memorable afternoon flashed past with dizzying speed, leaving me only a jumble of sharp impressions. I remember that, in the surge past the entrance to the racetrack, Harry and I did become separated, but not before he'd thrust a ten-dollar bill in my hand and said, "Velvet Glove is number four. Bet to win!"

A few minutes later I found myself standing indoors under a large electric board featuring all sorts of different numerals, while, over a loudspeaker, a harsh voice announced that the horses were nearing the starting gate. "Where do I make a bet?" I asked the man next to me and was rewarded with a look of amazement.

Eventually somebody came to my rescue, and I joined a long line of people shuffling slowly toward a small window behind which a man in shirtsleeves was taking money and punching a ticket machine. I had no sooner paid my ten dollars and received my slip of cardboard in return than a bell sounded, and I heard a roar from the crowd outside. People began running away from the windows and up the ramps leading, I gathered, to the track itself. I joined them and fought my way out into the open just as a knot of horses flashed past below me, and three people directly in front of me began jumping up and down and pounding each other on the back. Beside me a huge black man under a light-blue derby slowly tore a wad of tickets into shreds and began to curse loudly. "What happened?" I asked him.

"What happened?" he shouted. "The fuckin' race was fixed, that's what happened!"

I went back inside and found Harry at the bar. His ascot had come undone and he was sweating heavily. The racing paper, now beginning to look slightly soiled, was sticking out of his pocket, the black satchel was tucked under his arm, and his expression was ecstatic. "How about that?" he said, as soon as he saw me. "How about that? He paid better than five to one!"

"You mean Velvet Glove won the race?" I asked.

"My God, don't you know?" he barked happily. "Stayed in front all the way like I said he would!"

It was only the beginning. Harry's first five choices came in, all but one of them at odds of three to one or better. We spent most of our time standing in line—Harry at the hundred-dollar window, I at the ten-dollar one—either waiting to collect our winnings or to bet on the next race. After each triumph we'd meet again at the bar to embrace each other and toast our success.

After a horse named Apache won the sixth race by a nose and Harry came back from his window holding great wads of money in his fist, a crowd of watchful admirers began to gather around us. Harry quickly stuffed the money into his pants pocket and patted his black satchel. "I'm sure glad I brought this," he said.

"What's in there, anyway?" I asked.

Harry opened the satchel and shoved it under my nose. It was full of losing parimutuel tickets from all over and dating back several months. "They've got an Internal Revenue man sitting by the big-money windows," he said. "When I went back this time to collect, he asked for my name and address, and I just shoved the open bag under his face. I can prove I lost thirty thousand dollars last year alone."

"Say, mister," one of our fans piped up, "what do you like in the next race?"

Harry took out his paper and glanced over the entries as the watchers pressed in around us. He finally shook his head and handed me the sheet. "Maiden fillies," he said. "There's no sense even trying to handicap it." He winked at me. "You pick it, Billy."

"Me? I don't know anything about it."

"Just pick one, for the hell of it."

My first selection ever, an unsung filly named Que Hora, won by a neck and paid off at nineteen to one. Back at the bar, Harry was whooping and hollering and buying everyone rounds of drinks. "Good Lord," was all he said, "we could just throw the damn form away!"

Slightly dazed, I began to count my money. It amounted to several hundred dollars and seemed a vast fortune to me at the time.

"Well, how do you feel?" Harry asked as I finished counting my loot.

"Fantastic," I said. "Is it always like this?"

"Not always," Harry said. "I'll explain it to you later."

We left the track in a pink haze of glory without betting the last race of the day, because, as Harry put it, it was strictly for plugs and we shouldn't insult our luck. Our departure caused dismay in the ranks of our admirers, several of whom followed us as far as the exit gate in a vain attempt to persuade us to tell them who was going to win that last one.

As we rode back to town in a rented limousine, Harry explained the facts of life to me. "Not every day can be like this one," he began and went on to say that, over the year, he usually lost far more than he won. "If you bet every race," he concluded, "you can't help but lose. To me it doesn't matter because I can afford it and I like the excitement."

"You mean we were just lucky?" I asked. "There isn't any sure way of winning?"

It was then that Harry told me about Pittsburgh Phil, a gambler who had flourished in Chicago some years before. According to Harry, Pittsburgh Phil had made a fortune betting on horses. His system was to wait for a race in which his selection was almost certain to finish third or better, and then bet a large amount on his choice to show. "Betting to show usually pays less than even money," Harry said, "but it's safer. Of course you have to wait for the right race, sometimes for days, and you have to have some capital to make the bet worthwhile." He sighed and leaned back in his seat. "I could never do that," he said. "It's too boring."

That night we stopped first at their hotel to pick up Isolde, who had spent the day moving like a Mongol horde through the Fifth Avenue luxury department stores; then we had dinner at "21," paid fifty dollars apiece for tickets to a Broadway musical and sat at a ringside table for the last show at the Copacabana. When I finally got back to my father's place, I found him still awake. He was propped up in bed reading something light by Thucydides, in the original Greek.

"How did it go?" he asked.

"Oh, Harry made about fourteen G's and I took away a few hundred," I said casually. "I don't know why we don't do this all the time."

My father shut his book with a decisive little slap. "Of course you know that Harry loses a lot more than he wins," he said.

I yawned. "That's because he doesn't care. Pittsburgh Phil played safe and made millions."

My father stared at me. "Jesus Christ!" was all he said.

A couple of days later I went back to school, and several years passed before I finally had a chance to test Pittsburgh Phil's infallible system. I was always away, either at school or in the country, and my graduation was followed by fifteen inglorious months in the service. But it wouldn't have made any difference where I was, because I didn't have the capital to give the system an honest tryout. While still at school I contented myself by subscribing to one of the racing journals and making a careful study of its intricacies. I also read books on the subject, and for a long time I kept a notebook in which I recorded the outcome of all my imaginary bets at New York racetracks. Once, when my father wrote me another of his Horatio Alger letters, I sent him back a sheet of paper with a complete account of my most recent hypothetical winnings and a brief accompanying note in which I informed him that his theories about dedication to a chosen task were obviously outmoded; no one in his right mind would work hard to make money if it could be made easily.

Finally, in the fall of 1945, I was discharged from the service and found myself in New York with no prospects, no business ambitions, and several hundred dollars in separation pay in my pockets. My family wanted me to go back to college, but I wanted to study for the opera (I had a good lyric tenor voice) and find some way to support myself while doing so, since my father was utterly opposed to my going into any form of show business. My capital amounted to about five hundred dollars, not nearly enough, but I intended to be conservative and content myself, at first, with a modest income. What Pittsburgh Phil had done with tens of thousands, I would do with a few hundred.

My father was outraged. "Don't tell me you haven't outgrown that imbecile idea," he said.

"You like to do things the hard way," I answered. "I like to do them the easy way."

The next day I went out to the track, waited all afternoon in the rain to make one cautious bet and came home with a twelve-dollar profit. Both my fond parents were unimpressed, but I was filled with quiet elation. I went out faithfully every day after that, continued to play Pittsburgh Phil's system and invariably won. My earnings were meager (never more than eighty dollars a week and usually nearer fifty), but I consoled myself by thinking with glee of my friends, all of whom were either back in school or working at mundane jobs. I was absolutely convinced that I had solved the money problem and that I'd soon be earning enough to live, if not like a king, at least like a prince. It didn't bother me at first that I had no time to work on my voice, because that would come a bit later, when I could up the ante at the track a bit.

I had been doing things the easy way for about two months

when I came home one night and went to bed with a high fever. My father sent his doctor over the next day and was told that I had nothing more than a very bad cold. "He's run-down," the doctor said. "Maybe he's been working too hard."

"Working too hard?" my father snapped. "All he does is go to the track."

"Well, whatever he's been up to," the doctor said, "it doesn't agree with him."

During the week it took me to recuperate I had a lot of time to think over this curious diagnosis, and I began to wonder about Pittsburgh Phil and the life of ease. On a piece of paper I drew up a schedule of a typical day among the loafers:

10 A.M.–11 A.M.	Get up, instant coffee, scan paper for late scratches, leave house.
11 A.M.–11:30 A.M.	Subway ride to Penn Station, standing on crowded platform.
11:30 A.M.–12:30 P.M.	Train ride to track, reading form and standing on crowded platform.
12:30 P.M.–1 P.M.	Enter track, check odds, eat lunch standing at crowded counter.
1:15 P.M.–5:45 P.M.	Watch races while keeping track of odds, checking form, standing in ticket lines.
5:45 P.M.–6:45 P.M.	Train ride back to city, standing on crowded platform.
6:45 P.M.–7:15 P.M.	Subway ride home, standing on crowded platform.
7:15 P.M.–10:30 P.M.	Dinner break.
10:30 P.M.–2:30 A.M.	Buy next day's paper, handicap all races, soak feet.

When I added up all my figures, I discovered that, for an average net profit (before taxes) of $52.37, I had been working a six-day, seventy-two-hour week. Furthermore, I was excluded from all welfare benefits, such as Social Security, pension plans, profit-sharing, and health insurance. Worst of all, I wasn't having any fun.

I lay in bed and stared into my future—a succession of bleak and hopeless days, an infinity of servitude and unrewarded toil. I came to the conclusion that Pittsburgh Phil must have had the constitution of an iron ox and the dogged determination of Sisyphus. I said nothing to either of my parents, but on my first day out of bed, I went out and got a job in a book and record store. Eventually, my mother gave me enough money to go to Italy to study, and I never again went to the races with the idea of making a living there.

For a long time I never knew what had become of Harry. He and Isolde got divorced and I lost track of him. Some years ago, however, I spotted him in the Turf Club during the Santa Anita meeting. He had put on weight and aged, of course, but otherwise looked much the same and I recognized him immediately. He was sitting alone at a table covered with small mounds of losing tickets and was intently scanning the *Daily Racing Form*. I went over and said hello, but had to remind him who I was. "My goodness, Billy," he exclaimed, "how are you doing?"

"Not bad, Harry. What about you?"

He laughed. "I'm on the worst losing streak of my life," he said. "Say, Billy, can you make any sense of this race? I don't know these western horses."

I sat down beside him, looked at the *Form* and finally paid him back by picking him a winner.

3

STYMIED

"I never met a horse I didn't like better than most actors."
— Ed Friendly, TV producer

I NEVER saw in the flesh the first horse I ever fell in love with. His name was Stymie, and according to Joe Palmer, then the racing columnist for the *New York Herald-Tribune*, he was "the most average horse you ever saw. Not tall, not short, not long, not close-coupled. Good bone, good muscle, good chest—nothing outstanding, nothing poor." Bred in Texas, he was a chestnut with a crooked blaze who made his debut in a cheap twenty-five-hundred-dollar claiming race, ran once for a rock-bottom fifteen hundred dollars, and went to the post fourteen times before he finally won and so broke his maiden, also in a cheap claimer. He had no speed and so not much chance to win as a two-year-old, since most races for young horses are at distances of six furlongs, three-quarters of a mile or less. It wasn't until he aged, like fine wine, and the distances stretched out to a mile and more that Stymie established himself in New York as "the people's cherce," a competitor who came from out of the clouds to win. In 1945, when he was four, Stymie ran nineteen times between May 22 and November 30, won nine of those contests and banked $225,375, then a huge sum. He was the star of the handicap division.

He hadn't amounted to a great deal as a three-year-old, so I hadn't paid any attention to him. I also hadn't been around very much. The Second World War was being waged abroad, and I had stayed in school during most of 1943, including the summer, then had gone straight into college at Harvard that fall. In mid-August of 1944, at the age of eighteen, I reported to Fort Dix, New Jersey, to begin what was to become an inglorious military interlude in the U.S. Army Air Force, as it was then called. While still at Harvard, I had managed to get out to Suffolk Downs, near Boston, a few times, but otherwise my career as a budding horse degenerate had been put on hold. Wars have a nasty way of interfering with the more pleasurable courses of human events.

I spent the rest of that summer and fall at a noxious military base named Keesler Field, outside of Biloxi, a seaside resort town on the Gulf Coast of Mississippi. The first six weeks there were spent in basic training, which meant essentially learning how to perform a number of completely useless tasks, such as cleaning a carbine, picking cigarette butts off the ground, saluting my inferiors and marching about in formation under a merciless sun in one-hundred-percent humidity. Nothing that I was compelled to learn during this period had anything to do with what I thought I had enlisted some months earlier at seventeen to achieve, which was a commission as a second lieutenant with a license to either pilot a warplane, navigate one or drop bombs from it on helpless civilians. Nobody had told me that I was to be regarded for some length of time as human vermin, suitable only to be abused, sworn at and made to jump at the whims of red-necked ignoramuses with degrees in sado-masochism. I believed in the basic goal of our military effort, which was to crush our evil enemies, but as the product of a comfy East Coast, middle-class background and a private-school education, I hadn't been able to imagine the depths of depravity and idiocy the human race is capable of. "The world is populated in the main by people who should not exist," my favorite author, Bernard Shaw, had written. It took six weeks of horror to ram that basic truth home to me.

What I did receive from the army, however, was a great education in life. I had been brought up to believe in the basic goodness of man and to embrace a credo that stressed reliance on such virtues as honesty, self-sacrifice, trust, hard work, obedience, integrity, compassion, and honor. None of these admirable virtues were much on display at Keesler, where the only people who led bearable lives were the careerists and opportunists who had risen like scum to the top of this human cesspool by the sort of ruthless cunning and abuse of power that characterize the social structure of a pack of wild dogs. The first and only time I ever told the truth to a superior in the service, about inadvertently coming back a couple of hours late from a weekend pass, I was assigned to three eighteen-hour days washing pots and pans. I never made that mistake again. In fact, by the end of those first six weeks, though I still couldn't reassemble my rifle or march in step, I had begun to master the techniques of evasion that are necessary to sustain civilized life in a world dominated by tyrants, predators and the merely insane.

My chief ally and mentor through this difficult time was the guy who slept in the bunk next to me, a tough kid from the streets of Philadelphia whom I'll call Charlie Minelli. Luckily, Charlie liked me, for which I've been forever grateful. He probably took pity on me, because no sooner had I come back from my stint on KP than he set about wising me up. "The first thing you got to figure is that there's an angle to everything," he told me one night over a couple of beers in the day room. "They load all this bullshit on you and then you work an angle around it. Grease also helps."

"Greece? Are you Greek? What's that got to do with it?" I asked.

"Jesus, don't you know anything?" Charlie said, appalled. "I'm talking grease, as in moolah, bucks, *dinero*, *capish*? You understand?" He rubbed his thumb and forefinger together. "Actually, I'm Italian, see, or my folks were, but that's got nothin' to do with it. It don't matter where you grew up, it's grease that makes the wheels spin and don't you forget it."

Charlie Minelli not only knew angles; he had a talent he knew how to exploit. He could play the trumpet and he could play it well and very loudly. Halfway through basic training, he had talked our company commander into letting him form a section band. He asked me to join it. "I don't play anything," I said.

"Can you beat time?"

"Sure."

"Good," he said, reaching under his bunk to hand me a pair of enormous cymbals. "Show up at the day room right after mess. We're gonna practice. Just bang them on the beat, okay?"

I had no idea what Charlie was up to or why he expected his dozen or so volunteer musicians to be enthusiastic about putting in what seemed to us like a lot of extra time rehearsing, when we could have been drinking beer, shooting pool or just lying around, recovering from the day's atrocities out on the drill field. We soon found out, however, and Charlie became instantly elevated in my eyes to a status bordering on genius.

By the early fall of 1944, just as we were completing our basic training, the Nazi and Japanese air forces had pretty much ceased to exist, and our losses in the air war had become minimal, even though there was still a lot of serious fighting going on down below. The officer-training program I had enlisted in had been designed to keep our armed forces supplied with replacements for all the fliers expected to be shot down. As usual, our military planners had erred on the side of excess. Once the casualty rate dropped precipitously, the U.S. Army Air Force found itself with some eighty thousand young men for whom there was no longer any room or need at the various officer-candidate schools. We couldn't be simply switched over to the infantry or the other military branches where they could have used us, because we had volunteered while still underage and with parental consent for a specific program. We could have been discharged and then drafted, like anybody else, but the concept was too complicated for the bureaucratic military mind to absorb immediately (though eventually, and mostly too late, that's exactly what the loonies in charge did do), so we piled up at the various bases like refugees, disenfranchised and with nowhere to go.

The military solution to this boondoggle was first to make us repeat basic training, then to reassign us as indentured servants to the upper classes at various other air bases around the country. That was the situation Charlie had anticipated. When our section was ordered to repeat, day by day, the miseries we thought we had put behind us, the only ones exempt from the program were those who, for one reason or another, had already been assigned some specific function within the command structure. Obviously, a band fell into this privileged category. Our job was to march the boys to and from the drill field four times a day, which we did with admirable dispatch. We had mastered, in addition to the Air Force hymn, several other peppy tunes, such as "Toot Toot Tootsie" and "Wait Till the Sun Shines, Nelly," and saw no reason to expand our repertoire. Out we'd go and back we'd come, banging and tootling away, until we could escape into either the latrine, where I sat on the crapper and read, thus immune from having to stand up and salute the passing brass, or the day room, where we drank beer, shot pool and talked about sports or the possibility of getting laid without catching a disease at Gonorrhea Pier, the social center of Biloxi. It was a life devoid of culture and charm, but at least it had become livable, thanks to Charlie.

Unfortunately, like a lot of wiseguys I've met since, Charlie quite literally got too cocky and overreached himself. He had begun to run a couple of hookers in and out of the base and was caught with his pants down in the sergeant's quarters of our barracks one night. He was arrested and disappeared from my life, later to be discharged, I heard, but I never worried about him; he'd have found an angle in hell.

The next morning, I was called into section headquarters by our master sergeant, the only person in authority over me whom I respected because he was the only one who seemed to be even faintly competent at his job, which was essentially to cover up for and correct the blunders of his commissioned superiors. "Your buddy got shipped out today," he said, when I presented myself in front of his desk. "Did you have anything to do with that?"

"No," I answered truthfully, for a change. "I knew nothing about it."

"Okay, then, you're it."

"I'm it?"

"Minelli's gone, you're in charge of the band."

"Me?"

"You don't want it?"

"Oh, sure, sarge, sure, of course."

He leaned back in his chair and looked up at me as if I represented some form of lowlife he'd never seen before. "Get out of
here, Murray," he said, "and don't fuck up like your buddy, you
hear me?"

Which is how I became the only cymbals player in history ever
to lead a band.

Eventually, after going through basic training several times, we
were all shipped out of Keesler to other airfields where our services
as menials could be put to better use. I wound up at a base in
Alabama, a few miles outside of Montgomery, the state capital.
There I was assigned to be a parachute dispatcher, which meant
that at dawn I handed out parachutes to fliers about to soar off into
the wild blue yonder, after which I could lie down behind the
counter and go back to sleep until our heroes came back a few
hours later from their training missions. They would return their
parachutes, I'd stuff them back into their individual bins, then sink
out of sight again for another snooze. I wasn't having as easy a
time as when I played the cymbals for Charlie Minelli, but I wasn't
being overworked either. I was merely in danger of being bored
to death.

On my first afternoon pass, I hitched a ride into downtown
Montgomery, mainly with the idea of putting myself in touch with
a civilian urban civilization again, and there made the discovery
that lifted my military career onto another plane of achievement
and comfort. I found a bookie joint.

It was located on the second floor of a nondescript red-brick
office building in the heart of the business district and was entered
openly up a narrow staircase from the street. No one asked any
questions, and there were no secret doors or passwords, which
meant that the police and local authorities had been well greased;
gambling was then illegal in Alabama. Inside, I found myself in a
large, rectangular room whose walls were lined by blackboards on
which the entries, odds and results from tracks all over the country
were being chalked up. A hundred or so mostly middle-aged men
and a handful of military types like myself were milling about

tables in the center of the room that contained mimeographed lists of entries, scratch sheets, racing papers and betting slips, or walking to and from a counter at one end where a couple of clerks were accepting wagers and paying off winners.

As I stood there, enraptured by my first glimpse of this oasis of sanity and cheer, a rasping male voice piped up over a loudspeaker to inform us that it was now post time for the second at Jamaica, in New York. I picked up the entries for the day, persuaded a fellow player to let me look over his shoulder at his racing form, then made a mind bet on some animal in the first race to place, just as the announcer's voice came on again. "We now have the first from Jamaica," he said and then proceeded to call the race, describing it with a fine dramatic flourish just as if he were actually seeing the contest instead of picking it up off a wire service. My selection won the race, paying off at better than even money in the place hole, a result that inspired me to get active and join the festivities.

I had to be careful, of course, because I wasn't exactly swimming in money. My salary then, as a preflight cadet with an enlisted man's rank of private first class, was less than a hundred dollars a month, and I had only about thirty bucks on me until payday, still over a week away. Nevertheless, I saw no reason not to plunge in, and I took another look at my neighbor's form just as the announcer began to call another race, this one from New England.

I hadn't been following the horses, so I had no idea what animals to wager on. I decided to concentrate, instead, on trainers, since I knew a little about who the good ones were and their training styles. Almost at once my eye fell on the name of Hirsch Jacobs, a top conditioner whose horses won more races in New York, especially at the lower levels of the sport, than anyone else. And so it was that on that memorable afternoon, May 29, 1945, I bet ten dollars, one-third of my total capital, on his entry, Stymie, to win at odds of even money.

When the race went off, Stymie's name was prominent by its absence from the announcer's call. Halfway around the first turn in the mile-and-one-sixteenth contest, at least five other horses had been mentioned but not him. But then, as the leaders reached the quarter pole, I heard the announcer say, "And here comes Stymie!" He blew past the front-runners and won going away by three and a half lengths, quickly doubling my money.

I made only one more bet that afternoon, half of my winnings on a horse I liked in Chicago, and cashed again, this time at odds of three to one, which meant that I was able to return to the base, after a nice dinner at a nearby steak house, with a net profit of twenty dollars. More important, I had found a refuge and a means to escape from the rigidities and stupidity of my daily existence in a world I had come to despise.

Stymie was entered to run again four days later, in the Grey Lag Handicap at a mile and one-eighth, and he figured not to be the favorite, since he was coming back so soon and out of a cheap race. Nevertheless, I was certain he would win and I was determined to get into town to bet on him. Unfortunately, I had been assigned that afternoon to serve on a garbage detail, which meant having to stand waist-deep in trash emptying containers or heaving them up from the street to somebody else standing waist-deep in trash.

I remembered Charlie Minelli and studied the angles, then applied the principle of grease to solving the problem. I found a bunkmate who was off and eligible for a pass that afternoon and paid him five dollars to take my place. We switched dog tags and I rushed off the base and into town, arriving at the oasis just after the third at Jamaica. I waited for Stymie's race and bet twenty dollars on him to win. Once again the contest went off without his name being mentioned until the last quarter of a mile, when the announcer sang out, "And here comes Stymie!" He swept on to victory, paying off this time at three and a half to one.

Between June 2 and August 25, Stymie ran eight more times, at Aqueduct, Belmont and Jamaica. He won three of those races and finished second in three. His best win, from my point of view, was in the Brooklyn Handicap at Belmont, at odds of six and a half to one. Even in most of the races he lost I didn't do badly, since I had begun to back up my bets on him in the place hole. By the time the Saratoga Cup at Belmont rolled around, which he won by three lengths at odds of four to five, I had become an affluent member of my set, able on my winnings to grease my way out of the more noisome tasks the army assigned me to perform and treat myself to edible meals at Montgomery's better restaurants.

This idyll came to an end when, along with most of my group, we were suddenly shipped back to Keesler. I didn't know of a bookie joint in Biloxi and I was wondering where I could find a pair of cymbals, but I didn't have to bother this time. My mother had written me to look up some friends of friends of hers, a retired set designer and his wife, who lived in Pass Christian, a small town down the coast from Biloxi toward New Orleans. Somewhat embarrassed by its boorish treatment of our courageous band of patriotic volunteers, the local brass did not require us this time around to go back into basic training but assigned us to the sort of routine menial tasks we'd been carrying out for months elsewhere. I was told to report to a hangar, handed a screwdriver and instructed to tighten metal plates under the wings of airplanes, a duty a retarded chimpanzee would have had no trouble mastering.

Two days after my arrival, I called the people in my mother's letter, who invited me to a dinner party the following Saturday, when I'd be able to get my first pass off the base. I hitchhiked up the coast and arrived in Pass Christian at about dusk, just in time for cocktails. My hosts turned out to be charming, an elegant and sophisticated old couple who lived in a large two-story house with its own private beach and set well back from the coastal highway. Best of all, I was the only serviceman present, and for the first time in months I found myself having the sort of civilized, urbane conversation I'd become accustomed to while growing up. One of the other guests, a beautiful woman in her late twenties named Molly, seemed especially interested in me and introduced me to her younger sister True and their mother. When they heard my comedic account of my adventures in the military, they promptly invited me out for the following weekend, at the house they shared a few miles away, back toward Biloxi. "I'm not sure I can get a pass next weekend," I said, but Molly told me not to worry about it; it would all be arranged.

It turned out that she and True were both married to Air Force colonels, who were still overseas fighting for democracy, Molly's husband in Europe, True's in the Pacific. Their mother, furthermore, was the widow of a West Point colonel who had once been the base commander at Keesler. The angle was to have her telephone the present commander, an old personal friend, on my behalf. This was done the following Monday, and I was immediately given a weekend pass, from Friday afternoon to Sunday night.

I spent every weekend that fall with Molly and her family, who also lived in a beachfront mansion staffed with servants, one of whom was an old black woman who cooked the best gumbo and other Creole dishes I've ever eaten. Naturally, I fell in love with Molly, who assured me that her marriage was not a happy one. Neither True nor her mother seemed to disapprove of the arrangement and simply turned a blind eye to it. My bedroom was next to Molly's, connected to it (and everyone else's) by a veranda that ran the full length of the building facing the water.

For a hundred and thirty dollars, part of it money I had won betting on Stymie, I bought a 1932 Plymouth, which solved the transportation problem. Even my life on the base itself became more bearable, after a call from headquarters whisked me away from my duties at the hangar to reassignment at the information and education section, where I lectured to commissioned officers on European history and culture.

Until I bought the Plymouth, I had never owned or even driven a car. I knew the principles, of course, and inspired by romance, I soon mastered them on my own. I also knew about putting in gas and water, but nobody had told me about oil. Six weeks after I bought the car, I was happily tooling down the highway toward Molly's house when something called a piston rod hammered through the cylinder head and embedded itself in some other part of the engine. The damage, I learned, was irreversible, so I sold the machine for scrap for twenty dollars, after which Molly or True would come to pick me up at the Keesler main gate in the family convertible on Friday afternoon and drive me back Sunday night.

I forgot all about Stymie. In fact, I forgot all about the rest of my life. I wanted this new one to go on forever, which, of course, it couldn't. In mid-October, we were informed that, unless we chose to sign up again for three more years with our enlisted ranks (I was still a PFC), we would be discharged, and those of us with less than twelve months' active service would be drafted back into some other branch. I had been in fourteen months by this time and was safe, so I made a special request to be discharged at Keesler, in order to go on seeing Molly. It was not granted and I was shipped out a couple of weeks later to Westover Field in Massachusetts, where, after a few days, I became a civilian again.

Suddenly, everything in my former military life seemed different and very unreal and terribly distant. Back in New York, I called Molly a few times and we also wrote to each other, but I think we both knew it was all over. True's husband had come home from the war and Molly's was on the way. The last time I talked to her, she seemed a little cold, abstracted, too busy now with her own life and concerns to care about mine. We parted quietly and with relief.

One of the things I wanted to do as soon as I got back home was see Stymie run, but I didn't make it in time. He ran his last race in New York that year on November 3, in the Westchester Handicap, which he won. Then he shipped down to Baltimore to run three times at Pimlico, winning two, including his last race of the year, the Pimlico Cup. He horrified his field by eight lengths that day on a heavy track, after which he went south for a well-merited rest. By the following spring, when he returned to New York, I was gone, back at Harvard. But even today, the first thing I hear whenever I think back to my ludicrous military career is the sound of a disembodied male voice calling out, "And here comes Stymie!"

4

A LIFE, NOT A LIVING

"[Trainers] spend all their time looking for one thing. . . . They're looking for the horse."

—Columnist Brendan Boyd

"That's Roadtown," the trainer said, as a ghostly horse and rider galloped by. He turned and peered through the gloom to his left. "Now here comes Lake Moreau."

It was about five-thirty A.M. on a cold early-spring day in 1961, and I was standing at the rail of the training track at Belmont Park, watching a veteran horseman named R. N. Blackburn, whose small string was stabled there, put a couple of three-year-old fillies through their paces. I didn't realize it at the time, but I had just begun to find out what this game was really about.

It had rained heavily the night before, but overhead the sky was turning slowly blue, and in the distance, above the tops of trees, loomed the empty grandstand of the main course. The air was crisp and clean, the only sound the rhythmic slop-slop of the horses' hooves as they struck the muddy surface of the track. "I was going to breeze them," Blackburn said, watching the progress of his horses around the track, "but it's a swamp out there, so I just told the boys to gallop them out a mile and a half." He waited until the riders eased up and came trotting past us, then nodded and turned away. "They both moved all right. Come on."

On the drive back to his shedrow in Barn 33, the last in a long line of stables, we passed several cars, their headlights still on, heading for the track. "The clockers for the racing forms," Blackburn said, with a little smile. "If they want to time *my* workouts, they'll have to make it a little faster. I'm up at a quarter of four every morning, seven days a week."

I had been introduced to Blackburn by a friend a couple of weeks earlier in the grandstand at Aqueduct, where the horses were then racing, and I had asked him if I could hang around with him for a few days. Like most horseplayers, I had never been behind the scenes of a racetrack. I had been losing and at last I had become curious about what was going on back there. I thought I might learn something that might rouse me out of my slump. Blackburn had a small public stable and had been working around the New York tracks for about a dozen years. He was a small, trim-looking man of about fifty with a complexion reddened by outdoor work and set off by a pair of sharp blue eyes. He had a strong, square-jawed face and short, iron-gray hair. "I hope I can help you out," he had said. "And my name is Bob."

It didn't matter what he said his name was, because his wife, Rosemary, called him Robert and everybody else called him Pinky. His nickname should have been Swifty, because he flitted from task to task like a hummingbird, never remaining in one place for more than a few minutes at a time. Born in New York of English-Irish descent, he came from a long line of horsemen and had begun in the game as a rider. "I wasn't a good jockey," he explained. "It takes a special kind of touch to be a race rider, and apart from the weight problem when I got older, I just didn't have it."

I asked him at that first meeting how he liked being a trainer and he had looked away from me, as if trying for the first time to sort it out in his head. "A horse can injure himself a hundred different ways, and when you don't have too many horses—well, I can't complain," he had answered tentatively, then turned back to face me. "Hell, you know, it's my life, not just a living."

At the time I first latched up with Blackburn, he was trying to bring Lake Moreau up to her first race. He had bought her for his wife and his main owner, a man named Lou Doherty, for a modest price of thirty-five hundred dollars at the Saratoga Yearling Sales, but due to a series of minor injuries she had suffered, he had so far been unable to get her to the races. "As a two-year-old, she showed brilliant speed," he'd explained, "but I don't know. Her daddy, Bolero, was a pretty good sprinter, but the most you could expect now would be a useful horse. She ought to win a race or two, and I hope she does, because we've got too much money tied up in her." He added that he expected to run her in about ten days.

Around the stables that first morning, the atmosphere had changed considerably since my arrival. The sky had cleared completely, and the first faint rays of sunlight were striking the shingled roofs of the barns and slanting down across the dark-green sides and windows trimmed in white. It was cold and still damp, but the prospect of a fine spring day seemed to have brought the entire park to life. All around me there was a constant coming and going of people and horses: exercise boys in white-and-red crash helmets receiving instructions, mounting and riding off toward the training track; grooms, many of them black, leading horses into and out of the barns; trainers, on horseback and on foot, moving and talking in a solid, purposeful way.

At the entrance of Barn 33, Blackburn introduced me to his groom, a slender, gentle-eyed black in his late teens named Willie Washington, who, he said, was going to be a fine horseman one day, if he stuck with it. Willie smiled, then he and Blackburn went over and conferred with the exercise boys, who had just ridden up on Lake Moreau and Roadtown. Both fillies were medium-sized and chestnut-colored, and if Roadtown had not been wearing rundown bandages on her hind legs, I would have had a hard time telling them apart. After the boys had gone, Blackburn and Willie came back toward the barn leading the horses. "Stay on our left," Blackburn called out. "That way you won't get kicked."

In front of the stalls, the trainer glanced back at me. "Have you ever walked a horse?" he asked.

"No."

"You're going to now," he said, handing me Lake Moreau's bridle. I must have looked pale, because he added: "Don't worry, she's gentle enough. Stay on her left and give her enough room so she won't step on you. I've got to cool her out. My wife can't make it this morning, and I've got two other horses to take care of."

I spent the next forty minutes walking Lake Moreau counter-clockwise inside the shedrow. The horse seemed oblivious of me, though on one go-around somebody else's old selling plater stuck a head out of his bin and nipped me on the shoulder as I went past, probably because, in my city clothes, I must have seemed totally out of place. I needn't have felt self-conscious, however, because everyone in the barn was much too busy to even notice me. Down at one end, several grooms were sponging off their horses to the pounding beat of a radio blaring rock-and-roll.

After the horses had finally cooled out and been returned to their stalls, Blackburn, who had been occupied till then mostly with a wicked-looking filly named Falconine, went right to work on Roadtown. "We call this 'doing a horse up,' " he explained. "It includes everything you do, from sponging and currycombing to medication and protective bandaging." Roadtown, however, seemed anything but appreciative of his care. She bobbed her head up and down, fidgeted nervously from side to side, tried to reach back and bite, and once or twice tentatively struck out with a hind hoof, but the trainer anticipated her every move and continued nimbly with his chores, talking steadily and softly to her: "Now, mommy, you take it easy. This isn't going to hurt. Oh, look at you—mud from your ears to your toes. Now did that hurt? Did it? Oh, I know you. I know you like to be left alone. This won't take long now." Once, to avoid a particularly vicious kick, he was forced to grab her tail and leap to one side. "Hey now," he said, not raising his voice or pausing in his work, "what were you going to do, mommy? Kill me?"

When he had finished with her, Blackburn patted her affection-ately and gave her a carrot and a lump of sugar, then walked over to see how Willie was making out with Lake Moreau.

"This could be dangerous work," I observed.

Blackburn shrugged. "Not if you know what you're doing," he said. "Horses are like you and me, they have quirks. Roadtown hates being fussed over; she's very high-strung and wants to be left alone. This filly, on the other hand, a child of five could handle. But it's the nervous ones that can really run, and I wish she had a little more temper in her. Of course, some of them are real mean. You take that Falconine, for instance. She's crazy. And she can hate. You got to watch her all the time. Last week my wife walked her past that radio down there, when they had the music on, and she damn near tore the barn down."

"Maybe she's a critic," I said.

"In bringing one of these horses up to a race," Blackburn continued, gazing at Lake Moreau, "you have to be careful. Up to a point, you can train on a schedule, but as he actually nears racing condition, a horse, like a prizefighter, becomes even more of an individual, and what you do with him depends on how he's eating, how he looks. It's a delicate business, especially with fillies. One workout too many, a filly will blow her top and you can't catch her with a net. The main thing with a horse is to instill enough confidence into him and not abuse him, if you can help it. As long as you don't make the same mistake twice, you're all right."

We stopped by the track kitchen for a cup of coffee, then spent the next couple of hours running what Blackburn assured me were routine errands: he visited the stable of another public trainer from whom Blackburn tried to wangle a stall for an incoming colt; chased down an itinerant electrician and arranged to have him fix some faulty wiring at Falconine's end of the barn; asked one of the track veterinarians to come by and have a look at some horse's shins; stopped by a notary public and had some ownership papers notarized; haggled with a salesman over the price of a saddle; bought liniment for Lake Moreau's ankles. Blackburn seemed to move with unhurried nonchalance, but it was at the speed of light; by ten-thirty we were back at Barn 33 to supervise the feeding of the horses.

Of all the daily hazards of training, none, Blackburn informed me as we watched Roadtown nibble listlessly at her food, is as frustrating as getting a horse to eat properly. "You feed them three or four times a day," he said, "and you try to get ten quarts of grain and twenty pounds of hay into them, plus supplements—carrots, vitamins. Every trainer has his own pet ideas, of course. One fellow in this barn gives his horses honey every day, but the main thing is to get them to eat at all. When they're training hard, they're all wound up and too tense to eat. That phrase 'He eats like a horse' is okay for people, but it doesn't apply to horses."

Although it had become a balmy spring day, the stable, with its damp dirt floor and dark stalls, still held some of the earlier chill, and after a while, I left Blackburn to his chores and went outside. I sat down in a battered wooden chair and leaned back against the wall of the barn, feeling as if I had already put in a full working day.

I had been there only a few minutes when a rugged-looking man of about forty rode up on a roan pony, dismounted and walked briskly past me into the barn, spurs jingling. I smiled at him, but he barely acknowledged me with a cold, appraising glance, and I looked away in embarrassment.

I was just dozing off in the sun a few minutes later when the man suddenly reappeared with Blackburn, who could hardly contain his glee. Somewhat sheepishly, the newcomer introduced himself to me as Sid Watters, a trainer also berthed in Barn 33. "Pinky here told me you were all right," he said in a mild southern accent. "I saw you settin' there and I thought you were one of those goons from the Labor Relations Board. We had one of them around the barns a couple of weeks ago stirrin' up the help. Damn fool thinks we all ought to work an eight-hour day. Hell, this ain't a factory, I told him. We got animals here and we got to care for them. Mister, you're lucky Pinky told me who you were. I was goin' to pretend I didn't see you and dump a bucket of water on you."

"Sid's been having his troubles, like all of us," Blackburn added. "What help there is is hard to keep, when you consider that we all put in a fourteen-hour day. You can't just drop everything and walk away from a barn at some set hour. You have to have some feeling for the animals. If you don't have a feeling for them, you shouldn't be in racing at all." He glanced at his watch. "Come on, let's get out to the farm."

The farm turned out to be an old stable in one corner of somebody else's ten acres of pasture and woodland, about fifteen miles east of Belmont off the Jericho Turnpike, a heavily traveled truck route dotted with traffic lights and lined with used-car lots and gas stations. However, once we turned off the turnpike and arrived at the property itself, the setting became rustic and the city seemed distant. A narrow driveway, flanked by old trees and thick hedges, led directly to the front of the stable, beyond which I could see a large open field and the unbroken mass of a wood.

As we arrived, a slender, attractive blonde appeared in the doorway, followed by a canine welcoming committee consisting of a couple of Airedales and assorted spaniels. She introduced herself to me above the general ululation as Rosemary Blackburn. She was dressed in faded blue jeans and a man's shirt, and she was holding a pitchfork. Behind her, I could see a runway and a short line of empty stalls, and I had the sudden insane idea that this was all there was—that she and her husband lived in them. It wouldn't have surprised me, but I was set straight almost at once. "I'm sorry you find me like this," Mrs. Blackburn said, "but we have to clean out these stalls before lunch. Go around to the apartment and pour yourself a drink while Robert and I finish up here."

I left the Blackburns surrounded by leaping dogs and let myself into the apartment, which consisted of three tiny rooms at the rear of the stable. They were simply but comfortably furnished, and the chief decoration was a large framed photograph of one of Blackburn's past successes—a stakes-winning filly named Pocahontas. Two armchairs contained sleeping cats, and as I poured myself a whiskey, another cat emerged from under a table and stretched himself against my legs. Through a window I could see a colt trotting nervously around a large pen, and I began to have the feeling that, deprived of animals to care for, the Blackburns wouldn't know what to do with themselves.

I went outside again just as the trainer passed me under a staggering load of refuse, and I walked around to the front where Mrs. Blackburn was energetically forking huge loads of fresh hay into the stalls. "How many animals do you have around the place?" I asked.

"Oh, it varies," she said cheerfully. "Right now, I think we have five cats, but only four dogs. And the horses, of course. We've had as many as eight or nine dogs, you know, and we used to have a goat. We're stuck, I guess. We don't have any children, so we have animals."

After nearly an hour of work around the stalls, we went back inside, and Blackburn poured us all stiff drinks while Rosemary cooked lunch. I asked him what the afternoon would hold in store, and he explained that he would leave the farm at about one and drive in to Aqueduct, where he would try to enter Lake Moreau in a race, providing he could find one for her in the new *Condition Book*, a small pamphlet published every ten days by the New York Racing Association that listed the conditions of all the races to be run during that period. (Horses generally compete in their own categories, segregated by age, sex, distances to be run, number of races won and against what level of competition.) He would probably watch the first five or six races, then return to Belmont and his horses again. Most of the morning tasks would have to be repeated and the horses would have to be closely observed. "They'll tell me tonight how they worked," he said. "If there's anything wrong, they'll find a way of letting me know." He would be home by seven, have a few drinks, dinner, and then fall asleep by eight or nine, perhaps in front of his TV.

I remarked that he might as well be living a thousand miles from the city, since it seemed to have no direct influence on his personal life, and he agreed. "Rosemary and I don't get to town more than two or three times a year, usually in the fall," he said, "and then only to shop a bit and take in a couple of shows before we head south for the winter."

We were beautifully relaxed and about to eat lunch when the colt outside began to act up, neighing and tossing his handsome head angrily as he raced back and forth in his pen. Rosemary hurriedly put the food on the table and went out to him. "There's a filly in season next door," Blackburn explained. "It drives him wild." After fifteen or twenty minutes of wheedling, Rosemary succeeded in calming the animal and leading him into his stall, away from the atmosphere of potential romance. We then sat down and ate a large and excellent lunch, which Blackburn washed down with five or six flagons of ale and several cups of coffee.

Dazed by lack of sleep, an excess of fresh air and all that food and drink, I might have fallen asleep in my chair, but no sooner had Blackburn drained his last cup of coffee than he was on his feet. "Come on," he said, reaching for his jacket and heading for the door, "we'd better get over to Aqueduct."

Reluctantly, I rose and thanked Rosemary for her hospitality. She smiled understandingly. "Don't mind Robert," she said. "If any of our horses could move as fast as he can, we'd be millionaires."

A couple of weeks later, Lake Moreau showed up among the entries for the second race at Aqueduct, a six-furlong sprint for maiden fillies, and I went out to see how she'd do. Blackburn had told me earlier he didn't expect her to win, but was hoping she'd finish no more than five or six lengths behind the winner. Then, if she showed any ability at all, he'd drop her into an easier claiming race against cheaper horses and pop for the purse. (Most races, even at major racetracks, are "claiming" races, which means that the horses in them can be bought for their predetermined claiming price *before* the race goes off. The new owner acquires the horse *after* the race, even if the animal breaks down or dies during it. It's a way of allowing less talented animals to win purses, since obviously no one would risk a top horse for a claiming tag.) "She has the inside post," Blackburn had told me over the phone, "which isn't too good for a young horse. They get a lot of dirt kicked up in their faces in there, and some of them won't take it. But if the jock gets her out of the gate, she ought to do all right."

Sitting in a box with Blackburn over the finish line, while waiting for the first race to go off, I began to identify with the trainer, who was obviously tense. After arriving from Belmont, he had stopped by the receiving barn to make sure that everything was all right, then spent the next hour dashing about as usual, greeting people and drinking coffee. As long as he had been able to keep moving, he had seemed his normal agile self, but once immobilized in a chair, he had become silent. He was sure Lake Moreau wouldn't win, but like the producer of a Broadway-bound turkey, he couldn't help hoping for a miracle.

After the first race, a dull gallop for aging platers, we left the box and took an elevator to the ground floor, underneath the stands, where we joined a group of people standing by a ramp down which the horses would be led on their way to the paddock. While we waited, I looked at my program. Lake Moreau was one of ten entries in the race and was listed in the morning line, the track's estimate of probable betting odds, at ten to one. The hot tip in the contest was Hula Lou, quoted at six to one, but I had figured it was anybody's race and some of Blackburn's secret hope began to rub off on me.

When the horses filed down the ramp, led by their grooms, we followed them out into the paddock, which at Aqueduct was small and graceless and directly in front of the stands. Willie, resplendent in a scarlet windbreaker, walked Lake Moreau around and around the little ring with the other horses, trying to keep his filly moving and relaxed. Blackburn and I went over to the saddling stall and waited. Above us, several lines of hard-eyed speculators peered down at the activity, and behind us the electric tote board flashed the changing odds. Lake Moreau was now twenty to one. "Jesus, I hate this paddock," Blackburn said suddenly. "It's too damn small and too exposed. Some horse'll go crazy in here and kill five or six people one day."

About twenty minutes before post time, the grooms led their horses into the stalls, and the trainers set about saddling them. "All right, mommy," Blackburn said, "here we go now." He heaved a saddle onto Lake Moreau's back, tightened the cinch, checked the bit, the bridle and the stirrups. The jockeys, looking like Christmas decorations in their brightly colored silks, appeared from under the stands and fanned out toward their horses. Blackburn hastily made one more check of the equipment and patted Lake Moreau's neck, then turned to talk to his rider, a veteran named William Boland.

The jockey had a sharp, serious face with high cheekbones and a strong, prominent nose. He seemed tall and rather thin for a race rider, but he exuded an air of quiet professionalism that inspired confidence. Blackburn wasted no time on formalities. "She'll break good," he instructed him. "Give her her head and let her run, but don't abuse her; she may need the race. At about the three-eighths pole, give her a rap to keep her from bearing out. She's a nice filly and she'll give you whatever she's got."

Boland nodded and cast a quick, appraising glance at Lake Moreau. We chatted briefly about the weather and then the voice of the paddock judge rang out: "Riders up!" Blackburn gave Boland a leg up into the saddle and stepped aside. Lake Moreau took her place at the head of the line, and the horses moved out toward the track. We stood by the stall and watched them go. A drunk in shirtsleeves leaned over the rail as Boland passed and shouted, "Hey, ya bum, wake up for a change!"

"Well, I hope she beats at least one horse," Blackburn said, as we started back toward the elevators. "My wife can't stand it if I finish last."

Back in our seats, Blackburn picked up a huge pair of binoculars and followed the progress of the horses as they jogged slowly toward the starting gate, directly across the infield from us. "She's moving all right," he said, in a low, tight voice. "Yes, she's moving all right." When the horses reached the gate and began to file into their stalls, I stole a quick glance at the odds. Lake Moreau was now forty to one. The favorite was something called Holy Catfish, but the late money was going on Hula Lou. She had dropped to two to one and appeared to be the one to beat.

The start of the race was sloppy, as it often is with inexperienced horses. A longshot named Amber Sport broke through the gate and had to be brought back and eased into position again. "That's not too good," Blackburn said, still glued to his glasses. "She could fall asleep. She's standing in there like an old lead pony." Then there was an interminable moment as the horses seemed to strain against the barrier, poised for flight, and Blackburn moved to the edge of his seat. "Don't look at me, sweetheart," he murmured through clenched teeth. "Look straight ahead." When at last the gate opened and the animals burst into the clear, Blackburn jumped, then sank back into his seat. Lake Moreau had broken next to last.

She ran there all the way around, not making up any ground and not losing any, but she was at least twenty lengths behind the winner at the end. "I thought she was going to finish last," Blackburn said, standing up. "Come on." On our way out of the box, I stole a glance at the winning numbers; Hula Lou had come in second behind the favorite.

We rushed down to the paddock and watched Lake Moreau come back, sweaty and excited at last. Willie went out to meet her and Boland dismounted, unsaddled her and passed us on his way to the weigh-in scales. "She ran all right," he said, without enthusiasm. "But after what you told me about her breaking fast, I was up over her ears when the gate opened. She's not too green, I guess, but the dirt bothered her plenty."

Out on the track, Willie was now leading Lake Moreau away toward the receiving barn and we watched them go. He would cool her out there for half an hour or so; then she would be vanned back to Belmont and cooled out some more. I asked Blackburn what his plans for her were. He lit a cigarette and shook his head. "I don't know," he said. "I'll try to run her back in about ten days. I don't want to crowd her too much." He took two puffs and threw the cigarette on the ground, grinding it out with the toe of his shoe. "That was a bad race she ran, a real bad race," he said. "I just hope she comes out of it all right, that's all. Because in this business any day you get by without an accident is a good day."

5

EARS

Question: "What's the definition of a dead heat?"
Answer: "Two touts trying to borrow money off one another at the
same time."

THE TROUBLE with my friend Bender is that he can't stop listening to tips. He's been going to the racetrack for over forty years and still can't keep his ears shut. It's a weakness that has degenerated into a major hazard, because Bender would rather bet his money on a horse race than do anything else, except possibly breathe. In the mornings Bender hustles insurance for a living and in the evenings he's a devoted husband and father, but in the afternoons he's at the track. This has kept him in a permanent state of financial disarray and periodically puts a strain on his marriage, but it also provides him with those occasional golden days no one who goes to the races can ever forget—a handful of winners, some longshot coming in from out of the clouds, a giant daily double. And someday, Bender knows, just as surely as he knows the moon will wax and wane, he'll hit the ultimate Pick Six, a parlay wager in which the bettor tries to pick the winners of six consecutive races. It's about as easy to do with a modestly priced ticket as hitting the lottery, but the pots can be huge, up to a million dollars, and Bender is convinced he'll do it and be wafted above the herd into the ranks of the leisure class. If only the people he meets at the track, all those touts and hard knockers he knows, would stop telling him things.

It isn't as if Bender doesn't understand the game. He has few illusions left about it; he knows what the percentages are and that almost everyone who bets on horses loses. He likes to quote that old adage about being able to beat a particular race, but not the races. Betting into the house vigorish, the minimum of fifteen percent that is cut out of every wager, is like putting your money into a meatgrinder; folding green goes in and shredded parimutuel tickets come out. Bender knows this, but he doesn't let it discourage him. Like most horseplayers, he's the kind of person who believes he could fly, if he'd just flap his arms hard enough.

Bender likes to get to the track early, at least an hour before the first post. This gives him time to pick up the late scratches and jockey changes and make last-minute adjustments to his calculations. On a recent day not too long ago he showed up at Hollywood Park and allowed me to tag along after him, on the promise that I wouldn't use his real name in anything I might write about him. He seemed confident and he was feeling lucky, mainly because he'd sold a couple of medical policies that morning to a pair of ancients anxious to supplement their Medicare cards.

After parking his 1982 Toyota, a battered survivor of the L.A. freeways, in the lot reserved for trainers and owners, he swept into the premises by flashing a borrowed pass. (By the start of every race meet Bender has inevitably accumulated enough passes and parking stickers from his friends and touts in the grandstand to admit him into any part of the track, except possibly the Directors' Room.) Bender likes to start out in the Turf Club, which is for members only, partly because he likes to be right over the finish line so he can separate the noses in a photo without having to wait for the official picture. He wears a large pair of cheap binoculars like a yoke around his neck and reading glasses readily available in his left breast pocket. After all the years he has spent hunched over the tiny print of the *Daily Racing Form*, the horseplayer's Torah, Bender's eyes are not what they used to be.

The Turf Club is a beautiful scene, and it always warms Bender's heart to be there. Inside there's a comfortable dining area, a large bar and plenty of servile attendants. Glamour, style, chic, entrenched wealth, all conditions of life Bender aspires to and one day expects to achieve. Outside, the seats are directly over the track, one level above the grandstand boxes where most of the owners and trainers hang out. There are rows of tables where members can eat lunch and drink as they watch the action, but Bender never lingers there. It is customary to grease the headwaiter for a decent table, and Bender's whole style is to avoid all expenses not directly connected to the immediate business at hand, which is the selection of winners.

He began, as usual, by checking the scratches and jockey changes with the information in his program, then studied his *Form* closely for about ten minutes. He glanced at the tote board to bring himself up to date on the odds, and then he went outside to watch the horses in the first race come out onto the track. It was now about twelve minutes to post time and he'd been unable to make a firm selection in the first, so he decided to sniff around for what he calls "the edge," a useful tidbit of information from some person he respects that might enable him to locate the winner.

He walked down a flight of stairs into the grandstand area and almost immediately bumped into his friend Sid, another regular. Sid is fat, about fifty, wears brightly colored Hawaiian sports shirts and crepe-soled shoes. "The first is a bunch of broken-down cheap speed horses which you don't know whose turn it is," he told Bender, "but I heard that the four horse in the second is gonna go wire to wire."

Bender checked his *Form* and liked what he saw. The four horse in the second was a seven-year-old named Exotic Eagle, a veteran who had won eleven of fifty races lifetime and who had plenty of speed to get the lead. The only question about him was whether he was in form to do so, but he had won his most recent effort against similar competition, so Bender allowed himself to believe he would repeat, even though these old campaigners at the lower levels of the sport tend to be inconsistent. Bender went to a betting window and wheeled the six horses in the first race in ten-dollar doubles to Exotic Eagle in the second, then went outside to watch the first race.

One of his wheel horses came in at odds of nine to two, so now he had a pretty good double going, as Exotic Eagle figured to be a good price. Bender went back downstairs and permitted himself a sandwich and a cup of coffee, but then he began to worry because the odds on Exotic Eagle remained pegged at five to two. Bender reasoned that if his horse were as hot as he was supposed to be, his odds would have come down significantly. But then he told himself that he was indulging in bettor's paranoia. Just because the crowd seemed to be betting heavily on an outsider called Jogarob didn't mean his horse wouldn't win. Bender hadn't even considered Jogarob, who had drawn an unfavorable outside post position at the distance, was being ridden by an unsung apprentice and was trained by somebody he'd never heard of. He told himself that his double was all but banked, and he estimated he'd be two hundred dollars ahead after he cashed his winning ticket.

He was wrong. When the gate opened, Exotic Eagle showed brief speed, then disappeared. Jogarob bounced home first, at half his morning-line odds. Somebody had hit and hit big. Why had he listened to Sid? Having seen the action on the winner, Bender figured he should have bet a saver on him. The mustard on Bender's sandwich had begun to taste of bitter almonds. He was out sixty dollars and there was no way he could salvage it, either from the televised running of the New England Classic at Rockingham Park, a five-horse field dominated by two heavy favorites, or the third at Hollywood, a sprint for three-year-old maiden fillies with another obvious favorite. He went back to the Turf Club bar to admire the wealthy at play.

The so-called Merry Widows were all there, seated just beyond the edge of the bar, gigglers all. They are women in their middle years whose husbands have died or faded in the stretch, and they come to the track once a week, every Saturday, to bet tiny bits and pieces of their inherited loot on horses with cute names or on jockeys whose looks are darling. They also work variations on complicated betting systems based on astrological forecasts. Bender always knows when they've backed a winner, because they shriek like banshees. They did some screaming that afternoon, after the third race, when a ten-to-one shot named Northrops Bid ran second, thus providing the group with a nice exacta payoff.

Northrops Bid had been the first horse Bender had eliminated from his calculations as a possible contender.

Bender now went back to scanning the *Form*. He decided, first of all, to put in a small Pick Six, going three horses deep in the fourth so as to be reasonably sure of staying in action at least for a while. As he was sitting at the bar, making out his ticket, Goat passed him on his way to the windows to make some bets for a seated group of ancients too arthritic to heave themselves out of their chairs to wager. Goat got his nickname because he looks and smells like one. He likes to run errands for people because he usually picks up tips that way. Now, on his way back from a teller and just as Bender was preparing to make his own bet, he stopped by to confide in us. "They're playing the Robbins colt," he murmured, with a wink.

Bender again consulted his *Form*. The Robbins colt, Duke's Cup, was not one of his three horses. He had used the favorite, Silver Circus, a gelding named Green's Leader and a longshot named Broke the Mold. He had decided against Duke's Cup because he suspected the horse was unsound; it had once raced against much better animals but was in here for a claiming tag. Nevertheless, Bender decided Goat might be on to something, so he revised his Pick Six ticket by substituting Duke's Cup for Green's Leader, who was trained by a man Bender considered "a needle guy," someone who liked to inject sore horses with cortisone and other drugs, some legal, some not.

Duke's Cup ran out of the money and Green's Leader won the race, which meant that Bender was now out eighty-four dollars and dead in the Pick Six. He no longer felt quite so lucky, but there were still five races to go, and he informed me that he had never been a whiz in the early races anyway. He stuck his rolled-up *Form* into his pocket and wandered back into the grandstand area, taking up a position near one of the odds boards.

He was soon joined there by Beverly, a cocktail waitress at a poker club in Gardena; Harris, another insurance salesman; Wally, a pensioned high-school administrator; and Hugh, the ex-owner of a failed savings and loan who lived with his mother in a Pasadena mansion.

The friends did not greet each other with an excess of joy

because there wasn't a winner in the group. To make conversation Bender asked Beverly why she had failed to put in an appearance all week. "I was in Vegas," Beverly explained, "with Willie." Everybody nodded. Willie, a real-estate tycoon, had been Beverly's boyfriend for several years, ever since he'd picked her up one afternoon in the Santa Anita clubhouse. Willie was married to a woman who looked, according to Harris, "like a broad who's been hit in the mouth with a mashie." But he had no intention of getting a divorce, so he and Beverly got together once or twice a week and took occasional "business" trips. Nobody liked Willie, who was arrogant and considered Beverly's track pals a bunch of losers, but he was tolerated because everyone liked Beverly. She had wonderful legs and a great laugh, like the whoop of an amorous loon.

Silence reigned momentarily as the comrades studied their stats and tout sheets. It was broken by the arrival of Morris, a rich doctor who specializes in treating the ailments of elderly Jewish housewives wealthier even than he. He informed the group that he had so far won every race. Furthermore, he couldn't understand how Bender and his friends could have failed to pick each race as accurately as he. "That last one was easy," he said. "With McCarron up, how could he lose? And three to one was a great price on that horse."

He was swept away on a tidal backwash of loathing. "Someday I'm going to kick him very hard in the shins," Bender said, but Wally soothed him. "Don't let Morris get to you," he said. "He hasn't had a loser since 1966." Everyone knew exactly what Wally meant. Morris never bets less than five or six horses in every race, which means that he can come out of a day with six winners and a net loss. Still, it was aggravating to have to listen to him.

Bender decided to pass the fifth race, a sprint for two-year-old maiden fillies that figured to be won by an odds-on favorite. The last time Bender ever bet on a green two-year-old going off at that kind of price was sometime back in the Nixon era, and he was not going to make that sort of mistake ever again. He watched the favorite romp home on a TV monitor, then turned his attention to the sixth, another distance race on the turf. And now, at last, he came up with a winner.

Seattle Symphony, Bender's selection, scored for him at $19.20 for every two dollars wagered, making Bender a tiny winner on the day. Best of all, Bender had picked the horse himself, without asking for or listening to anyone else's opinion. From the statistics in his *Racing Form*, he had guessed that the horse would run well on the grass. I suggested that he might consider sticking to his own picks in future, and Bender agreed with me, but no sooner had he begun to look at the seventh than he was accosted by Snaps, one of the more aggressive of the grandstand touts. Snaps makes a living by acquiring information he then passes on to players who presumably will reward him if his tips win. He's a jumpy little man who wears garish sports jackets with ballpoints and odd bits of paper stuffed into his pockets. He has thin gray hair, watery brown eyes and seems to be in motion even when he's standing still, as if afraid someone may be gaining on him. He leaned in toward Bender and glanced quickly around, then whispered, "Big Wheels Rollin is money in the bank. I got that from a friend of the owner not ten minutes ago!" And he scurried away after another potential client.

"You know, I was going to bet that horse," Bender said, "but now I wouldn't touch him with a ten-foot pole." He went to the window and bet twenty dollars to win on Dark Ice, the favorite.

Big Wheels Rollin won, paying $13.40, while Dark Ice finished third. Bender was beside himself. "How could that be?" he said. "I was gonna bet him and then, just because Snaps liked him, too, I backed off him. There's no justice, none, in horse racing or anything else. How do you like that?"

I didn't like it much either, because I had also bet on Dark Ice, but I had to agree with Bender on the subject of justice. As we were standing there, commiserating with each other, Harris appeared beside us, frothing with rage. "Did you see that?" he said. "That fuckin' Gary Stevens pulled the favorite, wouldn't let him run a step, the little crook!"

I had seen no evidence of foul play and neither had Bender, but Harris, who has a low paranoia threshold, knew better. "These little gangsters!" he said. "These little Shakespearean actors! You ever see anything like it? That was a boat race out there! They ought to call it a regatta, and they should equip the jockeys with paddles instead of whips! You ever see anything like that? Did you? It's horrible even to look at, the little crooks!" And he rushed away to spread the news to a more receptive audience.

Matters did not improve in the eighth race. Bender's horse, Apollo, finished second, which made him a loser again on the day, to the tune of about seventy dollars. Bender's dream of a big day had faded, and now his sole concern became finding a winner in the ninth to bail him out.

Bender's horse in the ninth, a cheap sprint for California-bred maidens, the worst horses on the grounds, was Northern Bounty, who had drawn the extreme outside post, a liability, but had already shown some talent and was being ridden by Bender's favorite jockey, Patrick Valenzuela. Bender intended to bet the horse straight and box him in exactas with the morning-line favorite, George's Buster, and a six-to-one shot named Stanley Dard. All Northern Bounty would have to do is finish first or second to either of these two horses, and Bender would cash a nice ticket. The only question in Bender's mind was how wide Northern Bounty would have to go around the turn, but he decided that his rider's considerable skills would keep his horse from being fanned. As he headed for a betting window, Bender's confidence in his selection soared and he determined not only to get out of his losing day but to make some real money doing it. He was going to bet fifty dollars to win on his horse and forty additional dollars in the exactas.

As he was standing in line, waiting to make his bet, Bender was accosted again by the ubiquitous Snaps. "I told you," the tout declared. "Did you bet the eighth horse in the seventh?"

"No," Bender answered. "I didn't like him."

Snaps shook his head. "Boy, it's hard to help you guys," he said. "What are you doing here?"

Bender told him.

"Northern Bounty?" Snaps said, looking distressed. "I hear he's real sore. But I got a big push on the eight horse." And he flitted away to peddle his information elsewhere.

Bender again consulted his *Form*. The stats told him that the eight horse, Beyond Success, had no chance, but he also noted that the odds on the horse had dropped from twelve to one down to four to one. Somebody knew something, and in these cheap maiden races inside information sometimes paid off. So Bender decided to vary his action. Instead of backing up his straight bet on Northern Bounty in the place hole, as he had planned to do, he now added Beyond Success to his exacta play, boxing him with his selection.

"Your problem, Bender, is you've got rabbit ears," I said. "You listen to everyone."

"Well, he was right about that other horse, wasn't he?" my friend answered. "Besides, backing up horses in the place hole is basically a dumb thing to do. If my horse finishes at least second to any of the three others in this race, I stand to make some money."

On his way out to watch the race, Bender encountered Beverly, who looked distressed and needed a winner as badly as he. Bender told her about Northern Bounty. "I'm going to box him with Jake the Red," Beverly said, indicating a nineteen-to-one shot Bender had long ago dismissed from his mind.

"Jake the Red has no chance," he informed Beverly.

"The bartender told me he'd run good," she said.

"That's why the guy is a bartender," Bender explained. "If he knew anything, why is he tending bar?"

This reasoning failed to shake Beverly, who rushed away to make her bets. Bender and I went out into the grandstand to watch the race just as the horses were being loaded into the starting gate. Bender was feeling very confident. "No way this horse runs worse than second," he said.

He was right. Northern Glance did have to go wide on the turn, but Valenzuela brought him in a strong second. The only trouble was that of Bender's three exacta horses, only Stanley Dard did any running, finishing third. The winner was Jake the Red.

Without a word, Bender turned away and headed for the exits. As he passed the corner of the clubhouse bar, Beverly came running up to him and threw her arms around his neck. "Oh, my God, I'm rich!" she said. "Thanks for giving me that horse!"

"That's okay," Bender mumbled, his tongue apparently encased in some sort of fuzzy sweater.

Beverly looked at him in alarm. "Jeez, Bennie," she said, "you didn't play my horse? You know, you really should cool it for a while. You look terrible."

"I'm about to kill myself," Bender said, "but otherwise I'm all right."

So I watched Bender walk alone out of Hollywood Park that day through the usual sea of losing tickets, crumpled programs and soiled newspapers. After descending the stairs toward the parking lots, he stopped long enough to buy the next day's *Form*. He snapped the paper open as he walked and began to study the next day's entries. And suddenly, like all of us who go to the races regularly, he began to feel lucky all over again.

It's hard not to listen to information at the track. I try to have what my friend Sam calls stone ears, but it isn't easy, especially when some horse you do hear about comes bouncing in. I remember going out to Belmont Park one afternoon and deciding not to bet on a colt called Tronidor, going for the first time on the turf at a distance of seven furlongs, longer than he had ever run before. An acquaintance of mine urged me to risk a couple of dollars on him, at odds of better than thirty to one; he'd heard the horse was live. I knew better, because I had asked Pinky Blackburn, his trainer, what he thought of his colt's chances. "I don't know how he'll like the grass," the trainer said, "but I do know it's too long for him."

Tronidor not only won the race, but established a new track record for the distance. So much for stone ears.

6

THE SPORT OF STARS

Owner to trainer: "All you do is give me bad news about my horse. Can't you think of anything positive to say?"
Trainer to owner: "Well, you've got partners."

IT WAS in Europe that horse racing became known as the sport of kings, a tradition that was perpetuated in this country by our own patrician families—the Vanderbilts, Whitneys, Phippses, the aristocracy of the East. In southern California, however, the nobles who began to own and breed Thoroughbreds came from the unlanded gentry of celluloid. When Doc Strub opened his fancy new racetrack, he understood that to be successful he'd have to draw the movie celebrities to his emporium. This turned out to be fairly easy to do, because already on the scene as horse owners were Clark Gable and Bing Crosby, while others—Joe E. Brown, Walt Disney, Sam Goldwyn, Pat O'Brien, George Raft, Oliver Hardy—bought season boxes or became regulars. Charlie Chaplin used to drop in to bet two dollars at a time, while Mickey Rooney and Jimmy Durante wagered thousands, usually with disastrous results. In 1935, Louis B. Mayer, then head mogul at MGM, Hollywood's richest and most powerful studio, began to build a great racing stable and others soon followed. All that is required of a horse owner is plenty of loot and a compulsion to spend it flamboyantly, a sine qua non of the town's traditional life style.

The celebrities took to racing with the same élan they lavished on multimillion-dollar epics, palatial estates, fast cars and dumb bed partners. If you've got it, baby, flaunt it, and the winner's circle, out there in front of the packed stands, was as good a place as any to do that.

Mayer spent a fortune on broodmares, stallions and horses of racing age, including a filly named Busher, the Ruffian of her era. His example proved irresistible, because everybody in Hollywood wanted either to please him or to beat him, at the box office, the card table or the track. In 1946, three of the favorites in the Santa Anita Handicap, the country's first one-hundred-thousand-dollar race, were owned by Hollywood types: Triplicate (Fred Astaire), War Valor (Howard Hawks) and Be Faithful (Mayer). Frank Sinatra and Basil Rathbone were observed strolling about the walking ring, chatting with the owners before the race, and among the boxholders in attendance that day were Bob Hope, Cary Grant, Edward G. Robinson, Randolph Scott, Bing Crosby, Don Ameche, Betty Grable and Harry James. The event was won by War Knight, an outsider owned by Ethel Hill, a screenwriter who had once spent all but fifteen dollars of her life savings to buy her first racehorse.

Mayer eventually sold out, but many of his horses were bought by the Hollywood people he'd first lured into the sport, including Harry Warner, who acquired a fine race mare called Honeymoon from him and won a lot of races with her. During the Mayer era, Greer Garson and her husband, E. E. (Buddy) Fogelson, a Texas oilman, launched a very successful stable, and she is still in racing. Harry James and Betty Grable, after a series of disappointments and costly failures, came up with a winner in Big Noise, a handsome chestnut who took the 1951 Del Mar Futurity. Fred Astaire, who had dabbled in racing off and on for years, came up with a bargain-basement triumph in Triplicate, a horse that had won only once in fifteen starts when the dancer bought him but won the Hollywood Gold Cup in 1946. Astaire had then imagined himself retired, but after his up-and-down experiences in racing he observed, "I probably should go back into the movies for a rest." He did.

Even more influential than Mayer on the local racing scene was Bing Crosby, who not only campaigned a large stable of his own but launched a new racetrack. Crosby was living in Rancho Santa Fe in 1937 when he heard that the people building facilities for a San Diego County Fair in Del Mar, which was to include a mile racetrack on the premises, had run out of money. The crooner quickly organized the Del Mar Turf Club, held an election for officers on the Warner Brothers lot in Burbank and signed a ten-year lease with the Fair people. The fact that this new racing entity had to lend its landlord the money to finish the facilities they had leased didn't phase the directors. Nothing ever ruffled Crosby, who had surrounded himself for the venture with such associates as Pat O'Brien, Oliver Hardy, Gary Cooper, Leo McCarey and Joe E. Brown, a well-heeled and glamorous array of plungers. By the time opening day came around, on July 3, 1937, a lot of the paint on the premises was still a little wet, but at least a roof had been put on the grandstand, and the horses were ready to run.

Crosby and O'Brien were on hand to greet the fifteen thousand people who showed up that first day. They went down to the turnstiles in person to check in the first arrivals. Crosby was dressed, as usual, in slacks, a floppy sports shirt and yachting cap, though he later donned a bright-blue blazer, white pants and a straw boater for the official opening ceremony in the infield. "We hope you all enjoy the meeting and have a measure of success at the payoff windows," he told the crowd in his fanciest informal style. No one even complained when one of Crosby's own horses won the first race.

Under the Crosby-O'Brien regime at Del Mar, the tactic adopted to lure the public was to turn out the celebrities, on the reasonable assumption that people would gawk first and bet later. It was the same technique that had worked at Santa Anita and would also help to launch Hollywood Park, in 1938. Crosby even broadcast a half-hour radio show from Del Mar every Saturday afternoon. He'd stroll about the grounds interviewing the patrons, then retire to the premises of the Jockey Club from where he'd belt out a couple of songs. Later, after the racing, large informal parties took place at the Jockey Club until the wee hours, with such entertainers on hand as Al Jolson, Danny Thomas, Tony Martin, the Ritz Brothers, Donald O'Connor and Jimmy Durante, who always demolished his quota of pianos every season. Paramount even put on the world premiere of Crosby's latest movie, *Sing, You Sinners*, at the track. It was a management style that established Del Mar as the most relaxed and enjoyable place to go racing in America.

The Hollywood involvement in southern California racing persists and has attracted all sorts of entrepreneurs to the sport, with varying degrees of success. Producers Quinn Martin, Danny Arnold and Ed Friendly have all raced successful stables, while others have poured money into the game for years and have little to show for it. The odds against anyone remaining healthily in the black in racing are heavy. The horses are too expensive and too fragile, the operating costs are too high, the tax incentives minimal. The smartest and toughest show-biz racetracker I ever met was the late Martin Ritt, who directed *Hud, Sounder* and a fistful of other fine movies. Perhaps this was because he came into the game the hard way, as a horseplayer during the nineteen-fifties, when he found himself the victim of the notorious Hollywood black list. "I was living in New York then. This was in the McCarthy era, and I couldn't work. I'd been accused of being a Communist, so nobody would hire me," he told me. "So I began going to the track. It didn't take me long to figure out that most of the people out there don't know much."

Ritt learned fast. He supported himself at the track for years as a bettor until he could get back to work as a director. When he became an owner, he approached it with the same tough-minded unsentimentality with which he'd plucked winners out of the *Racing Form* in order to pay the rent. He had what he called an iron ass and could sit in his box all day without making a single bet, if he had to, a discipline that kept him from squandering millions on expensively bred bums. He claimed and bought and bred horses at all levels, but got rid of the ones who didn't produce and had no more feeling for the animals themselves than a trader in commodities. When I once asked him why he never went to the backside to see his horses, he answered, "Why should I? They don't know me."

This attitude is hardly what the English would call sporting, but it's fairly characteristic of the new breed of Hollywood entrepreneur, most of whom can't tell the difference between Secretariat and Ed, the Talking Mule. Bruce McNall, for instance, looks about as at home around a racetrack as a gringo in a bean field.

He is a short, chunky forty-year-old who laughs frequently in a high-pitched giggle and wears expensive slacks and sports jackets. When he walks the length of his shedrow, he steps gingerly through the dust, straw and manure and gets no closer to his animals than a visitor to a zoo. By his own admission, the only conveyance he rides supremely well is his Rolls Royce. "When I first got into owning racehorses," he says, "I just wanted to have some fun, but it's gotten a little out of hand." Over the past decade he has poured millions into the sport, alone and with partners, only a part of which he has recouped in purse money and sales. "My trouble is, I can't get into anything halfway," he explains. "Once I took up horse racing, I got just as involved as I did in my business. It's the only way I can operate."

Such commitment has paid off handsomely for him in the past. As a teenager growing up in Arcadia, California, next door to Santa Anita, McNall went occasionally with schoolmates to the track, but his real love was coins, a passion that overwhelmed him when he was nine. At the age of twelve, McNall got a part-time job in a small coin shop and read everything he could get his hands on about numismatics. By the time he was in high school, he'd started his own business, buying and selling and reinvesting his profits to build up his stock.

McNall was seventeen when he became the purchaser at auction of the world's most valuable coin, the Athens Dekadrachma, for which he paid four hundred and twenty thousand dollars. The coin is one of two known specimens in the world and the only one in private hands. McNall's acquisition of it was a shrewdly calculated risk, because he had sixty days in which to pay, during which period he resold the coin at a sizable profit. Since then, his Beverly Hills firm, Numismatic Fine Arts, has grown into a fifty-million-dollar enterprise, a success that provided McNall with enough ready cash and time to devote to his new passion—owning, breeding and racing Thoroughbreds.

About fifteen years ago, McNall found himself at a numismatic convention in Miami that turned out to be "some kind of boring." He and a colleague escaped to the races at nearby Hialeah, picked a few winners and had a lot of fun. For the next couple of years, McNall took to dropping in at whichever local track happened to be open. One day, author Joseph Wambaugh and a restaurateur, who owned a cheap but speedy colt named Bull Rullah, introduced McNall to the horse's trainer, Lin Wheeler. A soft-spoken Westerner then in his mid-thirties, Wheeler had spent his whole life working on ranches and at racetracks. "I had nine million questions to ask him, most of them ridiculous," McNall remembers. "Mainly, I liked Lin and I felt that I could trust him. I told him to get me a horse I could have some fun with."

Good horsemen are essentially conservative. It took Wheeler nearly five months to find a suitable animal, a two-year-old colt named Ruggedness that McNall, caught up in the excitement of an auction, wound up paying fifty-one thousand dollars for. His original intention had been to spend about twenty thousand and risk perhaps another twelve thousand for yearly stable and training fees while racing his purchase. However, this was the only horse in the sale he and Wheeler had determined to acquire, and the showy give-and-take of the bidding had hardened McNall's resolve.

"Coin auctions are stuffy affairs, with people lifting a single finger in almost total silence," he later explained. "At a horse auction, it's loud and glary, with this living thing you want to buy right there in front of you. I decided it was really fun."

He promptly went out and bought two more animals for an additional eighty thousand. He also began to do some homework. "When I get involved in something, I read everything there is to read about it," he says. "Not only the *Daily Racing Form*, but breeding magazines. I began to realize that if you took the whole thing seriously, it could become profitable."

In 1978, he spent a quarter of a million dollars for a colt named Maheras, then probably the second-best sprinter in the country. Maheras competed in important stakes races, which gave McNall a real charge. He became caught up in the glamour and excitement of the racing world, as he found himself among the rich owners and trainers of the top stables. He continued to pick up horses here and there, including one called National Flag that gave him his first big thrill.

Although Wheeler had had no intention of running National Flag, whose recent record had not been impressive, in a stakes race, McNall insisted, and at the last minute the horse was entered in a division of the Sierra Madre Handicap at Santa Anita, a six-and-a-half-furlong contest down the hillside turf course. While Maheras ran out of the money in his division, National Flag came flying in the stretch to win at huge odds.

After the race, McNall did a computer check on National Flag's career record and discovered the horse had once won a stakes race back in New York. "Class always tells," McNall concluded. "The experience convinced me that breeding and bloodlines were what this game was all about. I decided from then on to buy only top-quality horses. The best way to go in everything is first class."

McNall had made a lot of money selling Texas tycoon Nelson Bunker Hunt what had become one of the finest private collections of ancient Greek and Roman coins in the world. Hunt owned racehorses, and McNall felt that the least he could do for the noted silver hoarder was to buy some of *his* wares. Sy Weintraub, a movie producer, decided to throw in with McNall.

The two men went to the Keeneland Sales in Kentucky in July, 1979, and bought eighteen yearlings for a total of $6,430,000, all but two of the animals from Hunt. The Texan promptly offered to buy back a quarter interest in each horse, an offer that delighted McNall, who believes that "if you deal with the top people, a lot of times it rubs off."

Since that memorable plunge, McNall has been running horses not only in southern California but all over the world. He has brought other celebrities into the game with him, most notably hockey star Wayne Gretzky, and remains enthusiastic despite his discovery that the risks are huge, "bigger in the breeding shed than at the track itself." But risk, even in a costly sport like racing, is relative to entrepreneurs like McNall. "Compared to coins, it's much less high-powered," he once said. The attraction, apart from the gambling aspect and the ego trip, is the relaxed, casual atmosphere the track is famous for. "You can be dealing with Bunker Hunt one day and a Mexican groom the next," McNall points out. "The racetrack is a great leveler."

This adoption of the sport by celebrities and new money was one of the first differences I noticed between East and West when I moved to California in 1966. In New York and the East in general, the game was still firmly in the hands of the good old boys in the racing establishment, who dominated the Jockey Club, ran the racing associations by electing each other to office, failed to foresee and exploit the rise of off-track wagering, and enforced instead antediluvian codes and rules based on the English model. They regarded the California racing scene as boorish and the racing itself as inferior in every way, an attitude that still prevails there despite the incontrovertible fact that for the past decade California racing has flourished economically and dominated the national scene, with California-based horses winning a preponderance of the big races everywhere and in all categories.

Lately, the New York Racing Association has been making some attempts at reform, with Ogden Mills Phipps in the role of Gorbachev, but when Lite Light, the country's best three-year-old filly showed up in New York in the spring of 1991 to take on the eastern champion, Meadow Star, there was an absurd flap over the fact that her owners' silks didn't conform to Jockey Club rules. Lite Light is owned by a family group headed by M. C. Hammer, the black rap star, who has been known to appear in the paddock and the winner's circle dressed in little more than pants and suspenders. If Lite Light had been just another horse, she probably wouldn't have been allowed to run, certainly not in her own silks.

Celebrities are good for racing because they focus public attention on the sport, but too many of them turn out to be cheap sprinters—quick out of the gate but with no staying power. Telly

Savalas is a prime example, even though he had the sort of luck most horse owners dream about and never achieve. He bought into a horse, an unnamed, undistinguished yearling, simply because he happened to drop by producer Howard W. Koch's Beverly Hills house one afternoon in September, 1974, to consult on a script. A local trainer named Mel Stute was then trying to talk Koch into loaning him six thousand dollars or, better, buying this horse Stute had for sale. Koch, however, had been around, knew racing and didn't need the aggravation of another loser. But he liked Stute, who had trained horses for him in the past, and wanted to help him out. So it was Kojak to the rescue: Savalas offered to buy in on the spot, even though what he knew about horses could have been written on the back of a parimutuel ticket with enough room left over for the Gettysburg Address.

Koch tried to talk him out of it, then informed him that he himself usually bought horses in partnership with Walter Matthau. A quick call to that worthy thespian, however, revealed that he'd "had it with horses." That should have been the tip-off; Matthau is one of the great losers at the track, Las Vegas or anywhere wagering of any sort is tolerated. Savalas bought in for three thousand dollars and became half-owner with Koch of a gelded, slow-working animal they eventually named Telly's Pop, after the candy Kojak sucks on television. All the partners now had to do was wait for their horse to run, but the only one who had any confidence he'd amount to something was Savalas, who didn't know any better.

In May, 1975, Telly's Pop won his first race, at Hollywood Park. He went on to earn several hundred thousand dollars, was acclaimed as California's top three-year-old and became a leading candidate for the Triple Crown. Savalas became a trial to his associates, because, Koch reported, he'd sit in his trailer on the lot where his series was shooting and watch tapes of his horse's races over and over. "People like Telly, they love him," Koch explained, "but they're beginning to shy away from the dressing room because he makes everybody watch the races. He's really into it now."

Telly's Pop never won a Triple Crown race and broke down

later in the year, leaving Savalas with a huge profit on his investment but no desire to remain in racing. Who's to say he was wrong? For many celebrities, racing serves primarily as an ego trip; few make any money at it. And as bettors they are generally disastrously wrong. I once entertained a small fantasy of my own about making a consistent killing at the track. I'd go every day to the Turf Club and the grandstand box area to find out what animals the Hollywood crowd was plunging on and bet against them. I'd have gone broke going up against Marty Ritt, but I'd have gotten rich on the action of Matthau, Jack Klugman and Vince Edwards alone.

The latter, a surly and unpleasant loser, provided me with one of my happiest winning days. I had narrowed the ninth race at Santa Anita one afternoon to four horses. I decided to throw one of them out and box the other three in five-dollar exactas. On my way back from the betting windows, I passed Edwards and overheard him tell someone that a particular horse he liked couldn't lose. The animal happened to be one of three I had used. I turned around, went back to the window and exchanged my ticket, throwing out Edwards's horse and substituting the one I had discarded. My exacta hit for nearly three hundred dollars; Edwards's sure thing ran last.

7

WE HAD THE HORSE RIGHT THERE

"They all get beat if you run them often enough."
—Old racetrack maxim

"How'd you like to buy a piece of a good two-year-old?" the voice on the telephone asked.

I said no and hung up. I knew all about owning racehorses by this time. The costs are high and the risks extreme. Most of the thousands of foals born every year never even make it to the track, and only about four percent of them ever win an important race. Horses start running professionally as two-year-olds and seven out of ten of them buck a shin at one time or another, a minor injury that can nevertheless knock a horse out of training for weeks. There are dozens of other ailments that afflict Thoroughbreds, some of them serious enough to immobilize them permanently, and none of them are rare. Worse, a horse may not run well simply because he doesn't feel like it. The stables are full of morning glories who burn up the track in training moves and die in the afternoon. The trouble is, they don't really die; they go right on eating. It now costs about two thousand dollars a month to keep one of them in active training at a major track, and that's not including vet bills.

So much for the forces of reason. The fact is the phone call had caught me with my resistance down. The year was 1967 and I had just sold a novel of mine to the movies. I had a chunk of money I was anxious to keep the IRS from savaging, and I rationalized that, at worst, I could always deduct my losses. Also, I'd been living in Los Angeles for a couple of years, after having spent most of my life in the East and in Europe, and the balmy L.A. life-style tends to soften your brain. Back in New York, no one could have sold me any part of a horse; out West, blinded by smog and baked silly by sunshine, anything seemed possible. I called my friend back. "I'm still not interested," I said, "but tell me more."

Five of us bought the horse. He was an unraced two-year-old colt named War Flag, foaled in Kentucky at the Calumet Farm, a famous racing establishment. His sire was My Babu, a celebrated English stakes winner, and the mare's daddy was Bull Lea, one of racing's superstuds. The colt's credentials were impeccable. Best of all, his trainer, Willis Reavis, said he was only weeks away from his debut. We paid, including taxes and a reserve to tide us over the first couple of months, a total of thirty-five thousand dollars.

I never saw the animal until the day he ran his first race. He was stabled at Del Mar, about a hundred and twenty miles south of where I lived in Malibu, and I was too busy working on a book to get down there. However, a few weeks after we bought him, we heard he'd been entered in a race, the first one on the card that day, and I drove down for the event.

The whole experience remains pretty much of a blur, but certain vivid images stand out, in bright Technicolor. The way War Flag looked, for instance, when he was led out into the bright sunshine of the paddock. (My God, I'd bought the most magnificent horse since Pegasus, a great big solidly muscled paragon of a beast with a dark, gleaming coat and the noble head of an Elgin Marble!) The stupidly grinning faces of my partners and their wives and girl-friends as we all stood around staring at the horse. The shrewd, confident look on the trainer's face and the thoughtful, almost puzzled solemnity of the jockey, Dean Hall, as he listened to the trainer's instructions before being hoisted lightly into the saddle. The bright yellow lights of the tote board winking the odds at us and the growing confidence I felt as War Flag, who had opened at twelve to one, was backed down to become the favorite, at two to one. The hum of the crowd as the horses came out on the track and the scratchy recorded voice of Bing Crosby singing the Del Mar anthem, "Where the surf meets the turf down at old Del Ma-a-ar . . ." Someone muttering savagely, as the horses stood fidgeting in the starting gate, "Get them out of there!" And the horses exploding into the clear, War Flag tucked in along the rail and dropping back to fourth, then, at the head of the stretch, Hall taking him out to find running room. And the way, with all of us screaming at him, the big horse simply ran them all down.

War Flag won the race. According to the chart in the *Racing Form*, he "responded to light urging in the stretch to wear down the leaders and won going away while well in hand." It was only a six-furlong race for a modest purse against untried competition, but it could just as well have been the Kentucky Derby as far as we were concerned. I popped two buttons on my jacket, my wallet flew out of my inside pocket, and I smashed the unbreakable crystal on my wristwatch. But so what? I had my horse wheeled in the daily double to everything in the second race, I had my share of the winner's purse, and obviously it was only a matter of months before I'd be right up there, rubbing haunches with Ogden Phipps, Jock Whitney and Alf Vanderbilt. I remember somebody in our box saying that we ought to make reservations for Louisville right now, since hotel rooms get scarce there around Derby time, which, after all, was only nine months away. The words that will be forever engraved in my memory, though, are the ones Dean Hall spoke when he shook hands with us in the winner's circle after we'd all had our picture taken grouped around our champion. "I just tapped him once and that was it," he said. "You got a real nice colt there."

After we'd all spent some happy minutes at the cashiers' windows and reunited again in our box, the trainer, that man of genius, told us he'd race War Flag one more time during the meeting at Del Mar, probably two weeks later in a twenty-five-thousand-dollar stakes race on the infield turf course. Our winning share of that purse, we figured out, would be about fourteen thousand dollars, which bought a lot of hay. After that, War Flag would take it easy for a few months and wait for the winter meet at Santa Anita. "We'll be racing for big purses there," the man of genius said. "And if he comes along the way it looks now, we should do all right with him."

Doing all right was not exactly what any of us had in mind that day. We were an oddly assorted group, I realized. I was a writer. Al Rappaport was a physicist who also invented household gadgets and dabbled in oil. Howard Kosh was a stockbroker. Jerry Shanberg worked for an outfit that rented people furniture and party favors. Duke Waxenberg, who had first called me about the horse, was a Beverly Hills boulevardier and bon vivant. About the only thing we had in common was horse fever and the newly acquired conviction that we were all about to become very rich. What was bugging our genius of a trainer?

For the first time since I'd met him, I took a close look at Willis Reavis. He was in his mid-fifties, stocky, with a shrewd, leathery, good-humored face, small bright-blue eyes and a thick head of wavy iron-gray hair, a typical horseman; and typical horsemen are tight-fisted gamblers and vote Republican. It's all right, Willis, I wanted to tell him, you just go back to the barn, take care of the horse and play your Lawrence Welk records. Destiny calls, baby.

If destiny ever did call, the line must have been out of order. War Flag never won another race for us, and to this day I'm not sure why. To begin with, he did not run again at Del Mar. Something about the infield turf course being too hard for his tender feet, according to Reavis, or was it that he had bumped himself in his stall and limped around for a couple of days? Anyway, better not to take a chance with our champion, the trainer said, with the much more important and lucrative Santa Anita meet coming up.

What could we do but agree with the man? We sat it out for three months until Santa Anita opened, on December 26. The wait drained away the purse money we had won at Del Mar, but never mind. We never doubted we had a real good one in the barn, and maybe we were right. I went out a couple of times in the early morning to watch War Flag work, and he looked every bit as impressive as he had at Del Mar. But something Willis said to me in the track cafeteria one day, after War Flag had breezed five furlongs in good style, has stuck with me. He began by observing that he was sure War Flag would improve as the distances of his races got longer, then added, "But you can't never tell. I been around this business all my life, and the only good horses I ever had was geldings. You don't know what these studs are going to do, especially now with the mares coming into season. Just getting them to eat is a problem. Well, maybe we'll be lucky."

We weren't. On December 29, War Flag, with Dean Hall up, came out on the track for the seventh race as the seven-to-one third choice of the bettors. He broke well, then dropped steadily back and finished a dismal eighth in the field of eleven. We sat in our box, paralyzed by the disaster; Howard Kosh looked as if his favorite stock had just dropped twenty points. Willis, who had gone down to talk to the jockey, never did come back, and it wasn't until the next day that we found out what had happened.

War Flag, it seems, had popped a curb, which is a small bone about the size of a man's thumb just under the hock. It was seven weeks before he ran again. This time he broke last, threw his head to one side and swerved when Hall tried to make up ground by coming through on the inside at the turn. He finished ninth in a field of ten. A week later, with a new and stronger-armed jockey named Bill Harmatz in the saddle, War Flag ran about an eighth of a mile, then bolted for the outer rail as the other horses swept past him. Harmatz was forced to pull him up or risk ending in the parking lot. "Mean, mean," Reavis said, "he's so mean now he don't even want to be near other horses."

After that performance, the Santa Anita stewards barred War Flag from racing until he could prove in training that he wouldn't be a menace to himself and to everybody else. Reavis suggested we geld him. "He just don't like other horses," he said. "He wants no part of them and tries to get out when the gate opens. He's a stud, all right." The trouble was the five owners couldn't agree on what to do. Jerry was with Reavis, Duke disagreed and Al, Howard and I were undecided. "If we geld him, we've got nothing after his racing days are over," said Duke. "You've got nothing anyway, if he doesn't win," said Jerry. "Thirty-five thousand dollars' worth of nothing," said Howard.

We decided to try other, less drastic measures first. Reavis sprinkled saltpeter or something calming into War Flag's feed bin. Blinkers were added and a stronger bit was substituted. A specialist in handling fractious beasts coached War Flag in trials out of the gate. Nothing worked. After a couple of weeks, the stewards reinstated our animal, but in races he simply wouldn't run. "All right, cut his balls off!" Duke snapped one afternoon, just after Howard had observed sweetly that War Flag had just lost by only twenty lengths rather than the thirty we had become accustomed to.

War Flag's testicles hit the ground early one morning, and Reavis was full of wonder at the event. "They was just as big as coconuts," he announced. "How he could run with them things between his legs back there I just don't know. Must have hurt him something terrible."

He couldn't run too well without them things back there either, we discovered, when War Flag came back out on the track a couple of months later at Hollywood Park. Nor was it any consolation at all that he was now losing races by only ten and twelve lengths. "We cut him too late," opined Reavis gloomily.

"How can we get that message across to him?" Duke asked. "Singing telegrams?"

"Isn't it just possible that we bought an overrated horse?" I told Jerry one day. "I mean, his winning time at Del Mar wasn't that fast, if you want to be cold-blooded about it."

We got very cold-blooded about War Flag. After all, he was draining hundreds of dollars out of our pockets every month. We began entering him in claiming races and, as he continued to lose, moved him rapidly down the ladder. And the inevitable happened. War Flag appeared one afternoon for a price tag of sixty-five hundred dollars and somebody grabbed him. Interestingly enough, he ran his second-best race for us that day, making one real move at the leaders before dropping out of it again. I watched him being led away by his new owners, the red claiming tag dangling from his halter, with relief but a good deal of sadness and a nagging feeling that somehow the horse wasn't to blame; we had ruined him, all of us, Reavis included.

Over the next two years, War Flag, running in similar company and for a variety of different owners, won about thirty thousand dollars in purses. He ran far too often and never achieved anything but mediocrity. He became what is known in the game as a useful horse. The last time I saw him was at the fair grounds in Pomona, where he ran against real cheapies around the tight turns of the bull ring, as these half-mile tracks are called. By that time he had a knee that looked like a cantaloupe. I bet on him that day and he won, but I never heard of him racing again anywhere. I still feel badly about him and what we did to him. He was certainly not a great horse, but he might have become a good one.

By the end of the War Flag saga, three of the five partners in our stable decided they had had enough, took what remained of their money and went back to civilian life. Jerry Shanberg and I surveyed the debris that passed for our stable bank account and discovered that we had about four thousand dollars left. We decided, like true horseplayers, that we might as well go all the way. We began to look around for a cheap horse to claim from somebody else.

The one we selected had an interesting name, El Lobo, but, judging by his record, little else to recommend him; he hadn't even come close to winning a race in over a year. But Reavis picked one small statistic out of the *Racing Form* and indicated it to us, jabbing at it with a stubby forefinger as we watched El Lobo being saddled prior to the four-thousand-dollar claiming race he was entered in one day at Hollywood Park. "Look here," he said, "this sucker worked a mile in a minute and thirty-nine flat. Hell, he works faster than these other horses in here with him can run."

He didn't run much that day, finishing fourth against the worst horses on the grounds, but before the race we dropped our last four thousand dollars into the claim box and took him. "Well, that wipes us out," I said to Jerry, feeling an odd sense of relief, as if I'd suddenly become impregnable to further disaster.

About ten days later, El Lobo ran his first race for us. The distance was a mile and one-sixteenth, and he was in against slightly better horses than he'd just lost to. I gave him no chance, but bet fifty dollars on him anyway, because he was mine. I didn't pay much attention to the early part of the race, but as the field hit the last turn I suddenly realized that Harmatz had El Lobo rolling along the outside, picking up one horse after another. I began to shout. By the time El Lobo hit the finish line, a couple of lengths in front, I had lost my voice, but who cared? We had just won three thousand dollars in purse money and my fifty-dollar bet had been on the nose at a delicious sixteen to one. "What did you do, Willis?" I asked, as we rushed for the winner's circle. "Just changed his shoes is all," said the trainer. "The dumb bastard that had him had the wrong shoes on him. He couldn't even walk in 'em."

Eight days after that, El Lobo came out again in his new shoes. He was up a notch in company and at the shorter distance of seven furlongs, which didn't figure to favor his late-running style. I didn't care; I had returned to the true faith and I'd have bet El Lobo that day against a Ferrari. I banged it in on him at nine to one.

Once again he started late and finished like an express train, zooming past the front-runner, a game and still talented ex-stakes horse, to win by a long neck in excellent time. Jerry and I threw our arms around each other and danced the wild fandango to the cashiers' windows.

It had to end, of course. Reavis gave El Lobo a well-merited rest, then took him down to Del Mar for the summer meeting. He entered the horse in an eight-thousand-dollar claiming event at a mile. The field was short, with only six horses in it, and two of them were ailing but classy beasts being dropped down in company in an effort to win a purse. "I wouldn't bet him in here," Jerry said. "He doesn't figure to beat these two top horses, the odds with the short field will be low, and we stand to pick up a piece of the purse anyway. He should run third."

Jerry proved to be a seer. El Lobo finished a very respectable third, but it was the last race he ran for us. He was claimed out of the race by Farrell Jones, a trainer with a huge public stable whose horses won more races in California year after year than anybody

else. It figured. Trainers like Jones are always looking for improving animals, horses "on their way up," to claim for their many
owners. But could I complain? Hardly. In six weeks, between
purses won, doubling our money on the original claim price and
bets, I had recouped all of my losses with War Flag. Still, I wanted
Reavis to watch for a chance to get El Lobo back from Jones. "I
wouldn't," the trainer said. "He ain't that sound, and Jones'll run
him into the ground."

El Lobo never won a race for Jones. The last time I saw him on
the track, some months later, the hairs on his front legs were
tightly curled, indicating he'd probably been standing for hours in
ice, and he walked as if tiptoeing on glass. So the first two horses
I'd ever had anything to do with wound up their racing careers as
cripples. But horse racing, I had discovered, was more of a business
than a sport.

The highest gambling wisdom is knowing when to quit. El Lobo,
however, had scrambled my brains. I was like a man panning for
gold in a riverbed who's just found a big nugget and some ass
comes along, waving his arms and shouting that the dam upstream
is about to burst. Do you get out of the water? Of course not. So
over the next eighteen months of my career as a horse owner came
the deluge.

There was, for instance, the case of Quita Dude. He was a
nine-year-old gelding we took out of a cheap claiming race at Del
Mar because Willis thought he could win with him. He had had the
horse years before, when he was good and had won a couple of
important races. But that had been a long time ago, and nine is
ancient for a racehorse. "It don't matter," the trainer said. "I know
how this big sucker likes to run. He should beat this kind walkin'."

Quita Dude was a monster. Not only was he the biggest horse
I'd ever seen, but he was easily the fussiest. Here are Reavis's
instructions to Alex Maese, the journeyman jock who rode him the
first time for us: "You got to take a big hold on him out of the gate
and pull him back away from all the other horses or he's going to
fight you and try to run with 'em. He's got one move in him and

it's exactly three-eighths of a mile, not one goddamn foot more and not one goddamn foot less. You got that? Good. Now let him drop back and get all relaxed. It don't matter how far he drops out of it. Just don't let him run. Then, when you hit the three-eighths pole, let him go. He'll come like a damn hurricane."

Maese stared at Reavis as if the trainer had just tried to peddle him a platinum brick. "There's another thing I didn't tell him," Reavis added, as we watched Maese guide Quita Dude toward the starting gate. "This horse won't run on the inside neither. He don't like the dirt kicked up in his face and he hangs."

"Why didn't you tell Maese that?" I asked.

" 'Cause what I told him is bad enough," the trainer said. "Hell, you can't ask no rider to take back thirty lengths and then tell him to go wide on the turn. He'll think you're crazy."

Evidently Maese didn't believe a word of what Reavis told him, because he ran Quita Dude up with the leaders for the first half-mile and wound up last. We tried a couple of more times with different riders, but the conditions were never met. Either the jockey would not take Quita Dude far enough out of it, or he'd move him too soon or too late or try to come through on the inside. By the time the Del Mar meeting ended and the horses moved to Pomona for the traditional two weeks of racing on the grounds of the L.A. County Fair, I'd given up hope, especially as I felt sure Quita Dude would never get up in time around the tight turns of the bull ring, which favor front-running speed horses.

Miguel Yanez, the Mexican jockey who rode Quita Dude at Pomona, listened to Reavis's spiel with the stony impassivity of an Aztec carving. He mounted and rode off without a word or even a nod, and Reavis observed that he probably didn't understand English. Naturally, I bet lightly. So, of course, Quita Dude won, at astronomical odds and just the way he was supposed to, coming from a mile out of it and looping the field on the turn. "Sure he understands English," I said, clapping Reavis on the back. "No, he don't," said the trainer. "The horse had his head turned when the gate opened, so he got left. And with these tight turns there ain't no way you can come through on the inside. There wasn't nothin' Yanez could do to cock us up."

"Maybe we should let the horses run on their own," Jerry said thoughtfully.

Two weeks later, Quita Dude hurt himself in training and we eventually sold him for a fraction of what we'd paid and put into him. But by this time we had nothing but losses to add up anyway. There was Climb Across, a three-year-old who won one race for us at Del Mar in glacially slow time and moved speedily on to oblivion. There was Camaro, a horse I distrusted from the first because he was named after a car and who never won anything for us before he, too, injured himself and was sold at a tidy deficit. And there was Parlay Time, who turned out to be the world's champion windsucker. He'd gnaw for hours on anything solid within reach and, while doing so, suck in great gulps of air, bloating himself so he couldn't eat or train properly. I gave him to a lady who wanted a saddle horse, and she had to put him in a metal stall charged to give him a shock every time he went to work playing with himself. I hope she cooked him.

Last, but certainly not least, in the freak parade was Irish Friendship, a six-year-old male with his sex organs intact. "That's good," I said. "If we still have him when he's through racing, we can use him as a stud. He's got some breeding."

"No, you can't," Willis answered. "This horse don't like mares. He only likes ponies. He just loves them ponies. You get him near a pony and he'll mount him. On the track the outriders all know about him. He's kind of a joke."

"Christ," Jerry said, "we got us a fag horse."

He could run, though. Unfortunately, he was bad-legged and the problem was keeping him sound. He won the race we claimed him out of, then he picked up pieces of purses for us here and there while Reavis tried to find just the right spot for him. Before he could do so, Irish Friendship stepped into a depression in the track while training and bowed a front tendon. Next to a broken bone, a bowed tendon is the most serious injury that can overtake a racehorse. It requires a minimum of six months to heal, and even if he does get back to the races, the horse is rarely ever as good again and will generally not be able to run more than a few times at most.

Irish Friendship received the best of medical care and was shipped off to an expensive ranch to convalesce. Jerry and I, by this time, were struggling to get out from under our other losers, but we decided we'd wait for Irish Friendship to come back. "We'll take him down to Tijuana and run him there," Jerry said. "He'll have been away at least nine months and his workouts never show much. We should get a big price on him and that way we can get some of our money back. This horse has so much class that on three legs he can beat what they got running down in Mexico."

It took fifteen months for Irish Friendship to come back. His training was taken over at Agua Caliente, the little track on the other side of the border, by a plump, pink-cheeked Munchkin named Bobby Warren. "Look at the belly on him," he said when he first saw Irish Friendship. "This horse must drink more beer than I do."

Warren got some of the belly off our horse with workouts and by galloping him a slow two miles as often as possible. "He's got some problems," he confided to us, "but he can run, all right. Only you may lose him. If he shows anything at all, somebody here will claim him. There's a group comes up from Mexico City every weekend looking for studs."

"That's all right," Jerry said and told Warren about our horse's predilection for ponies. "Anyway, we don't care. Just hold him together for one race, that's all we ask."

The great day finally came, and Jerry and I brought six hundred dollars, the last of our stable's bank account, down to Tijuana. Irish Friendship was entered in a sixteen-hundred-dollar claiming race at a mile and a sixteenth against pigs he'd have eaten alive the year before. Best of all, it was a quinella race, meaning that you could win a goodly amount of money by picking two horses in the field to finish one-two in any order. We coupled Irish Friendship with every other horse in the race; all he had to do was run second and we stood to pocket a heartening bundle of green.

"This horse ain't been out in a long time," Bobby Warren told our jockey, an American gnome who wasn't good enough to make it up north but who was considered one of Caliente's top riders. "He'll be a little short, so don't move him till the half-mile pole. And don't worry about having to come on the outside because he'll outrun all these others. Just don't get boxed in and don't make him run too early."

The race went off and Irish Friendship, at seven to one, dropped behind the leaders around the first turn. As they straightened out in the backstretch, however, he suddenly began to move so fast it looked as if the other horses were running on a treadmill. "Look at him go!" I shouted. "It's too early," Jerry said. "That mother's making him run from too far out."

When they hit the stretch, Irish Friendship was two lengths in front, but already he was beginning to shorten stride and the field was closing on him. Still, all he had to do was finish second and we'd be big winners. Jerry and I screamed encouragement, but a few yards from the end Irish got caught. He finished third.

Warren, who had also bet on him, was livid. "What the hell was that dumb bastard of a jock thinking about?" he said. "I don't want to know," Jerry said. "If a man had any brains he wouldn't want to risk his life on the backs of dumb animals anyway."

Irish Friendship did not come out of the race well, and Warren informed us the next day he didn't think he had more than another outing or two left in him. "Drop him down to the bottom and let's unload him," Jerry said. So a week later, Irish Friendship was entered for a thousand dollars at the same distance.

He won easily that day, but Jerry and I couldn't bet on him. The odds were too low and there were no quinella or other exotic betting propositions to hook him into. We stood by the rail near the finish line and silently watched him come home in front, and I think the same thought was going through our heads. We had started out with a thirty-five-thousand-dollar horse at a glamorous track with a win and dreams of the Kentucky Derby. Now here we were, two and a half years later, ending the adventure with another victory, but this time with a crippled plater at a third-rate track and no dreams at all. Also no money; the six-hundred-dollar purse we picked up with Irish Friendship just about bailed us out of our stable bill with Warren. We went north empty-handed. I figured out later that overall I had dropped a total of about twenty-five thousand dollars as a horse owner, which is the kind of tax deduction only writers like Sidney Sheldon and Mario Puzo can afford.

Irish Friendship was claimed out of his winning race by the outfit from Mexico City. As a courtesy, Warren dropped by his new owners' stable to inform them of their horse's peculiar proclivities. He was cut off early. "We know how to handle horses," said the sour Texan who functioned as stable foreman. "We don't need no advice." Warren shrugged and left.

The next time Irish Friendship came out on the track he was accompanied by an outrider on a honey-colored pony. And right there, in front of the packed stands, Irish Friendship threw off his rider and mounted the beautiful pony. They scratched him from the race. We heard about it from Warren, and I wish I'd been there to see it.

8

SOUTHLAND SARATOGA

"I had a great day, I got a ride home."
—Joe Frisco, at Del Mar

EVERY DAY at the races in Del Mar was a great day for Joe Frisco, a night-club comedian who wouldn't accept an engagement in any town without a racetrack. Frisco loved Del Mar and became a fixture there during the Crosby regime. He also allowed Crosby to loan him money so he could stay in action. Frisco was one of the great losers of all time, and Del Mar is a great place to lose money. One of the local sayings, attributed originally to a professional handicapper on his way out to the parking lot after a particularly dismal afternoon, is, "Well, just another shitty day in paradise."

I found this out for myself during the summer of 1966, when I drove down from my home in Malibu and checked into a seedy motel on the public beach, about twenty miles north of San Diego. I'd heard about Del Mar, of course, and a horseplaying acquaintance of mine named Action Jackson had touted it to me as a "veritable Southland Saratoga," but as a cynical transplanted New Yorker, I reserved judgment until I could check it out on my own. So I brought along my two daughters, Natalia and Julia, then aged ten and six respectively, and spent a week I will never forget.

My first glimpse of the track, through a sudden gap in the hills, immediately lifted my spirits. The modest little plant, lying on flat land close to the ocean and between two low-lying ridges, then still largely undeveloped, looked as if it might have been built by Spanish monks. There was even a bell tower, from which, I presumed, the faithful could be summoned to daily worship at the windows of chance. I found out later that the two local architects who designed it, Sam W. Hamill and Herbert Louis Jackson, had intended to evoke an era of Spanish Colonial grandeur, with bits of Venice and Versailles thrown in. They ran out of money, which is probably just as well. "The theme was on a gay, happy note," Hamill recalled years later, "calculated to recreate the carefree days before taxes, freeways and tract houses. Our conception tried to recapture the spirit of the viceroys, the rancheros and land owners and the gifted Franciscans." In this respect they failed, but what they did create was a racetrack high on pure charm.

The horses ran around a one-mile dirt oval and an inside turf course, usually in warm sunlight, while the Pacific broke gently against a long white beach visible in the background. In the early mornings, horses would be led from the barn area to the beach and allowed to gambol in the surf or gallop along the hard, flat sand at low tide. In the afternoons, between races, families picnicked in the grassy infield, lovers strolled about the ponds, the beautiful young people set up camp in beach chairs along the rail and guzzled beer and wine as they cheered their favorites home. This wasn't like any racetrack I had ever been to before; it was a celebration of the golden California life-style.

Every morning my girls and I breakfasted on the open terrace of a restaurant and night club called the Fire Pit, right next to the motel. We'd spend several hours in the surf and on the beach, after which I would head for the track, knowing that the girls would be safe under the supervision of the local lifeguards and the motel manager's kindly wife. I'd get back in time for a twilight dip, then take the kids out to dinner somewhere along the coast. Evenings were spent handicapping, while my children, stunned by sun and surf, fell asleep watching TV.

It wasn't entirely idyllic, of course. The motel itself was a slum, with a noisy and unreliable plumbing system and furniture apparently salvaged from a flophouse. Showers were risky, because every time a nearby toilet flushed you had to flatten yourself against the wall to avoid being boiled. At two A.M., curfew time for public boozing in California, the Fire Pit would disgorge a horde of revelers into the adjacent parking lot, from which they would depart over the next half-hour in a great clashing of fenders, screaming, laughter and clattering beer cans. Then, at five A.M., the garbage trucks would rumble onto the scene to grind up the day's trash. My children slept through everything, but I did a lot of catnapping on the beach.

None of these drawbacks mattered. Not even the fact that I couldn't seem to pick a winner mattered. I was totally hooked on Del Mar, and I made it a point to come back every year, usually for several long weekends during the traditional seven weeks of the meet, from the end of July until the second week in September. In 1975, I spent a whole summer inhaling backstretch gossip from a motel across from the stable area, while researching a behind-the-scenes account of a season at the track. Six years ago, with my children grown and out on their own, my wife and I moved from L.A. and bought a house in the hills east of Del Mar, about three miles and a couple of head bobs from the finish line.

It isn't only that we crave the action at the track; we like the surroundings. Despite a tremendous building boom that has sparked an influx of about thirty-five thousand new residents annually into the greater San Diego area, the town of Del Mar has remained pretty much the same as when I first saw it. There are many new houses, including our own, on the slopes around it, but the business area looks the same—a few blocks of small shops, restaurants and modest commercial structures fronting on the old coast highway. A hotel and a new shopping center have been built, but both projects were grudgingly approved by the voters only after the developers agreed to scale down their original proposals and to conform to the overall architectural motif, best defined as California Tudor. Furthermore, Del Mar, with its fiercely elitist defense of the local environment (franchised fast-food emporiums and garish advertisers are kept beyond the pale), has inspired the neighboring communities along the coast to organize in their own interests. A Maginot Line of slow-growth ordinances now confronts the bulldozers from the Mexican border to the Cape Pendleton marine base north of Oceanside.

And where environmentalists linger, can the super-rich be far behind? Rancho Santa Fe, once an isolated horsy community of so-called ranchos, mainly estates half-hidden among orange and lemon groves a few miles inland, is now surrounded by other equally fancy developments, some with palazzi opulent enough to have pleased the Medici. Interspersed among them are elegant shopping centers, private golf courses and tennis clubs, and even a polo field, where matches are played regularly between rows of parked Rolls Royces, Bentleys, Ferraris and other expensive toys.

Though it was never our intention to sneak in among the swells, I have to admit that the position has its advantages. Where the plutocrats play, no one is likely to convert the corner lot into a gas station or open a Jack-in-the-Box across the street. The entire scene, in fact, conforms to a vision of existence I would like to see perpetuated at the racetrack. "What this is, it's more of a mood, a way of life," a sportswriter named Oscar Otis once told me about Del Mar. "It's racing, all right, but with this important difference—it's a great place to relax."

Del Mar has never been a great place for the professional horse-players, most of whom regard it as a difficult track at which to break even, much less make money. Essentially, this is because it's a so-called horse-for-course emporium. "When they can run here, they run like hell, or they can't run at all," is the way Charlie Whittingham, a trainer of legendary accomplishments, once put it. This factor may be due to the configuration of the racing oval itself, with its tight turns and short stretch. Some people think the climate may be to blame or the rising and falling of the tides under the track itself. Del Mar's early-morning mists are credited with keeping the racing surfaces moist, presumably making it easier on some animals' feet. Then there used to be a speed bias favoring fast horses on the rail, but that vanished in 1980, when heavy winter storms flooded the plant and all but washed out the main dirt course. When racing resumed that summer, the inside speed bias had disappeared, apparently never to return.

What probably bugs the pros more than anything else is the inconsistency of the speed figures upon which most of them rely. Horses run one set of numbers elsewhere, then show up at Del Mar and either zip along like stakes contenders or wallow in a slough of despond. The best and boldest bettor I know is Andrew Beyer, the racing columnist for the *Washington Post* and creator of the Beyer Speed Figures (generally referred to as "the figs"), a computer-based method for isolating the fastest horse in the race that has proved its efficacy at every other major racetrack in America. At Del Mar, the figs are still a useful tool, but often the fig horse will find himself lumbering helplessly in the wake of some plodder computed to run ten lengths slower but transformed at Del Mar into the second coming of Secretariat. Beyer, whose aplomb as a handicapper is matched only by his grace as a loser, has yet to have a winning stay at Del Mar, which he once referred to, in a fleeting moment of exasperation, as "this quirky little track." He is not alone in his frustration, but that can hardly be much consolation to him or to any of the other punters whose wallets have been emptied on the premises.

I can't recall a single winning day during my first visit twenty-five years ago, but I've learned since then to adapt. Often, I toss my own figures away and go on hunches or scatter two-dollar bets among what I call the Cloud Cuckooland horses, nags with nothing to recommend them but their long odds. Enough of them come in to have made it possible for me to show a modest profit at this track in five of the past seven years. And I once hit a Pick Six here with a two-dollar ticket I selected by cutting a deck of cards. Del Mar is not a place for the serious horseplayer, but calls instead for imagination, verve and plain dumb luck.

Horses, of course, can always find new ways to lose, and at Del Mar they become creative. I once bet on a filly named Why More Worry, who opened up a comfortable lead on the grass and seemed headed for an easy win, when she suddenly bolted through the inner hedge into the infield with less than fifty yards to go. Then there was the day I put money on a two-year-old filly named Leal's Jewel, only to watch her pull up in the stretch when her jockey's pants came apart.

Some animals here have trouble making the tight turns. Years ago, Joe Frisco had been betting on a fast sprinter that always went to the lead by the turn, but would then try to come home through the parking lot. The comedian looked up the trainer and suggested that he insert some of the lead weights normally carried in the saddle cloth into the horse's left ear to keep him on course. "Very interesting, Joe," the trainer observed, "but how do you propose to put the lead into his ear?" "With a .38," Frisco said, in his familiar gentle stutter.

Picking winners, however, is not really what racing at Del Mar is all about. Some of my favorite times have been spent in the barn area, especially up in the guinea stand (so named because two hundred years ago winning English owners used to tip their stable-hands a guinea, a gold piece then worth about five dollars) over-looking the backstretch to watch the workouts or around some trainer's shedrow during the routine of a working morning or in the backside cafeteria having coffee with the men and women whose lives have been spent around horses. I hear great stories and a lot of very unreliable information about which animals are going to do what in their next races, most of which I've learned to ignore.

All of this may change in the next couple of years. The 22nd District Agricultural Association, a public entity that administers the fairgrounds for the state of California, is lavishing about eighty million dollars on a new plant designed to seat fifteen thousand people. There's no denying that improvements had to be made, because the charming old structure was really a decaying wreck, but the new project seems to be another manifestation of the American obsession with wiping out the past in the name of progress. Although the fans have been assured that "the charm and atmosphere of the original Spanish Mission-style grandstand will be preserved," the old paddock, with its fifty-one-year growth of ivy, will be destroyed and the whole complex looks, in an artist's rendering, like a Hilton hotel. Needless to say, no part of this appropriation has been allotted to improving the lot of the under-paid backstretch help, some of whom still sleep in unsanitary wooden shacks planted like packing crates between the dusty shedrows. But then who cares about housing people properly in this country, when there's a buck to be made elsewhere?

The management style at Del Mar has always been relaxed to the point of torpor whenever it came to improving the daily lot of either the employees or the horseplayers, so one could argue that any change has to be for the better. I won't mind what they do, so long as the horses still come out for the first post parade every day to the tune of Bing Crosby warbling the ditty he, Johnny Burke and James V. Monaco wrote for the original opening day: "When the turf meets the surf/ Down at old Del Mar/ Take a plane, take a train, take a car/ There's a smile on every face/ And a winner in each race/ Where the turf meets the surf . . ." My wife calls it our song.

Whatever may happen over the next few years, the setting will still be the same and my daily routine unvaried—the backstretch, some writing, some beach time, occasionally some tennis, and then to the races. Some years ago, a handicapper I know thought up "the wine ceremony," which consists of a twilight session on the beach with towels, a blanket, a bottle of chilled white wine, glasses, and friends. A sunset dip in the surf followed by a little alcohol and good conversation can restore one's faith in the human condition. In his book *A Moveable Feast*, Ernest Hemingway wrote eloquently about the pleasures of a summer spent going racing in France. I reread it recently and wound up feeling sorry for him. He had never been to Del Mar.

Some horseplayers, of course, are impervious to ambience. I got into a conversation one morning in 1975 with an old man in the lobby of my motel. He was wondering what to do about his dirty laundry. Usually, on Tuesdays, he informed me, the only dark days of the meet, he would drive back up to L.A. for clean clothes. "But maybe, if they got a laundry here," he said, "I might stay. A cleaner's, you said?" I explained to him that these services were available in the town of Del Mar.

He had been coming to the races for five or six years, he told me, and staying in this motel about a mile from downtown, but he had never visited it. "What's to see?" he asked.

I told him, but the old man seemed uninspired by my pitch. "Listen," he said, "I lived in New York City for forty years and I never went up the Empire State Building or went out to that statue they got out there in the harbor. Then I lived in Miami for twelve years, but I never went on no boats. I don't know towns. I know racetracks."

9

THE SPORTSHOLIC

"You go between two horses for money, not for fun."
—Eddie Arcaro

WHEN JOCKEY Bill Shoemaker finally retired on Saturday, February 3, 1990, the management of Santa Anita threw him a party. They also named a special race, "The Legend's Last Ride," in his honor and let him pick the horse he wanted to mount in it, then wrote a number of other conditions into the scenario to make sure that, no matter what happened, he'd have a good chance to win it. Having paid Shoemaker a hefty sum, perhaps as much as a hundred thousand dollars, to show up, and having promoted themselves into a lather, with ABC's *Wide World of Sports* on hand to immortalize the event, track officials committed themselves to a venture that had little to do with pure sport but everything to do with money. As such, it promised to be but one more manifestation of the American genius for self-serving hype and a somewhat inglorious way for one of the finest athletes of our time to make his exit, but then that seemed to be the way he wanted it.

Shoemaker was fifty-eight years old and, by his own admission, no longer a top athlete. Like all jockeys, he had survived serious, incapacitating injuries that had, along with age, eroded his talents. His knees hurt and he could ride only a couple of horses a day, and he hadn't the physical strength anymore to take full charge of a

Thoroughbred—a headstrong beast powerful enough to maim and kill any human being incautious enough to get on him. Jockeys are badly hurt and die every year in accidents, and being a rider is the only profession in the world in which an ambulance follows you around while you're working. Like most sports, it's an occupation for the young, and those of us who had watched Shoemaker over the years thought he should have hung up his tack a decade earlier.

But he had always fooled us. Every time we'd written him off, back he'd come, flashing some of the old magic at us, with those great hands, that clock in his head, that coolness and patience and delicacy that had made him seem an indispensable part of the animal under him, as essential to its success as its heart and lungs. Nobody rode with more style and poetry than Bill Shoemaker, when he really wanted to. He was to riding what Astaire was to hoofing—the consummate pro, a living embodiment of grace in action. And he'd put up the numbers to prove it: 8,883 wins, over $120,000,000 in purses, and more other records than any other race rider in history.

That's why it had been sad for me to watch him that last year promoting himself at racecourses across the world in a series of farewell appearances for which he was being paid sizable fees. At Del Mar, where he'd scored many of his most memorable victories, the occasion was accompanied by a ruthless hustling of products—T-shirts, trinkets, pictures, assorted gewgaws—that left a sour taste of commerce in the mouth. Several writers, especially in the East, had taken him to task for all this and pointed out that the tone of these promotions was questionable. Paranoia is rampant at the racetrack, and anything that smacks even faintly of a fix tends to erode public confidence in what is, essentially, a far more honest enterprise than banking and the stock market.

The rumor was that he needed the money. He'd had a couple of expensive divorces and, like many athletes, made some incautious investments. But if he hadn't, why should we take him to task for wanting to cash in on his fame? It was all show biz anyway, wasn't it, and the tracks were making money, weren't they? On the day *The New York Times* cluck-clucked over the whole business, Will Clark signed to play baseball in San Francisco for about twenty-three thousand dollars a game, and hardly anyone gives away a free autograph anymore. Shoemaker was entitled to whatever he could get; the only celebrity who isn't on the take these days is Mother Teresa and she doesn't have an agent yet.

Jockeys are not the most graceful of athletes. In most other countries, where the races are longer and almost exclusively contested on deep turf, the emphasis is on endurance, and riders can weigh up to a hundred and thirty pounds. In the United States, three out of every four races are sprints, run over dirt courses. American riders are expected to "make the weight," which means having to compete at a hundred and seventeen pounds or less. Many of them, consequently, are odd-looking little men who can appear ridiculous in their multicolored silks, porkpie helmets and white breeches. Even on horseback they can seem awkward, all hunched up on the shoulders of their mounts, spindly legs tucked under them like precariously perched monkeys. Perhaps this is why they're never taken seriously when the barroom talk gets around to discussions of greatness on the athletic fields. The feeling among the uninitiated seems to be that it's the horse that does the actual running, not that high-riding speck up there holding on for dear life. Even many quite sophisticated bettors believe that a good jockey can indeed help a great horse achieve his potential, but that most of them are merely along for the ride.

Shoemaker was one of the few who looked as if they belonged nowhere else but in the saddle. At four feet eleven and his normal weight of ninety-three pounds, he was smaller than most race riders, but well-proportioned and with the hard-muscled body of a superbly conditioned athlete. In a race, with his mount in full stride, Shoemaker seemed to blend with the animal, to become a part of him, the guiding force that would extract every ounce of talent and heart the beast had in him and bring him home a winner. Like a few other great riders—Braulio Baeza, Eddie Arcaro and Angel Cordero come immediately to mind—Shoemaker was beautiful to watch in action, nearly as beautiful as the magnificent animals he rode. He belonged to that category of great athletes who made whatever they did seem easy. He was to horse racing what Joe DiMaggio and Willie Mays were to baseball, Bill Tilden and Alice Marble to tennis, Arnold Palmer to golf, Sugar Ray Robinson to boxing—the consummate professional whose special quality was once defined by Ernest Hemingway as grace under pressure. It is possibly the only claim to genius any athlete can ever make.

What was even more astonishing about Shoemaker was his longevity. By the time he retired he had been around as a top rider for forty years and held every record in the books for money and races won. Although he competed mainly in southern California, he rode everywhere and won races all over the world. While still in his mid-forties, after recovering from a series of injuries, Shoemaker put himself through a testing program devised by the National Athletic Health Institute. He was listed among the top ten percent in "muscle strength, power and endurance," along with such much bigger and younger men as Wilt Chamberlain, the basketball star, and Ron Cey, the third baseman of the Los Angeles Dodgers. Furthermore, his reflexes and overall abilities were found to be those of a man at least twenty years younger. "He's a true phenomenon," Dr. Robert Kerlan, an orthopedic surgeon and close friend, observed at the time.

As for his riding ability, Charlie Whittingham, who put him up on many of his best horses, was never able to spot any weakness in him. "At least I don't know of any," he once said. "The first time I saw him, up at Golden Gate in San Francisco, I knew he was a natural, like Arcaro. I took him on right away, because I could see he was the best."

Billy Lee Shoemaker was born prematurely on August 19, 1931, near the small town of Fabens, Texas, about thirty miles from El Paso. He weighed only two and a half pounds at birth, and the doctor who delivered him told his parents that the child probably wouldn't make it through the night. His grandmother kept him alive by putting him in a shoe box, tucking him in the oven with the door open and turning on the heat. This improvised incubator almost certainly saved his life, though he was to remain forever undersized.

His father worked in a cotton mill in Fabens, then later drifted from job to job in different parts of the state; it was the Depression and steady work was hard to find. When Billy Lee was seven, he and his younger brother Lonnie went to live for three years with his grandparents, who managed a cattle and sheep ranch in Winters, Texas, not far from Abilene. The boy enjoyed ranch life and rode his grandfather's horse every day to pick up the mail, an event he still remembers as "my big thing for the day."

During this time, Shoemaker's parents divorced. His father remarried and in 1941 settled in suburban Los Angeles, where he went to work in a defense factory and then sent for his sons. Shoemaker, who weighed only eighty pounds, took enthusiastically to the comprehensive sports programs offered by the California public schools, first in Baldwin Park, then at El Monte Union High School. Too small to play football or basketball, he went out for the wrestling and boxing teams and never lost a match. Then a girl he had met as a freshman in high school and who was herself dating a jockey told him he ought to consider becoming a rider, a possible career that had never occurred to him.

Without telling his father, he quit school and went to work at the Suzy Q Ranch, a Thoroughbred spread in nearby Puente. "It's the best way to learn all about horses," he wrote years later, in his book *The Shoe*, "what to do with them in the beginning, and to get a real good feel about them. That's not just like coming to the track and getting on a horse and then a year later you're riding races. You really don't know what the hell the horse is all about." By the time his father discovered his son's defection from academe, it was too late to do much about it, even had he wanted to. At the age of sixteen, Shoemaker went to live on the ranch, for seventy-five dollars a month plus room and board. He loved the life and everything that had to do with horses. "Right from the word go, I just knew I wanted to be a rider."

A year later, in 1948, he and a friend named Bill Roland, who also worked on the ranch, decided to go to the races at Bay Meadows, near San Francisco. The boys went into the stable area and walked around, inquiring about work. A trainer named Hurst Philpot put the seventeen-year-old Shoemaker up on a fractious mare he knew would run off with him, then, as some compensation for this mischief, took the boy on as an exercise rider and hot-walker.

Philpot's regular jockey at the time was Johnny Adams, one of the best in the country, and Shoemaker learned a great deal simply by watching him. "I was probably the best exercise boy Philpot ever had," he said later, "but I didn't know much about race riding—how to cross the reins, how to really get down on a horse, things like that. Nobody could do those things better than Johnny, and I studied his every move. After a while, I couldn't wait to get out there myself and show what I could do."

Philpot had two other young apprentices working for him whom he considered better riders than Shoemaker. "He'd decided I was too small to become a good jockey," Shoemaker recalled, "so he wouldn't put me up on his horses in races." Many trainers, here and abroad, feel that ideally jockeys should weigh about a hundred and fourteen pounds. Otherwise the weight conditions in most races would necessitate the use of what the horsemen call dead weight, in the form of small strips of lead inserted into pouches in the saddlecloth. The theory, a dubious one, is that horses, in such circumstances, not only are harder to control in the early stages of a race, but will not respond at the finish with that essential extra effort a great jockey riding "live weight" can elicit from his tiring mount.

Convinced that Philpot would never give him a chance, Shoemaker quit his job the following summer, at the end of the Hollywood Park meeting, and went down to Del Mar, where he went to work for George Reeves, a trainer who saw something in the boy that Philpot had missed. "He was little, all right, but, boy, he sure could sit on a horse," Willis Reavis remembered years later. "George was a friend of mine and we both noticed what good hands Shoe had. The hands, that's what makes for a rider. They was always real still. And horses liked him. They didn't run off on him or fight him none. They settled down and did what they was supposed to. Hell, you can't make that kind of talent. You either got it or you ain't." Reeves signed Shoemaker to an apprentice contract and told the boy he'd soon put him on "something live."

Shoemaker did not ride in a race at Del Mar that season, but continued to learn and went north with Reeves in the fall. That winter, during the first few days of the 1949 Santa Anita meeting, Reeves introduced his apprentice to Harry Silbert, an experienced jockey's agent from New York who had moved to California and was then booking mounts for Bill Passmore, an established rider. The trainer urged Silbert to take the new boy on, and the agent, who knew that Passmore would be leaving him soon to return back East, answered that he'd keep the prospect in mind, though he wouldn't commit himself until he had actually seen Shoemaker ride in a race or two.

On March 19, 1949, Reeves finally put his apprentice rider up on an experienced old race mare named Waxahachie, in a six-furlong sprint at Golden Gate Fields in San Francisco. She finished fifth. Silbert's wife was ill that day, so the agent was unable to attend, but a week later he showed up, had a look at Shoemaker's second effort, a fourth-place finish on a ninety-to-one shot named Soonuseeme, and took the boy on. The deal was concluded by a handshake, the only contract the two men ever had between them, and Silbert remained his agent until he died in 1987. "Shoe's a great man," he once mumbled, around his omnipresent cigar. "He does the riding and he let's me do the picking."

Shoemaker rode his first winner on April 20, 1949, at Golden Gate. She was another experienced old race mare named Shafter V., who had won as the favorite in a race the week before with a well-known jockey on her back. Because no one knew much about her new rider, this time she left the starting gate at odds of nine to one. Shoemaker then promptly won seven more races that week, the start of a year in which he was to bring in a total of two hundred and nineteen, second-highest in the nation.

Silbert, a gruff but fatherly sort, practically adopted Shoemaker, who moved in with him and his wife and grew up with their children. The agent, however, was not only a warm family man, but a tough-minded horseman, with a talent for figures, persistence and an iron sense of loyalty. Despite his new client's early successes, he knew very well that his boy was still raw. Every year talented young apprentices, who benefit by special weight allowances to compensate for their inexperience, flash across racing's horizons, capturing headlines and winners because owners and trainers, who want the least weight possible on their good horses, are quick to book them. Once they graduate to journeyman status, however, and lose their "bug" (the asterisk denoting a weight allowance beside an apprentice jockey's name on a racing program), most of these flashy young comets, thrown into competition for good mounts with the best of the older riders, have to settle for mediocrity or, in quite a few cases, complete oblivion. "The bushes are full of old bums who used to be stars," Silbert once said. "They win twenty, thirty races, they think they got it made. You got to earn it every day you ride and you'd better know what you're doing out there."

That first year, Silbert sent his new client south on Sundays to Agua Caliente, the dusty little track across the border in Tijuana, Mexico, that used to conduct year-around weekend racing, and so had his boy riding seven days a week. "The more you ride, the better you get," Shoemaker once explained. "Harry knew there were a lot of things I was still doing wrong. It takes a year or so before you mold yourself into the style that's right for you. Most kids emulate a top rider—then it was Arcaro, a terrific hand-and-whip rider—but everyone's different, everyone's built differently, so you have to develop your own style."

It was during his first two years with Silbert that Shoemaker became a real race rider. He mastered all the physical skills required of jockeys, and the experience of riding every day taught him about tactics—how to get out of the starting gate cleanly and get position, when to move with a horse, how to get the animal to relax and change leads, when to come through between horses, avoiding going too wide on tight turns, how to judge pace and how to reserve something extra for the finish. And it soon became clear to almost everyone in racing that this new bug boy, with his quiet hands and short stirrups and his way of moving in perfect harmony with his mount, had established himself as one of the best the world of racing had ever seen.

Shoemaker's greatest asset, however, turned out to be not his physical skills, but his temperament. He had all the attributes of a great competitor, so tough-minded and chilly that a sportswriter once compared him to a bucket of ice cubes. "If you get beat," Shoemaker once said, "control your emotions when you have to, when you need to. That's the key." This unflappability, however, masked a competitive spirit so acute that it often surprised rivals, who found themselves beaten just when they thought they had the race won. (A favorite Shoemaker tactic in a distance contest, for instance, was to sneak out to an easy lead, give his horse a breather, then come on again with an extra all-out effort in the last few hundred yards; it often caught opponents napping.) One old friend once summed up Shoemaker's basic attitude this way: "There's got to be a winner, so why shouldn't it be me? The tactics are those of a good poker player. He sizes up his opposition and adjusts to the changing situation, with the self-discipline of the born winner."

In 1951, Shoemaker rode in New York for the first time and divided his efforts between both coasts. Eddie Arcaro, then the nation's top rider, had never heard of the new kid, but he was among the first to appreciate his talent and recommend him to racing people. It opened doors everywhere for him. "Arcaro was the greatest rider I've ever seen," Shoemaker once observed. "When he said I could ride, it really meant something."

By 1953 Shoemaker and Silbert were piling up the statistics. That year alone the combination brought home 485 winners, a new world's record that was all the more impressive because there were fewer races and shorter seasons in those days. In 1954, Shoemaker won 380 races out of 1,251 mounts, for a winning percentage of .304, the highest of any rider in this century.

He rode many of the country's best horses, including Gallant Man, Round Table, Olden Times, Buckpasser, Damascus, Candy Spots and the filly Cicada. In his later years, he was up on Exceller, Spectacular Bid and Ferdinand, on whom he won the Kentucky Derby with a weaving ride through traffic that was acclaimed as a masterpiece. "The first really good horse I ever rode," Shoemaker once recalled, "was Swaps, only at first I didn't know what I had under me." Swaps belonged to Rex Ellsworth, a breeder and owner then just beginning to establish a reputation in 1954, when the jockey won his first race on the colt. It wasn't until the following spring, however, when Swaps easily defeated a good field in a stakes race at Santa Anita, that Shoemaker realized he had been put up on "the kind of horse he turned out to be."

Swaps won the Kentucky Derby that year, when the colt to beat was Nashua, ridden by Eddie Arcaro. In the paddock before the race, Mesh Tenney, Swaps's trainer, left it up to his jockey as to how this feat was to be accomplished. "You're supposed to be a good rider," he told him. "Use your judgment."

Shoemaker took Swaps out to an easy lead on a relatively slow pace. By the time Arcaro realized what was happening and moved on Nashua, he found himself chasing a fresh horse. Shoemaker simply clucked to his mount and pulled away to win handily. Later on Nashua humbled Swaps in a match race and was probably always the better horse, but Shoemaker's ride in the Derby only proved what a difference the jockey could make in a race. He established himself that day as probably the greatest judge of pace alive and against the man, Arcaro, of whom people said that he had a clock in his head.

Even the best riders, of course, can make disastrous mistakes. In the 1957 Kentucky Derby, Shoemaker had the race all but won on Gallant Man, but he misjudged the finish line and stood up in the irons about a sixteenth of a mile from home. By the time he realized his mistake it was too late, and Gallant Man lost by a nose to Iron Liege. The incident caused a furor and got Shoemaker suspended for fifteen days. He came back on Gallant Man that year to win the Belmont Stakes, but few remember that today. His mistake in the Derby became one of sports' most celebrated boners, right up there with Dodger catcher Mickey Owen's ninth-inning passed ball against the Yankees in the World Series and Jim Marshall's touchdown run in the wrong direction for the Minnesota Vikings.

Like most jockeys, Shoemaker had his share of crippling injuries. He once shattered his right hand and was out for two months. Then, early in 1968, at Santa Anita, he fell and broke his right leg because another jockey miscalculated and tried to go through a hole that wasn't there. As Shoemaker went down, his horse kicked him and broke his femur. Dr. Kerlan, whose specialty is patching up damaged athletes, operated and inserted a metal pin from the hip through the thigh in order to help the healing process. Nevertheless, it was thirteen months before Shoemaker came back to the races. His right leg had withered and his knee stiffened; he had to put in months of physical therapy to rebuild the muscles and loosen the knee joint. The accident left him with a long, thin scar on his right thigh.

Finally, on February 11, 1969, at Santa Anita again, Shoemaker came back. Silbert had put his client up on three horses that day. The first one won and earned the rider a standing ovation. In the feature race, Shoemaker brought a sprinter named Racing Room home a winner and helped the colt break the track record for six and a half furlongs while doing it. In the ninth, he made it three for three with still another win. At home that night, Shoemaker cried. He hadn't realized what it had meant to him to ride horses. "I'd never questioned my talent or my luck before," he explained.

Two months later, he was hurt again in a freak accident at Hollywood Park. A skittish filly flipped over backward on him in the paddock, shattering his pelvis and rupturing his bladder. The pain this time was worse than anything he had experienced before, and as he lay in a hospital bed with tubes protruding from his stomach, he didn't think he would make it back a second time.

Once again, however, he climbed back into the saddle. For weeks he exercised to build himself up and galloped horses in the early mornings. When he went back to race riding this time, he didn't win first crack out of the gate, but it didn't matter to him that much. He knew how lucky he had been not to have been badly hurt earlier in his career. "It was enough just to be out there," he said afterward. "It felt real good."

The severity of these accidents led to some speculation in the press that Shoemaker might soon want to retire, but he himself had never actually considered the possibility seriously. "You know you're going to have to do it someday," he said, "but you don't want to think about it. If physically I couldn't ride or mentally didn't feel like it, if I didn't have the drive to go out and win, well, then I'd probably do it. Some lose the drive early, some lose it in the middle, only a few still have it late. I'm one of the late ones."

At Del Mar the following summer, Shoemaker rode his six thousand and thirty-third winner, breaking a record set by Johnny Longden in forty years of riding. Shoemaker had been competing for only twenty-two. In 1971, he won forty-six stakes races to break Bill Hartack's record of forty-three, set in 1957. In 1972, he passed Eddie Arcaro as the record-holder in career wins, ending that season with 577 for the year. At meet after meet, year after year, Shoemaker kept winning. As he aged into his forties, he seemed to get better, like fine Bordeaux. And outwardly he remained much the same sort of man he'd always been—very quiet, reserved, loyal to his old friends, unflappable and ruthlessly single-minded about his profession.

His personal life, however, was in turmoil and finally it began to affect his performance. Shoemaker's first marriage, in 1951, had ended in a costly divorce. His second one, to a glamorous society belle, was reportedly now unraveling, and it was rumored that there were financial complications as well. Characteristically, Shoemaker refused to discuss any aspect of his private life with the press, but gossip about the situation persisted. Whatever the truth may have been, the fact was that for the first time in his career the jockey seemed to be riding with less than his usual verve. He still won races, but observers noted that he was five pounds overweight, looked pale and a bit flabby. He also didn't appear to care as much or to be trying quite as hard, and he made mistakes. As an old friend put it at the time, "What the hell's the sense of trying when, no matter what you earn, you're spending more?"

The marriage ended in divorce and it was rumored that Shoemaker, after all those years and all those winners, was nearly broke. However, it didn't seem to matter to him. He suddenly began to ride with his old zest. It got so that every time he posed in the winner's circle it established a new record, and well into his fifties the end of his career seemed nowhere in sight. "As you get older, you do have to pay more attention to keeping fit," he observed. "The strain is on your legs and back and it gets harder to keep in shape. When I'm not riding, I run two miles a day and I don't vary my routine all that much. The point is, I still have the desire to do it and to do it right."

He married again, to Cynthia (Cindy) Barnes, the daughter of a retired brigadier general. She was a tall, leggy California blonde in her late twenties who had grown up around horses in the Del Mar area and loved racing. She showed up at the track every day with her husband and talked about him, to anyone who would listen, with unqualified enthusiasm and admiration. Her only complaint was that he had never seen her ride and apparently had little interest in discussing the finer points of the sport with her.

Cindy's own total involvement in the world of horses was regarded by the jockey's oldest friends as a boon, because Shoe-maker seemed to have no outside interests. His working day began at six-thirty A.M., when he'd get up, put on boots, pants, a turtle-neck jersey or sweater and a helmet and head for either Santa Anita or Hollywood Park, a half-hour away by car from his home in Beverly Hills. He'd work or gallop horses for Charlie Whittingham and a few other trainers, the ones Harry Silbert had contracted with for mounts. Between nine o'clock, when the workouts ended, and post time at midday he'd remain in the jockey room, where he'd get a massage and play a cutthroat three-handed game of pinochle with his old cronies. The game would go on intermit-tently all afternoon between races and was played by Shoemaker with the same fierce concentration he brought to his profession.

Except for visits with a few old friends, all of whom were connected in one way or another to racing, and attendance at the sport's official functions and parties, the Shoemakers rarely went out, especially after the birth of their daughter, Amanda. Their place in Beverly Hills was an unpretentious split-level ranch house, comfortably furnished and well stocked with riding trophies, but without even a pool or a tennis court. The couple spent their evenings playing gin rummy or watching sports events on TV. Aside from reading an occasional historical romance and playing a graceful game of social tennis, the rider seemed to have no outside interests. "This doesn't make him a great human being and I can think of a lot of people who are more fun to have around than

Shoe," an old friend remarked a few years ago. "Basically, Shoe's a fanatic, a real sportsholic, but he's also a steady, dependable friend, as loyal as they come, and right there when you need him every time. Look at all the people who are great at what they do. Usually, outside of that, they're just plain bores. Shoe's world is all-consuming. It's locked into its mystique like that of the circus or a traveling carnival. But in that world he's the best there is."

I was one of about sixty-five thousand people who showed up at Santa Anita for "The Legend's Last Ride," which was run as the fifth race on the program in order to accommodate ABC, and we were treated to a prerace ceremony apparently dreamed up in Disneyland. The Legend himself, attired in the red silks of his newly formed racing stable, marched out in front of the stands behind a swirl of Scottish bagpipers. Jim McKay introduced him to the crowd, as his fellow riders straggled in behind him, dressed in the colors of some of the important owners Shoemaker had ridden for. The calls of some of his most notable rides were broadcast over the PA system, and then there was a message from George Bush. "You've thrilled us all," the president said, in his usual inspired rhetoric, after which the crowd was introduced to the parasitical notables and politicos who infest these events.

Shoemaker got the only laugh of the afternoon when he began his thank-you speech by noting that he was "glad to hear the president's a horseplayer." Then the band played "Auld Lang Syne," and a skydiver came plummeting to earth under a parachute emblazoned with the Stars and Stripes and flying a banner proclaiming, "Thank you, Shoe." The surrealistic quality of this ceremony was ultimately dignified by the single tear the usually stoic Shoemaker shed at the first sight of his colleagues lined up on the podium behind him.

As for the race itself, it turned out to be a thriller. It was contested at a mile on the turf course, and the hundred-thousand-dollar purse attracted a highly competitive field of good second-rank animals, the sort of horses that don't win the major stakes and handicaps but can run. Shoe had chosen for his mount a tough, seven-year-old hard knocker named Patchy Groundfog, who rarely put in a dull effort and won his share of events at meet after meet. Listed at two to one in the morning-line odds, Patchy Groundfog figured to be just the kind of horse Shoemaker could still ride fairly well, a competitor with enough speed to get a good position early in the race and the heart not to quit in the stretch.

The crowd, out of both sentiment and cynicism, knocked Patchy Groundfog down to one to nine in the early wagering and eventually sent him off at the prohibitively low odds of three to five. It was a heaven-sent opportunity for the professional horseplayers, who were getting terrific prices on everything else in the race. When it finally went off, Trevor Denman, the track announcer, called it as if it were an exhibition and even shouted, "Come on, Shoe!" as the horses turned into the stretch. Patchy Groundfog had the lead at that point but couldn't hold it, as three horses swept past him at the wire. The winner, Exemplary Leader, ridden by Eddie Delahoussaye, paid an inflated $26.80, impoverished the cynics, and confirmed the basic integrity of the sport.

It may have been the only time during his long career that Shoemaker was cheered for finishing out of the money on a favorite. Jockeys are used to being booed. In fact, Shoemaker was booed more than most, partly because, like all jockeys, he didn't always ride to win and partly because he never abused an animal he knew had no chance to win merely in order to finish in the money. Trainers sometimes use races as workouts or preps for other races and tell jockeys not to try too hard, usually by such euphemisms as "he'll need a race" or "he'll be a little short." Strictly speaking, every horse in a race should be trying its best to win, but the procedure is an accepted part of the game. Shoemaker followed orders, but this did not make him popular with the hard-core gamblers. When I asked a friend of mine from Del Mar, who hadn't had a kind word to say for Shoemaker for the past twenty years, why he had come up for the great day, he answered, "I want to make *sure* he retires."

During his long career, Shoemaker rode in 40,351 races and galloped and worked several hundred thousand other horses in the early mornings. Any one of these animals could have killed him or incapacitated him for life. He survived them all, only to be done in by a machine.

Late on the afternoon of April 8, 1991, while driving home from a round of golf and a couple of beers with his old pal and riding rival, Donald Pierce, he lost control of his Ford Bronco. The car tumbled down a freeway embankment near San Dimas, rolling over several times. Shoemaker had his seat belt on, but the accident crushed and twisted his spine so badly that it has left him a quadriplegic, without the use of his limbs or lower abdominal muscles. He can now breathe and talk, but it's unlikely that he will ever regain the use of even a finger and will be confined to a wheelchair the rest of his life.

Nevertheless, as I wrote these words, he was looking forward to getting back to the track to supervise the management and conditioning of his string of horses. "Sure, I've been dealt a bad hand, so I'll just have to play it," he told a reporter for the *Racing Times*, who went out to see him at the medical facility in Englewood, Colorado, where for over five months he had been undergoing therapy and training. "I'm luckier than most," he also said. Class and courage, two qualities Bill Shoemaker has exemplified from the day he was born.

10

FAIR AND FOUL

"This is a race for pigs."
"Yeah? How come my wife ain't entered?"
—Overheard in the stands at the Alameda
County Fair

I NEVER even knew they had horse racing at county fairs until I moved to California. Nor was my first experience with the form reassuring. I found myself one September afternoon in the mid-sixties in the grandstand at Pomona, during the annual Los Angeles County Fair, inhaling great clouds of smog while trying to make sense of what was happening on the half-mile dirt oval below me. The early races were contests for quarter horses, Appaloosas and Standardbreds, the latter trotting or pacing along while pulling fat old men in two-wheeled carts behind them. The Thoroughbreds, who showed up for the remainder of the card, races five through twelve, were not an inspiring bunch. Most of them seemed to have been imported for the occasion from bush tracks all over the state, as well as from Arizona, Wyoming, Oregon, Washington, and Mexico. Their riders, too, were mostly unknown to me, regulars from other fair meets who rode like cowboys, whipping and slashing as they jerked hard on the reins to wrench their mounts around the tight turns of the bullring. I prudently risked very little money on these contests, but failed to cash a ticket. It wasn't until a horse I had an interest in, Quita Dude, showed up to run and win at Pomona the following year that I began to appreciate the benefits of the so-called fair circuit.

Fairs are big business in California, ranked among the top sixty industries in the state, and they share one primary function, that of a trade center. As one fair official once explained to me, "they create a market and stimulate business in their communities." There are now about eighty county, district and citrus fairs in the state every year, and the larger ones attract more than fifty thousand people a day on weekends and holidays. Not just because of the racing either. There are glitzy amusement zones with Ferris wheels and game booths, big-name entertainers, junk-food stands. And then there are the displays—all those animals, vegetables, fruit, flowers and home-made items, most of them for sale. A fair, I discovered, is a cornucopia of goodies and a place to compete, a yearly wingding in which the ordinary citizen can win himself a moment in the public spotlight and take home a handful of blue ribbons.

Horse racing is only one facet of this operation, but continues to thrive because the success of the fairs as a whole guarantees a purse structure for the horsemen that is the most generous in the nation. Even the cheapest claimers on the grounds at Pomona (now officially known as Fairplex Park, since its conversion a few years ago from a half-mile to a five-furlong track) compete for prizes worth nearly twice the value of the horses themselves, which makes it possible for their owners and trainers to stay in business the rest of the year. The circuit of ten meets operates from early June until mid-October, beginning in Stockton and ending in Fresno, with the horse people shifting locales every two weeks like carnies.

Some horses compete only on the fair circuit and are exhumed every spring to earn enough loot to get their connections through the winter, though most of them will show up the rest of the year at Agua Caliente, at the smaller tracks in other states, or in the cheaper events at the Bay Area hippodromes. I've learned to bet on these animals with caution, although I've also discovered that some of them favor certain racing surfaces and will win year after year over their favorite ovals. I have an acquaintance in L.A. who keeps a complete record of such matters and who can't wait for the fair circuit to get under way every year. He disappears from Hollywood Park in the spring and shows up again at Santa Anita in the fall, halfway through the Oak Tree meet, much refreshed and enriched. "In almost any race at any fair you can throw out at least half the field and sometimes all but two or three horses," he maintains, a handicapping edge that can prove invaluable to a fearless player and compensate him for having to live in motels four months out of the year.

My favorite fair is the one they put on for two weeks, in late June and early July, in Pleasanton, an old California settlement about forty minutes by freeway southeast of Oakland and San Francisco, in the so-called Tri-Valley area. The old town, which dates back to the Gold Rush, was built along the railroad tracks on flat land between gentle hills and is sheltered by large trees from the oppressive heat of summer. Many of the older wooden-frame houses have survived, as well as some of the original commercial buildings along Main Street, with their high false fronts that symbolize, to me at least, the braggadocio of the Old West. Some of them, like the Pleasanton Hotel, have been converted into restaurants and boutiques, while others still function as saloons and old-fashioned stores. A banner strung up over the street welcomes visitors to the "Home of the Alameda County Fair, Family Fun for Everyone," and the atmosphere retains a reassuring quality of uncompromising rusticity.

It is, of course, no more authentic than the false storefronts that now shelter establishments catering to weekend visitors and a more urban permanent population. Like most of the once rural communities within easy driving distance of the Bay Area, Pleasanton has been booming these past few years from an influx of middle-class fugitives from the cities, with new homes, condominiums, shopping malls and an industrial park ringing the historic center. More and more of the ancient establishments on Main Street are being converted to trendier uses, and the ranchers and Latino farmhands, who once dominated the downtown scene, today find themselves competing for sidewalk space with nattily attired business people on the make and thirtysomething couples pushing strollers.

Luckily, the fair, with its tawdry carnival games, animals and outdated displays, preserves much of the town's original raison d'être, which, after the madness of the gold fever, was based on agriculture. People still grow things in this countryside, and during the fair they all converge on what for them is still the year's most important public event. Coastal Californians and city dwellers tend to forget that we are still members of an essentially rural community, with roots deep in the soil, and I always find it an enlightening experience to be someplace where I'm surrounded by citizens who obviously spend most of their lives outdoors. "Now, Wendell, you hush up," I once heard a mother at the L.A. County Fair admonish her small boy, who had begun to cry at the explosion of light and sound at the opening of a rock concert. "This don't mean nothin'. It's just Hollywood."

"I come here every year," a gray-haired woman told me at another fair some years ago. "I've kept on coming, even though my kids have grown up and stopped showing. I guess it's because this fair brings the whole area together once a year. It tells us who we are and what we're up to. I like that."

They've been racing horses in Pleasanton since 1858, when one Augustin Bernal, a descendant of the early Spanish settlers, built a track and put on some sort of meet. This was six years before the opening of Saratoga and has caused some local boosters to claim that Pleasanton is the oldest racetrack in America, a bit of chauvinistic stretching of the truth. The first Alameda County Fair was held in San Leandro, about fifteen miles to the west, in 1859, and it wasn't until 1912 that the operation moved to its present location on the outskirts of the old town, when a group of prominent citizens banded together to sell stock in the venture and built a grandstand and track on private land.

It was a hit-and-miss operation that limped along until 1932, when the Junior Chamber of Commerce put on a Fourth of July celebration that included a parade, the election of a hometown beauty as the "Goddess of Liberty," and horse racing. The original grandstand had burned down, so the fans sat on borrowed folding chairs to watch the action, and at night most of the town's eighteen hundred residents turned out for an open-air street dance.

The event was such a success that it inspired the local authorities to keep it going, and by 1938, after the passage of a state law two years earlier that made public funds available to promote fairs and educational activities, it became established as an annual county fair. When parimutuel wagering came in the following year for the three-day meet, the occasion was dramatically acclaimed by the *San Francisco Chronicle* as "the revival of East Bay racing . . . on the same spot where horse racing had its birth in California more than seventy years ago when the Spanish Dons built the first track here." Hyperbole has always been characteristic of reportage in the Bay Area.

Today, about half a million people attend the fair, which sprawls over 266 acres and includes a museum housing a collection of ancient agricultural implements, while enshrining the achievements of the area's rustics. The horseplayers, as is their wont, tend to ignore such sideshows and head straight for the grandstand, a high, square concrete structure overlooking a one-mile track and a nine-hole infield golf course. The view of the racing is unobstructed and the crowd of several thousand people in the stands on an average day tends to be cheerful, a family affair, mostly, with small children running up and down the aisles. Several times every afternoon, the announcer and race caller, an affable Irishman named Dick Riley, who's been doing this sort of thing for years, has to remind the kids to get off the rail. "Thanks for coming to the races," he says at the end of the day, "drive home carefully and stay off the fence."

The racing itself can hardly be called first-rate, but a few talented animals do put in an appearance, usually from elsewhere, for the richer purses. Most of the horses are stabled in parallel rows of ugly stucco or stone barns outside the fair itself and file onto the grounds along an overpass leading directly to a graceless dusty paddock halfway down the stretch. "Ascot this ain't," a friend of mine observed one day, as we leaned against the rail watching the entries for the feature race come out on the track, "but it's fun, isn't it?"

Yes and no. Too many peculiar things happen at the fairs, especially in the cheaper races, for me to bet with any confidence. At Pleasanton, the old hands, whom my friend refers to as the "legendary handicappers," sit on the very top row of the grand-stand, just below the press box, and they set standards of behavior the average bettor would do well to emulate. I spent part of one day up there with three of these old duffers two years ago and watched four races go by before any one of them made a move toward a betting window. When I got up to go and risk exactly two dollars on a sprint featuring Arabians, one of them, a pink-cheeked, slender old man wearing a short-sleeved plaid sports shirt out of which his arms protruded like leeks, looked up from under his blue cap at me and said, "You're gonna bet? Fella, bettin' on Arabians is like bettin' on potato-sack races." He grinned at me. "They're sure pretty, but they can't run worth a fart."

I agreed with him, but told him I had never seen a race for Arabians before and felt that a token two dollars would probably not endanger my action in the later contests. "We had one good Arabian here one time a few years back," the old man told me, when I returned to my seat. "His name was Raf Oak. He won his first race by fifteen or twenty lengths. Then he won about five more before anybody looked up his breeding, and they found out he was part Thoroughbred. Hell, if an Arabian can run five furlongs in a minute flat, he's like Secretariat."

Not only didn't my Arabian run five furlongs in anything close to a minute, he was at least twelve lengths off that time and came lumbering in next to last, looking gorgeous, with his nostrils flaring and his white mane flying, but about as agile as an arma-dillo. His performance set the tone for my day, which I recall as a minor disaster in which I failed to cash a ticket in ten trips to the betting windows. (Most fair meets card an average of twelve races a day.) "You got to be patient here, fella," my legendary handicap-per informed me. "You got to wait for the right race. Some of these here trainers work all year on settin' a horse up to make one big score. That's what you got to wait for. Them races ain't all that hard to spot, see."

Still, though a lot of things can go wrong at any racetrack, they do seem to go wrong more often at the fairs. A couple of years ago, a trainer named Art Sherman was nursing a cheap colt called Ryan Baker up to a race on opening day at the Solano Fair in Vallejo. The horse had lost its previous two races by a combined total of thirty-five lengths, but after a long rest recovering from bucked shins, he was ready to run and had been training well. Sherman entered him in the third, bet on him to win and also coupled him in a daily double with a filly in the next race trained by a friend of his, who had told him he expected her to win.

Ten minutes before post time for the third, a transmitter blew up, shutting down the power for the whole fair. At any other racetrack, the proceedings would have come to a halt until the punters could get down, but most of the betting at fair races is done at off-track wagering facilities elsewhere in the state, all of which were functioning normally. So the race went off as scheduled. Needless to say, Ryan Baker won, at odds of seven to two, as did the filly in the following race, for a nice double payoff of $38.60. No sooner had the results been posted than the power came back on.

Electricity figured in one of my own misadventures at a country fair, this one in Elko, Nevada, about twenty years ago. I had gone up to Elko, then a town of about five thousand people in the northeastern part of the state, to write a story about the area for a travel magazine. I arrived at the start of the Labor Day weekend, when the place was packed not only with tourists but with visitors from the surrounding area, in for the annual four-day county fair. Elko is located in cattle and sheep country, not far from the Ruby Mountains, where prospectors still roamed hunting for uranium and gold. Many of these people, most of them men who hadn't seen a woman in weeks, came to party, and the atmosphere in the streets, as well as the bars and casinos, was Dionysian. Luckily, the county sanctioned legalized prostitution, in the form of half a dozen licensed whorehouses, a service that kept the hookers off the streets and out of the bars, defused potential violence and lowered the disease rate.

Not the least of the weekend's attractions, I discovered, was horse racing. When I asked the clerk at my hotel what kind of horses were on the premises, he asked me where I was from. I told him Los Angeles and the clerk grinned at me. "It ain't like your type of racin', mister," he said. "They ride right down to the nuts here."

I wasn't sure what he meant by that, but I went out the next day, sat in a box the hotel maintained for its guests, and found out. The horses competed over a half-mile bullring, in a great cloud of dust that all but hid them from view until they turned into the stretch, lurching arthritically for the finish line. Even the quarter horses seemed slow and the Thoroughbreds appeared to be the battered survivors of far too many arduous campaigns in happier climes. They came home in glacially slow time and seemingly without reflecting the posted odds, which were chalked up by hand on a giant blackboard and related to the betting action, as relayed from the windows by jeans-clad teenagers sprinting back and forth. At one point, having spotted a horse in a race that looked as if it might remain alive during the contest and risked ten dollars on it, I watched the odds plunge in one change from five to one to eight to five. He turned out, however, to be the wrong horse, like all the others I bet on that day, and finished out of the money.

I did notice, however, that a few people around me, mostly prosperous-looking ranchers, appeared to be doing pretty well. They seemed to know all the horses and what they were capable of, despite the absence of any sort of published racing form, and I soon realized that my only hope of cashing a bet depended on my ability to get next to someone who knew something. When I communicated this impression to my hotel clerk that night, he advised me to get up early the next morning, go to the stable area and talk to a couple of people he knew.

I had intended to go to bed early that night, but a colleague of mine from a news magazine, whom I'll call Jack, insisted that we do some gambling before going to have a look at one of the local fleshpots. A man we met during an inglorious session at a craps table offered to act as our guide. He represented himself to us as an upstanding citizen and member of the Chamber of Commerce. "Nobody's going to hustle you," he assured us. "We'll just go in, explain what we're doing there, buy a few drinks and leave. No problem, you'll see."

We walked a couple of blocks from the hotel to a nondescript one-story house with a small neon sign out front saying, "Lucky Draw." A plump, elderly black woman dressed in gingham, with a knotted red handkerchief on her head, opened the door, bowing and smiling at us. "Evenin'," she said. "How you gentlemen doin'? Come right on in and make yourselves to home." I thought at first she might be putting us on with an imitation of some character out of a nineteen-thirties Hollywood movie or an Aunt Jemima pancake ad, but she seemed genuinely grateful for the dollar our guide slipped her as we entered.

She led us down a short corridor, opened another door and ushered us into the social center of the establishment, a long, narrow room with a bar and a blaring jukebox. A rip-roaring party was in progress, with country sounds bouncing off the walls, couples dancing, ten or twelve men lined up at the bar, and a large, motherly-looking woman cheerfully dispensing libations. Our guide quickly explained to this lady that we had nothing on our minds except having a few drinks, then turned to us and said, "No problem." Jack and I bought a round for the house, which endeared us to the company at large, and settled in at the bar to enjoy ourselves. "You know, that woman doesn't look like a madam," Jack said. "She looks like a Sunday School teacher."

"That's exactly what she is," our guide assured us and proceeded to explain that the bartender was not the madam, but the madam's sister from Minneapolis, who spent every summer vacation from her teaching duties back home tending bar at the Lucky Draw. "It's a nice change of pace for her, the girls and the customers like her, and she helps her sister out."

We must have spent an hour in the Lucky Draw, watching couples disappear from time to time into the inner recesses of the establishment as we socialized with the other guests, and nobody hustled us. I have to confess I wasn't tempted, not out of an excess of virtue but caution, and also because none of the seven or eight working girls at the Lucky Draw, though affable enough to chat with, could have qualified as Miss Universe contestants.

I made the mistake of communicating this opinion to our leader, who promptly insisted that we leave immediately and pay a visit to another house called Sue's, "the really classy place in town." It was late and I wanted to go back to my hotel, but Jack insisted, so I tagged along to Sue's, an establishment another few blocks away.

Several big moving vans were parked outside, which explains, I suppose, why it takes weeks to move one's furniture and belongings across the country. Inside, however, the place was silent and seemed to be empty. We strolled into a large room with a bar from behind which a small, angry-looking woman of about fifty gazed impassively at us. As we approached, she reached up behind her and pushed a button on the wall. A bell rang loudly and six scantily-clad females promptly filed in and lined up against the far wall like pieces of meat on a butcher's rack. By this time, our guide had launched into his spiel. "And all we want to do," he concluded, "is have a few drinks and a couple of laughs."

The woman ignored him and looked past us toward the employees. "All right, girls," she called out, "do it the hard way!"

Three of the women left, as the others came up to us and began to hustle, flinging arms around our shoulders, draping naked legs over our laps, thrusting various other body parts toward us. "No no no!" our guide protested. "You don't seem to understand! We—"

"Fuck or get out!" the woman said.

We took the second alternative and quickly disentangled ourselves. Out in the street, I looked at our guide, who seemed nonplused. "I don't understand it," he said. "Something must be bothering Sue."

"Let's go back to the Lucky Draw," Jack suggested. "I don't need a classy place."

I excused myself and went back to the hotel.

After a refreshing two and a half hours of sleep, I got up at dawn and went out to the fairgrounds, where I looked up the hotel clerk's pals and soon got to talking to the horsemen, though mostly I just listened. By post time that afternoon I had every race narrowed down to two or at most three contestants. I swept the card and proceeded to do nearly as well the next two days. I limited myself to betting no more than five or ten dollars at a time, in order to keep the odds from plunging, but even so I found myself about five hundred dollars ahead for the weekend.

One race in particular, however, struck me as peculiar. An aged gelding I had wagered ten dollars on in a distance race on the second day had opened up a big lead and then began visibly to tire on the final turn for home. Two horses swept past him and I kissed my money goodbye, but to my amazement he had suddenly come on again and managed to get up just in time along the rail, for a nice payoff of better than three to one. "Juice," I heard a man behind me say. "A little juice, that's all."

I'd been around the track long enough by then to know what he meant. The jockey on my animal had apparently resorted to a buzzer, which is an electrical device consisting simply of a small battery with a hot wire attached to it. The rider on a tiring mount gives his animal a jolt with it, usually on the neck, and exacts a second effort from him. The practice is heinous, but not that uncommon at the bush tracks, where the purses are tiny and the horsemen have to rely on cashing bets in order to stay alive. (Far worse things are done to cheap and ailing horses at the larger tracks under the euphemism of "medication," but even so, offenders should be set down for life, not merely fined and suspended, sometimes for no more than a few months, as they are today.)

In the sixth race of my final afternoon, I bet ten dollars on a scrawny filly owned and trained by a sheriff from Montana known to me only as Boyo. He looked the part, a ham-fisted big man with a stomach protruding over his belt and a purple-colored face under his cowboy hat. "Son, this filly of mine has a world of speed, but she quits like a dog," he had informed me over a cup of coffee on the backside that morning. "Today, son, she ain't gonna quit."

Boyo's speedball went off at five to two and quickly opened up seven or eight lengths out of the gate. She soon started to shorten stride, however, and the field caught up to her at the head of the stretch. I waited confidently for her to draw away again, but instead she began to buck and threw her jockey, who miraculously escaped unhurt as the other horses swept by her.

On my way out of the premises after the last race, I came upon Boyo leaning against a wall behind the stands. He was nursing a bottle of beer and looked disconsolate. I asked him what had happened. "Aw, she didn't like that buzzer none," he said.

11

VENUS ON HORSEBACK

"Horses are more important to me than most people."
—MARY BACON, jockey

I'M A city boy myself. I was brought up in Rome and New York, and until I moved out to California, all I knew about these animals was what I'd gleaned from having bet on them and spent a little time hanging around Pinky Blackburn's shedrow. Horses were large and very beautiful and very strong, but they were also unpredictable and dangerous. It wasn't until I found myself living in a rented house in Malibu, on several acres of flat, fenced-in land with stables and a riding ring, that I had any direct contact with them. And that happened because my older daughter Natalia, then only eleven, fell in love with one.

Along with our lease, we had also agreed to adopt the three horses on which our landlord's children had learned to ride. Two of these animals were long in the tooth. Quitan was a gentle twenty-six-year-old Appaloosa, whom my children immediately nicknamed The King because of his royal bearing and whom Julia, then age seven, took over. Ginger was a sour-tempered Indian pony whom nobody could ride and who had a nasty habit of biting. Shorty, the third of our borders, was a chunky bay gelding of about ten who immediately became the center of Natalia's universe, though it was some time before I realized the full extent of her commitment.

I was first and most forcibly struck by it on a summer afternoon a year or so later, when I found myself sitting on our back patio watching Natalia and two of her girlfriends, who were boarding their own horses with us, galloping about under the tall trees that shaded the corral next to the house. The girls were lean and brown, their long hair blowing behind them in the late-afternoon breeze as they swept past me, riding bareback in shorts and T-shirts, the animals under them seeming to be merely extensions of their own vitality and grace. I was entranced by the spectacle, because I thought I had never seen anything quite so beautiful, as if the scene had been created for my enjoyment by a great artist. It was my first direct exposure to one of history's great love affairs, the relationship between women and horses.

It took me a while to warm up to it, mainly because, like most love affairs, the romance proved to be expensive. Horses eat almost all of the time and not only hay, which is relatively cheap. They munch on grains and guzzle noxious elixirs guaranteed to make their coats shine and keep them frisky. And they need equipment—bedding, boots, breeches, bridles, brooms, buckets, bits, and endless items from other letters in the alphabet, none of them cheap. The saddle alone, especially if ordered from some fancy emporium like Hermès in Paris, could wipe out your credit cards. After Natalia began to take lessons, got into shows and won a few ribbons, I had to consider taking out a bank loan. It was a vast relief to me when, after a couple of years, she suddenly opted to go back to informal trail-riding, galloping up and down the beach or swooping about Indian-style with her friends. I relaxed. At least we hadn't had to buy the horse.

Then, Shorty got sick. Natalia found him standing head down in his stall one afternoon, his stomach badly swollen. He had colic, a form of indigestion that can be very serious in a horse because he can't throw up; if the air inside the animal can't be released in the normal way, the pressure can cause a rupture and infection that will kill him. Our local vet administered antibiotics, but informed us that we had to keep Shorty moving and on his feet; he must not be allowed to lie down.

For two days we all took turns nursing Shorty. We walked him endlessly and cheered every time he relieved himself. He seemed to be improving, but when I went out to see him early in the morning of the third day I found him lying on his side, dead. I then had to go into my daughter's bedroom to wake her up and tell her.

Natalia was inconsolable for several hours, but later that afternoon she and her mother walked out to see Shorty and say goodbye. Nat put her cheek down against Shorty's neck and talked softly to him for a while, then sat beside him until it became dark.

Disposing of a dead horse is a gruesome business, especially because of the animal's size. Shorty was hauled away by two men in a truck with a winch and donated to a zoo, where he provided nourishment for the carnivores on the premises. It seemed to me a useful end, not unlike what would have happened to him in the wild, but it was a long time before I told my daughter what had become of him. She simply came home from school that day to find him gone. It was many weeks before she went near the stable area.

"Nat's riding again," my wife informed me one evening, then went on to tell me that they had found a sweet little mare for sale. "Nat's ridden her and likes her. It's only three hundred dollars."

The mare's name was Chris. She was a frisky, alert-looking, inelegant little animal, part Morgan and part quarter horse, who immediately replaced Shorty as the most important thing in my daughter's life. No sooner did Natalia come home from school than she'd disappear to the stables, where she'd spend hours washing and combing and brushing Chris. On weekends and holidays, she and her friends lived back there and out on the riding trails, and we wouldn't see them from dawn to sunset, except for occasional glimpses of them trotting off somewhere or coming back, occasionally with Julia, who was less involved with horses in general, bringing up the rear on The King.

Both the girls were doing very well in school, so I didn't worry at all about Natalia's obsession. I did wonder why only females seemed to be interested in riding; I hardly ever saw a boy on a horse at any of the shows I attended, and none participated in our own equine world. The situation was exactly the reverse of the racetrack scene I was familiar with, and I wondered why.

.   .   .

It was at about this time, during 1970, that I first began to notice the presence of women on the backstretch, not merely as wives and girlfriends but as active participants in the working routine. Until then the role of women at the track in general had been almost nonexistent. The trainers and jockeys and all the backside employees, from the exercise riders to the lowliest hot-walker, were all men. In New York, the stablehands had been mostly poor whites and blacks, with a sprinkling of Puerto Ricans and other Latinos. In California, the help consisted almost exclusively of Mexicans, many of them illegally in the country but ignored by the immigration people and other authorities because they performed a necessary service with very long working hours and for very low pay.

The stable areas of racetracks in this country are one of the game's dirty little secrets. Until fairly recently, no one cared very much how the hands lived back there, in the gimcrack free housing the tracks provide for the impoverished help, and the industry as a whole has ignored the problem. The men who took care of the horses, even the most valuable ones, were regarded as little more than serfs to be exploited and eventually discarded when they became ill or too old to go on putting in the brutally long hours that taking care of such animals requires. Some feeble attempts to unionize the workers here and there were easily beaten back, and except for the occasional lone voice raised in protest, usually by a reporter or some other outsider, no one did anything to alleviate the situation.

Today, even at the richest tracks, conditions are still poor, though some progress has been made. In California, the state has tried, often ignorantly and heavy-handedly, to enforce basic laws regarding employment, and the industry itself has begun to provide some services, such as drug and alcohol counseling and occasional free testing for such ailments as tuberculosis, AIDS, and venereal diseases. A few racetrack managements have even tried to improve living conditions on the backside, by constructing new housing and refurbishing old buildings, but the priorities remain skewed. At Del Mar, for instance, one of the wealthiest and most successful racing operations in the country, about eighty million dollars is being spent to construct a new grandstand and other frontside amenities, while another fifteen million has gone into the creation of an off-track wagering facility catering to the several thousand people in the area who like to bet year-around on horses running elsewhere in the state. Meanwhile, such a relatively small amount of money has been spent on improving the backside, mostly by the Del Mar Thoroughbred Club (which only leases the facilities from the state), that during the racing season of 1991 some people were still being compelled to sleep in airless wooden shacks, little more than large boxes, lined up between the rows of stables. The only horseman with any clout to protest publicly about the situation was trainer Bobby Frankel, who arrived with his string from Los Angeles to find that some of his help, deprived of living quarters by the erection of the new off-track palazzo, were sleeping outside on cots. The management was compelled to provide a couple of trailers, but not until Frankel's employees had been forced to spend several nights outdoors, then in a storage space hastily emptied to accommodate them. No one around the track seemed to be overly disturbed by the event, but then no one in racing has ever paid much attention to any aspect of the game not connected directly to the care and welfare of the horses first, with the bettors a distant second. It's a rich folks' world, as every humble hot-walker finds out very quickly.

It's no secret, in California at least, that the appearance of women on the backstretch coincided with some improvement in working and living conditions. I remember going out to Santa Anita for the workouts one morning that winter of 1970 and being suddenly struck by the number of women doing everything from exercise riding to mucking out stalls. With the local economy booming and as it became harder to find even undocumented aliens willing to work for the low pay and brutal hours the race-track imposes, trainers and owners began hiring women. And what woman, even if she didn't spend the night on the backside, would tolerate unsanitary food and filthy restrooms? The mere presence of women around the stables served to shame their male employers into providing, for them at least, an atmosphere a little better than that of a Dickensian charnel house. It was easy to accommodate them, because, as the men who ran racing soon realized, women loved the horses so much that they would accept the low pay and barely tolerable working conditions simply in order to be around them.

The roots of this love affair go back into legend and history. Nearly everyone knows about Lady Godiva, who rode naked through the streets of Coventry in eleventh-century England to compel her husband, the Earl of Mercia, to lower taxes. (The grateful populace promised not to peek, all except for one boor, who thus immortalized himself as the original Peeping Tom.) Godiva is usually portrayed as a demure lass with long golden tresses and riding sidesaddle. The image remains embedded in our consciousness probably because it connects to our earliest myths and fairytales, worlds in which longings and dreams assumed the guise of tales enacted by figures of heroic proportions and supernatural talents. In Greek mythology, for instance, the goddess Demeter transformed herself into a horse in order to escape the unwelcome wooing of Poseidon, the lord of the oceans. Pegasus, the winged steed, was born of the blood of Medusa, the snake-headed Gorgon sister slain by the hero Perseus.

Every culture seems to have its quota of lady-and-the-horse tales. In Africa, for instance, the Mossi, a tribe living along the Volta River, tell the story of a strong-willed beauty who tamed a copper-colored stallion no one else could ride, a feat that inspired the Mossi warriors to win all their battles. One day, however, the lady disappeared on her stallion, then showed up a year later obviously pregnant. She gave birth to a sturdy lad with coppery hair who grew up to become a great chief. Since that day, however, no Mossi woman has been allowed to ride, which seems a bit churlish on the part of the lads, not to say ungrateful.

The sexual implications are obvious. The horse is a splendid-looking beast with at least as many muscles as Arnold Schwarzenegger, and it doesn't talk back or like to hang around bonding in bars. Some psychiatrists have pointed out that women can masturbate on horseback, and the Freudians see the horse as a symbol of male potency. (Consider the centaur—half man, half horse, all lust.) Some young girls might find in their love for a horse a way to sublimate incestuous feelings for their father. "Many women who ride will admit to enjoying the sense of power they get from being able to dominate and manage a large animal," a psychiatrist informed me a while back. "Some of them feel horses represent strength, and if they can dominate a horse, they are powerful people in life. I can even cite you a clinical instance of a woman actually having an orgasm while controlling a difficult horse." The desire to dominate, the doctor maintained, "is an almost classic example of penis envy. A young girl's interest in horses often peaks during her pubescent period, before she's really aware of herself sexually. The most fundamental fantasy is that the horse itself is a penis, a phallic extension of the girl's own body."

Freudians aren't the only people who can become ponderous on the subject. I once came across a behavioral psychiatrist in Los Angeles who claimed that women got up on horses to be "admired for the way they look. Women who ride are, to a certain degree, exhibitionistic—they crave being looked at and put themselves in a position where they're sure to be noticed. It's all very ego-serving." Horses also bring out a woman's maternal instincts, this doctor maintained, because women "feel an intense need to care personally for their animals. Not only does a horse thus fulfill a woman but it serves as transportation to take her places while acting as the object of her fantasies."

Too much of this sort of analyzing tends to take the fun out of everything. I'm more sympathetic to the way a young actress once put it to me. "I love horses because they're so beautiful and honest," she said, "and still haven't been automated, motorized, economized, sterilized, mechanized nor stripped of romance." A riding instructor named Dan Tipton, whom Natalia took lessons from in Malibu, also pointed out to me that "a horse takes patience and it's a loving thing. It's something a woman can relate to." Men dominated the world of the horse, he continued, until the invention of machines. "There's no love in a machine, just use and play. And until the advent of machines, men kept women riding sidesaddle just so they wouldn't have to compete with them."

. . .

It would be nice to be able to report that women in racing today have achieved equality with men, but the sad fact is that the racing industry is still a fortress of male chauvinism. No racetrack in this country could operate today without the participation of women, but they have been relegated almost completely to subsidiary positions. On the frontside, they can be found as office help, waitresses, nurses and clerks; on the backside, they labor as assistants of one sort or another, exercise girls, grooms, hot-walkers, outriders, pony girls, and kitchen help. A few have become executives and trainers, and a relative handful, mainly in the East, have made it as race riders, most notably in recent years Julie Krone and Karen Rogers. Hardly a day passes in racing without evidence of male obtuseness in regard to the role of women. As I write these words, the National Turf Writers Association, of which I'm a member, is embroiled in a struggle with the Jockeys' Guild over access to the locker room after important events, such as the Triple Crown races. Jerry Bailey, the president of the Guild, has declared that one of the reasons for denying reporters entrance is his membership's concern about women back there.

As a typical horseplayer, I never paid much attention to such matters. I saw no reason why eventually women wouldn't break through in the sport, especially as executives and trainers. It had never occurred to me, however, that they could also become jockeys, mainly because I accepted the prevailing male judgment of them as riders—that they simply weren't physically strong enough to handle Thoroughbreds in competitive situations. When Robyn Smith, a former Hollywood starlet, appeared on the southern California racing scene in the early nineteen-seventies and brought in a few winners, no one, including me, was impressed, and she soon faded from view anyway, after marrying Fred Astaire. The conventional male judgment was that she had done it solely for the publicity and to hook a rich, celebrated and much older sugar daddy.

Long after women riders had established themselves in the East and proved that they could ride competitively with men, if they could just get up on horses good enough to win, the California scene remained dominated by males. Most California tracks are only a mile in circumference, with tight turns and lightning-fast racing surfaces demanding the utmost in strength and agility to get horses out of the gate and in position early. That, we were told, was why women jockeys would never make it in the West, as opposed to the East, with its bigger tracks and more leisurely running styles. Like everybody else, I accepted this estimate as accurate, even though I had before me the examples of such riders as Bill Shoemaker and Chris McCarron, two of the best jockeys in the world, who depended for success on finesse and timing and intelligence and rapport with their mounts, all qualities in which women riders excel. It took a tough blonde named Mary Bacon to wise me up, and she ultimately paid with her life for the career she attempted to carve out for herself.

I first became aware of her during the summer of 1975, at Del Mar, when she showed up in the first race on the opening-day card and brought her mount, an undistinguished five-year-old plater named Silver Salute, in third. I was impressed because I noticed that she refused to let her animal, an established quitter, give up and kept him going long enough to pick up part of the purse, something a lot of other jockeys wouldn't have bothered to do.

After that, I kept an eye on her, which wasn't hard because she was easy to look at. She had platinum-blonde hair that she usually wore pulled back into a ponytail, a lovely face and figure, and a deep tan usually set off by large hoop earrings. Her flowered panties were visible through her white riding breeches, and she knew exactly how to make an impression. When she came up to the press box to be interviewed that first afternoon, she was cradling a Dr. Seuss doll called Mr. Cat and sucking on a cherry lollipop. "I'm here to win races," she announced. "The fact that I'm a woman is just a fact, nothing else. So what if I look like Snow White with the Seven Dwarfs out there in the paddock? When I win a few races here, I'll just be one of the boys again."

The racing reporters, all male in those days, paid little attention to her riding skills, but wanted to know mainly why she had recently attended a Ku Klux Klan meeting. She'd gone as a sort of lark, she said, and the press had blown it up way out of proportion. She knew she'd made a mistake and all she wanted to do now was ride, if they would let her. "This political crap is over," she declared.

She was then in her mid-twenties and she had a baby daughter named Susan from her marriage at fifteen to a sixteen-year-old jockey named Johnny Bacon, from whom she had split almost at once and from whom she received no financial help. She'd learned to ride all kinds of horses on bush tracks all over the Southwest and she'd had more than her share of injuries; she'd broken her back twice, her pelvis once, various ribs, and she'd had to battle blood clots. But nothing deterred her. "It don't matter what I ride," she said. "I can ride them as fast as they can run."

Unfortunately for her, that wasn't fast enough; almost nobody put her up on a live mount. Finally, twelve days into the meet, she brought home a winner, a South American plodder named Cumpa, at odds of twenty-three to one. The animal was probably the worst horse in trainer Henry Moreno's string, but the win didn't help her much. The prevailing attitude in the stands was that the other riders had thrown her the race. I knew better, and all season long I continued to cash tickets on her in the place and show holes at big prices, from fourteen to forty-five to one. She was always a good bet, because she never gave up and she'd get the best out of the worst horses on the grounds.

She pretty much disappeared from the local scene after that summer and eventually dropped out of sight completely. She surfaced in the news again in 1982, after she took another bad spill, at Golden Gate Fields in San Francisco. She was in a coma for eleven days and never quite regained her alertness and quick wit. By that time she'd broken thirty-nine bones, and it didn't look then as if she'd ever get on a horse again. She tried, mainly because it was the only life she cared about, and horses were the only living creatures she trusted.

By 1989, she was back and riding at a small track called Pocono Downs in Pennsylvania, where she and her agent, also a woman, were reportedly briefly kidnapped one day at gunpoint. The incident later resulted in a long jail term for one of the men involved, who was arrested two years later in the bathroom of her hotel room in Louisville, Kentucky, with a gun on him. The story was odd and didn't quite check out, but then almost everything Mary Bacon did and said seemed a bit askew, as if her very life itself had been warped by her early misadventures and her struggles to succeed.

Then, early in the summer of 1991, she made the news for one last time by locking herself into a Fort Worth, Texas, hotel room and putting a bullet through her head. She had ridden her last winner, of the more than three hundred she had brought in during her career, at Bandera Downs, near San Antonio, the previous fall. Supposedly, she had cancer, but she hadn't mentioned it to anyone at the track, where she'd been getting up on two or three horses a day and had talked about staying in Texas. She was in her early forties when she died, and she asked that her ashes be scattered over Belmont Park.

In southern California today, only one woman is race riding with any regularity. Her name is Christine Davenport and from time to time she brings in a winner, always at good odds. She can ride, the boys say, but, well, hell, you know—she's a girl. . . .

My marriage began to fall slowly and painfully apart in the early nineteen-seventies and I spent most of 1972 in Italy, working in Rome and Milan. When I got back late that fall and went out to see my children in Malibu, I found the horse scene greatly changed. Ginger and The King had both died and only Chris and one boarder were left, looking forlorn in the otherwise empty pens. Natalia, now sixteen, had pretty much given up riding regularly. She and Julia were far more interested in a number of repulsive-looking rock stars and pimply boys than in horses. Eventually, Chris was sold to another family with a horse-crazy girl, the kids and their mother moved into a new house in Malibu that had room only for dogs, and I realized that a love affair had ended. Nothing is forever, not even horses.

12

CALIENTE FLASH

"Claiming horses is like trying to make a living by going through garbage cans."

—LEFTY NICKERSON, horse trainer

THE WORST horse I ever owned was named Parlay Time. I picked him out of a race at Agua Caliente one day in the spring of 1970 mainly because a friend of mine, whom I'll call Dick Baron, had convinced me that most horse trainers were boobs and that we could do better buying horses on our own than by relying on the wisdom of people who voted for Richard Nixon and thought Lawrence Welk was a great entertainer. "You can read the *Racing Form*," he said. "Pick out a nice cheap horse we can have some fun with. Then we can get one of these dummies to condition it and we'll tell him what to do."

I looked for a three-year-old who hadn't had too many races and who might improve. I also wanted one who could run farther than six furlongs, on the theory that horses going a distance of ground tend not to break down as readily, and they compete for bigger purses than the speedballs, most of whom fall apart under the stress of having to go all out from start to finish in sprints.

Parlay Time was by a cheap California stallion and out of an equally undistinguished mare, but I reminded myself, with that capacity for self-delusion that sooner or later afflicts almost everyone in the game at all levels, that Stymie had once been a cheap claimer and that the Kentucky Derby had been won fairly recently, in 1961, by a colt named Carry Back, sired by something called Saggy and out of a nothing dam named Joppy. Furthermore, Parlay Time had run only a handful of races, had already broken his maiden and was competing at distances of a mile or more. In every race, he showed enough lick to get position, then usually a little closing move that had enabled him to pick up pieces of purses every time he had competed. When the horse's name came up again, entered in a lowly twenty-five-hundred-dollar claimer at a mile and a sixteenth, I called Bobby Warren, told him that Baron and I had decided to claim the horse and asked him to take him over for us. Without actually saying so, I made it clear to him that we weren't interested in his opinion of the animal, but simply wanted him to train him for us and see what he could do with him.

"You sure you want this horse?" Warren asked us, on our way into the track on the afternoon of the race. "I got a nice little maiden filly that can run some you could get for maybe four thousand. She's got some speed and the owner's kind of hard up right now."

We didn't want a speed horse, Baron informed him; we wanted a winner going long. Warren looked at us a little oddly, but said nothing, then left us to put in the claim. Baron and I went to the paddock to look at our potential acquisition. I have to confess that I wasn't impressed. Parlay Time was long and rangy, but also too thin, with ribs showing and a rather dull chestnut coat. He walked around the enclosure with his head down, like a prisoner in an exercise yard. Baron, however, reminded me that numbers don't lie; the horse had established form and that counted far more than whether he could win a beauty contest. "Warren's got a horse he's trying to unload on us," he said. "Why listen to him? Let him train *this* horse, that's what we'll be paying him to do."

When the race went off, Parlay Time broke well enough, then settled in five or six lengths behind the leaders. We waited confidently for him to make his usual move as the field turned into the stretch, but instead he began to drop steadily back and came home well-beaten by a dozen lengths or more. I looked at Baron. "Forget it," he said. "Warren will improve him. Remember what he did with Irish Friendship."

Parlay Time was beyond improvement. Warren did the best he could with him, but I remember now that he also never spoke a single encouraging word about him. We'd ask how the horse was getting along and he'd say, "He's doing what he can," or, "Just about what you'd expect, I guess." Meanwhile, every couple of weeks, he'd enter him in a race and we'd drive down across the Mexican border to watch him run. I'm not sure that "run" is the right word to describe what Parlay Time did. He would break well enough from the gate, drop back to fourth or fifth around the clubhouse turn, then slowly continue to fall back until by the end of the race he'd be ten or twelve lengths behind.

"What's the matter with him?" I asked Warren, after the third such performance.

"Well, for one thing," the trainer said, "he's just about the worst windsucker I ever seen. He gets himself so full of air I can't get him to eat and I can't train him."

Parlay Time was a cribber, I explained to Baron, who knew less about horses than any other human being alive. He would clamp his front teeth on anything near him and then proceed to suck in air, thus bloating himself. Until Warren could find a way to keep him from doing that, Parlay Time would remain a gaunt, bloated shell unable to compete at any level. Baron thought that over and said, "Well, maybe we could float him over the track and sell ad space on him." After three months of stable bills and no purse money coming in, I began seriously to consider this possibility.

Over the next few weeks, we discussed a lot of other things we might eventually do, all of them lethal, with Parlay Time, or the Caliente Flash, as we now referred to him. Eventually, however, I decided that we ought to remove him, at least temporarily, from the racetrack, on the assumption that he could use the rest and might eventually be able to get back to the races refreshed, cured of his cribbing habit and ready to start winning. Warren agreed and arranged to ship Parlay Time north to us in Malibu.

He arrived midafternoon a few days later, and the event struck awe into my children, who stood around watching Parlay Time being unloaded from the van parked next to the corral. "Look, kids, this is a Thoroughbred," I said, as the horse emerged and was led down a ramp toward the stable area. And to Parlay Time's credit, he was impressive-looking, at least compared with the odd assortment of equine denizens, then numbering six, in our own personal backside. Thoroughbreds, even the worst of them, are living testimonials to creative evolution and Parlay Time was no exception. I instructed the children not to ride him, but to take good care of him. One day, rested and healed, Parlay Time would go back to the racetrack and show us what he could really do.

I hadn't had much luck with horses I owned at Agua Caliente, but my misadventures with Irish Friendship and Parlay Time had at least served to make me appreciate the place, mainly as a bettor. When I started going racing across the border, the track had fallen on hard times and was considered by the California horsemen and most horse owners as merely a third-rate facility to send untalented and broken-down nags to in order to compete for tiny purses in races often decided by skulduggery. It is important to remember that the general rule about honesty in racing is that matters are more likely to be on the up-and-up if the purses being competed for are large enough to sustain life as we know it. At Caliente, although the living, in terms of costs, was easier, the purses were such that cashing a bet was just about the only way anyone could remain solvent. It was not a place to wander into trusting solely in one's handicapping skills, based on the statistics published in the racing papers.

Horseplayers, however, will put up with almost anything, so long as they know what the rules are and have confidence that they're being administered with some consistency. At Caliente, the smart punters pretty much ignored recent form while keeping a wary eye on the tote board. Underlaid horses, animals bet early and late and going off at odds considerably under their morning line, won a disproportionate share of the contests. The trick was to hook these overbet steeds with longshots in various exotic combination wagers, such as quinellas, trifectas and exactas, so as to ensure adequate payoffs. The paranoia factor at Caliente seemed to be lower than at other hippodromes I'd attended, if only because expectations were firmly rooted in the conviction that honesty is at best a relative virtue. If some overplayed nag showed a startling reversal of form and won off by himself at inexplicably low odds, the general attitude at Caliente seemed to be that it was his turn and that a smart player would have known how to profit from it. If, conversely, some impossible outsider came romping in from out of the clouds at astronomical odds, well, that was all right, too; a man had to live and a nice ticket could have been cashed simply by scattering a few two-dollar wagers on the longshots. I found this attitude relaxed and refreshing, after the grimmer grind of picking winners up north, and it also saved me the trouble of having to spend a lot of time poring over numbers. I was freed to enjoy the lighthearted ambience of the place, its excellent food and, if I so chose, the raunchier pleasures of Tijuana itself, a town not noted for its adherence to puritanical codes of behavior.

Racing in Tijuana has a colorful and glorious history. An American gambler and speculator from San Francisco named Sunny Jim Coffroth built the first track in 1916, just across the border, and put on a handicap in his name for a purse of fifty thousand dollars, a huge prize in those days. Coffroth was squeezed out of the operation when Caliente opened on its present site, a few miles farther south, in 1929. Three years later, the great Australian champion Phar Lap showed up to win the hundred-thousand-dollar Caliente Handicap, then the richest prize in racing history. Other good horses competed there as well, including Seabiscuit, Gallant Sir and Exterminator. Such celebrated jockeys as George Woolf, Johnny Longden, Jackie Westrope, Johnny Adams, Bill Shoemaker and Eddie Arcaro came down to ride them. The track pioneered a number of innovations that have since become standard everywhere—an announcer to call the races, fireproof stables, goggles and safety helmets for jockeys, the daily double and other forms of combination bets, including the Pick Six. And the glamorous clientele included a roster of Hollywood personalities.

The glory days are long since over, mainly because of the return and proliferation of racing north of the border. The only claim to importance in racing Caliente can now make is that it has provided a relatively inexpensive facility for developing a few promising young horses, most notably in recent years a brilliantly fast filly named Melair and Snow Chief, the California-bred colt who won the 1986 Preakness. What hasn't changed is the congenial atmosphere, and the new lure is a dazzling variety of wagering on both live and televised events that not even a Las Vegas casino can match.

The resurgence at Caliente coincided with its purchase in 1985 by a thirty-year-old entrepreneur from Mexico City named Jorge Hank Rhon, who immediately announced an ambitious program of restoration and expansion. The most important development was the creation of a number of satellite wagering facilities, one very close to the U.S. border at San Ysidro, at which bettors could play not only the horses but other sporting events all over the globe. These newly created so-called Race and Sports Books are patronized primarily by visitors and they carry the losses from the live racing operation, which has been in the red for years.

Hank's ambitions encompassed not only the racetrack but the city of Tijuana itself. No sooner had he arrived on the scene than he began to invest heavily, providing jobs and donating to charities, activities that established him in many people's eyes as a true benefactor in an area of unemployment and poverty. His goal, he said, was to make his racetrack operation, which provided employment for a couple of thousand people, an intrinsic aspect of the city's daily life.

Unfortunately, his extravagant personal style and aggressive maneuvering on all fronts made him enemies as well, including Tijuana's most popular newspaper columnist, Hector Felix Miranda, known locally as El Gato (The Cat). Felix wrote a weekly column for a newspaper called *Zeta*, in which he ridiculed Hank Rhon as a spoiled rich brat, who was squandering money on a number of losing ventures while also leading a highly suspect social life full of drugs and sex. He nicknamed him El Pirruris, after a character, created by a Mexican comedian, who is a stupid daddy's boy. Hank's father, Carlos Hank Gonzales, is one of the wealthiest and most powerful men in the country, holder over the years of various ministerial portfolios in the national government. Hank Rhon, according to Felix, had been an embarrassment to his father and had been, in effect, banished to Tijuana and given the racetrack to play with.

Felix had a poisonous pen and had attacked almost every big shot in town, so it was no surprise to many people when he turned up dead on April 20, 1988, having been gunned down in his car not far from his home. Slaughtering outspoken journalists has long been a Mexican pastime, but Felix's death caused a public outcry. Hank Rhon himself was never considered a suspect by the investigating authorities or even questioned by them, though it turned out that the murder had been committed by two of his racetrack security guards. And he has continued to maintain his innocence ever since, even though the general feeling in Tijuana seems to be that the two killers would never have acted on their own, and *Zeta* has continued to appear every week with a whole page devoted to the affair in which El Gato cries out from the grave, listing the power brokers the paper considers prime suspects and inquiring of Hank Rhon why his bodyguards committed the deed.

The uproar put a severe crimp in Hank Rhon's activities, soon compounded by a *mano a mano* with the racetrack labor unions. The latter objected to many of Hank's innovations at the track and his attempts to cut costs, especially with the live racing operation. They struck and shut the track down for about seven months. When it finally reopened on May 23, 1991, with many of the basic issues largely unresolved, the operation faced greatly increased competition from the off-track wagering facilities just across the border, and the future of live racing in Tijuana remains in doubt.

This is too bad, because over the past five years I've had more fun going racing at Caliente than almost anywhere else. There is, first of all, the new Race and Sports Book at the track itself, which has replaced the old Foreign Book. It is located in a huge rectangular room that used to be part of the main grandstand, and the action there gets under way at about nine A.M., with racing and other sports beamed in by satellite from the East. The bettors sit or mill around the floor under banks of TV monitors and around a huge bar area. The scene is not an excessively gracious one, and by the end of each racing day it has achieved a truly Hogarthian level of sordidness, with the losers shuffling out glumly over a toxic dump of losing tickets on their way back to the border crossings. The Sports Book is open every day except Christmas and there are several hundred aficionados, mostly Americans, who show up regularly and haven't seen a live sporting event in decades.

This depraved spectacle is not for me, and I usually look for a seat somewhere else in the main grandstand, which looks like an enormous Aztec temple. The original structure, a much homier affair, was destroyed by fire in 1971 and was rebuilt, in a burst of misplaced optimism, as a four-story facility to handle up to thirty thousand fans. Over the years since, the average attendance on the two weekend race days was about four thousand, but has shrunk to much less than that recently.

This is fine for those of us who like to go racing in comfort and be entertained, an attitude complemented by a number of Hank Rhon's eye-popping embellishments. The entrance to the Turf Club, for instance, is now graced by floor-to-ceiling glass-enclosed cages containing exotic birds, wolves, big snakes, cheetahs and tigers. A portion of the infield has also been converted into a zoo. "Señor Hank is an animal-lover," a member of his public relations staff once informed me and confided that his boss also kept boa constrictors in his office. "You hope everything's locked up in there."

From anywhere at Caliente, whether from behind glass in the snootier sections or out in the open, the viewing is easy and the food, by racetrack standards, excellent. My personal favorite is a Mexican hot dog, a spicy sausage tucked under a mound of onion slices and chile peppers that is absolutely guaranteed to make a man of you, regardless of your sex. And best of all, the track offers a wide variety of betting options, with exotic combinations available in every race and no deductions taken on the spot for the IRS, if you happen to hit a big one.

Not too long ago, I invited a hard-knocking friend of mine down for a weekend from Los Angeles, where he had been limited to nine races a day, with half-hour waits in between. After a couple of hours of more action than even he could handle, with his binoculars alternately glued to a race in progress on the track itself and another being run simultaneously at Santa Anita on a distant TV screen, he was drenched in sweat like a decathlon contestant. "Man, this isn't a racetrack," he murmured, beaming. "It's an orgy."

Parlay Time never made it back to the races, at Caliente or anywhere else. No sooner had we settled him in his outdoor pen than he began to clamp his teeth on the nearest available surface and suck in air. We tried every method suggested to us to break him of the habit, including lining the railings of his stall with Cayenne pepper, but nothing worked. He'd stand there, hour after hour, gnawing and gulping, a spectacle I eventually equated with being compelled to watch someone masturbate. We all developed a healthy loathing for the animal, even though we knew it wasn't his fault. Someone somewhere in the horse's early life had mistreated him and turned him into a psychotic wreck.

I persuaded a friend of mine named Tom Blincoe, a trainer with a small public stable, to come out and have a look at him one morning. I reasoned that Tom, a Kentuckian born and raised in horse country, might be able to suggest a cure. He arrived to find the horse gnawing away, as usual, at one of the fence posts; but to my surprise, he ignored that phenomenon and dropped to his haunches to inspect the animal's front legs. I started to explain again about the cribbing, but Tom was too busy feeling Parlay Time's ankles to pay much attention to me. Then he went into the pen and made the horse move around, his eyes still focused on his limbs. "The cribbing's one thing, but it's not the problem," he said at last. "This horse has foundered."

I stared blankly at him, not having the faintest idea what he meant. The trainer proceeded to explain that Parlay Time had gone lame, either from having been poorly treated by his previous connections or because he might be suffering from laminitis, an inflammation of the sensitive part of the hoof caused, possibly, by overwork. "He's not in good shape," he concluded his chilling little analysis. "He might be all right eventually as a saddle horse, maybe, but I don't think he'll ever run again."

I relayed the grim news to Dick Baron, who promptly washed his hands of the whole business. He informed me that I could do whatever I wanted with the horse, but that he had no intention of squandering another dollar on him for any reason whatever. "You can keep whatever you can get for him," he added, indicating that he fully expected me to turn him over to a dog-food impresario.

We hung on to Parlay Time through a troubled summer, with my home life slowly disintegrating around me. My wife and I managed to keep most of our troubles hidden from the children, but I was away a lot, partly for work and partly in order to escape. The welfare of the horses was the least of my concerns, though I knew they were all being well cared for under Natalia's dedicated supervision.

I was home one weekday morning in late September, having a coffee on the back patio, when my wife appeared in the kitchen doorway. There was a brush fire burning on the other side of Malibu Canyon, she informed me, and there was some danger that, fed by the dry desert wind known as a Santa Ana, it would come through the canyon almost directly east of us toward Malibu. I stood up and looked at the hills, clearly outlined against a bright-blue sky and seeming to shimmer in the clear, hot air. The wind had not yet begun to blow and there seemed to be little risk of anything happening. Anyway, we reasoned, it would take hours at least for a fire to get through the mountains separating the coast from the inland valleys and we decided to proceed normally. The children had been sent off to school and we waited, not yet alarmed but with the radio on and tuned to a local news station. We had lived in California for only about five years, but we knew about brush fires and the devastation they could cause, once they got going.

By noon we realized we were in trouble. The Santa Ana had begun to blow hard and the radio reported that the fire was out of control and rapidly on the move toward the coast. I began to gather up our valuable belongings, including a couple of large paintings, and load them into one of the cars, while my wife set about rounding up the children. Natalia's school was far enough up the coast to be out of the immediate path of the blaze, so we decided she would be safer up there, and my wife went to pick up

Julia and our son, Billy, then only seven, from the nearby grammar school.

By the time she got back with the kids, early in the afternoon, smoke was rising from the hills behind us and the smell of the fire was everywhere. We had all the sprinklers on and I had watered down the house as well as the land around it, but I could have saved myself the time. The Santa Ana was blowing full force in gusts of up to forty or fifty miles an hour and the searing wind dried the water up instantly, nor was there enough pressure to make the sprinklers effective as a shield. The wind blasted the fire toward us, as if someone had opened a huge furnace door, turned on gas jets and blown the heat at us through a wind tunnel. As my wife, the children and our dog climbed into her car to make a getaway, the flames topped the rise of the hill behind us and began to leapfrog down the mountainside toward us. The sky was black overhead, and everywhere on the slopes houses were burning. On an adjacent hilltop, the Serra Retreat, once a large private estate since converted into a religious center, went up in flames like a miniature Valhalla.

I stayed behind to try to save the horses, as well as our cat, Gatto, who seemed to have disappeared; I couldn't find him anywhere. I ran out to the stables, where I was joined by the teenage son of friends of ours who had providentially figured I might need help. Between the two of us, we managed to get the seven horses on the premises out, leading them two by two down the road, then along the dried-up creek bed under the coast highway and out to the beach, where we turned them loose to join a growing herd of equine refugees from the surrounding area. It took both of us to handle Parlay Time, who alone among our group of animals was showing signs of panic. I remember hoping, when we finally got him to the beach, that he would swim out to sea and disappear from my life.

When I finally drove away from the house, several of the stable buildings, the fences and a huge mound of hay I had just bought were burning brightly. Trees were exploding into flames all around me, and I was certain the house would go as well, but I had no time for regrets. I fled and drove south along the coast. It was late afternoon, but the sky overhead was still black. The sun, already low on the horizon, glowed dully through the murk, casting into dramatic relief the enormous herd of horses now assembled on the beach. They stood quietly together, with the ocean flat and still behind them, a picture out of a doomsday vision.

I caught up with my family, except for Natalia, in Santa Monica, where we spent the night in a motel. Oddly enough, as I lay there in the dark, with my wife and children and dog, I felt a curious sense of relief, not at having escaped with our lives from this holocaust, but at the prospect of having now to start over, as if the loss of possessions had wiped a slate clean, freed me to begin again.

We talked our way through the police roadblocks early the next morning and drove straight to the house to find it untouched. Our landlord, an engineer, had apparently designed it to withstand just such a catastrophe and built it low to the ground, with a slanted fireproof roof that extended several feet out from the structure. We had lost part of the stable area, but the fire had burned around the house, then jumped it before puffing itself out in the flat fields of the ranches and flower-growers west of us. And when I opened the front door, we were greeted by a hungry and very annoyed Gatto, who had apparently, with the innate cunning of his species, taken refuge in the chimney and was now miffed at our having abandoned him without food or water.

After Natalia returned, having spent the night with friends, we set about over the next few days finding out what had happened to our horses. They had been taken, along with dozens of others, to Hollywood Park; the racetrack had dispatched its big vans up the coast to rescue as many of them as possible. Furthermore, the animals had not only been fed, but also exercised and groomed. As the oldest horse on the grounds, The King had immediately become a track favorite and a minor celebrity by the time Julia spotted him, his regal head protruding contentedly from somebody's shedrow.

Only Parlay Time was missing; he seemed to have vanished completely, as if my fantasy about him had come true. Then, about a week after the fire, he was found tethered to a hydrant at the foot of Sunset Boulevard, where it joins the Pacific Coast Highway about six miles to the south. Somebody had ridden him hard through the charred countryside, because he was pretty well beaten up by the experience. We brought him home and set about nursing him to health again, while he continued to chomp away and suck in air.

A few months later, we gave him away to an experienced horsewoman, who was certain she could break him of his habit and make a useful saddle horse out of him. I don't know if she ever succeeded, but I have to confess that I remember him only with distaste and regret at my own folly. He remains identified in my head with everything else that was going wrong in my life at the time.

13

WINNER TAKE ALL

"Never trust a trainer whose last name ends in a vowel."
—A horseplayer at Aqueduct

TRAINER BOBBY Frankel talks affably to anyone these days, even the press. This is probably because he has nothing left to prove. He works for rich owners who believe in him, and his shedrows in California are full of good horses who compete successfully, in every category, at the top levels of the sport. He has even begun in middle age to look avuncular, the sort of wily old uncle who knows more than you do and is perfectly willing to share his expertise with you, even if it costs him something. You would think, if you met him today for the first time, that he's a low-keyed, confident sort of chap, perhaps not entirely presentable at the grander functions patronized by racing's bluebloods, but still over-all not a bad sort. And quite a good horseman, too, evidently; he always wins his share of the big races and then some, even if he doesn't get the publicity of a D. Wayne Lukas or a Charlie Whittingham. Still, invite him for dinner to the Phippses? Well, hardly.

Frankel wasn't always liked, or at least tolerated, especially by the game's aristocratic types. When I first met him, a decade or so ago, he didn't exactly come on like a Marlboro ad. He was in his mid-thirties but seemed younger, with brown eyes, black curly hair and a long, slightly pendulous lower lip—the Semitic good looks of a New York sidewalk dude. His habitual expression was dour, sometimes sullen, and he talked like a wiseguy from a big-city slum, about as far geographically and metaphysically as you can get from Kentucky blue grass and the genteel world of millionaire horse owners like the Vanderbilts, Hunts, Whitneys and Mellons, none of whom found Frankel presentable in their tack rooms, much less their foyers. It was bad enough that Frankel, who couldn't even ride, won more races than anyone else in their world; the man also had a mouth on him. "I'm no genius, know what I mean?" he said to me early one morning, as we stood by the outer rail of the main track at Del Mar and watched two of his horses work a crisp half-mile. "But here you don't have to be. I'm lucky I got out of the fourth grade, and look at me."

Bobby Frankel isn't modest and in those days he wasn't kind about the competition. He was also ruthlessly honest about the game he was in, and his assessments of himself and the world in general tended to be definitive, uncomfortably absolute, often foulmouthed, and utterly without redeeming social graces. "Your trouble is you don't deliver," I once overheard him say to a colleague down on his luck. "You have to win races and you don't win. What do you expect?"

Frankel won a lot of races and couldn't tolerate losing. This was because he saw the world as populated exclusively by winners and losers, and he knew exactly what category he belonged to and where in the pecking order, right at the top. He'd have no trouble moving on to greater triumphs, he felt, if only his owners would write him some blank checks and turn him loose to buy and claim all the horses he wanted. "That's the only thing about New York I miss," he said. "Back there they got guys who'll let you go, man. Here I got to talk to three, four guys before I can get the money to take a horse, know what I mean?"

I certainly did. So-called claiming races are the sport's bread and butter, and without them the tracks couldn't stay open. In these contests the conditions stipulate that each horse is entered for a price, which in southern California can range from ten thousand dollars to as much as a couple of hundred thousand. The basic idea is to even out the racing and make it possible for even very poor horses occasionally to win some purse money, since obviously no one with a Sunday Silence or an Easy Goer would risk losing him by putting him into a claiming race. Without claiming events, only the very best horses would win all the races and put ninety-five percent of the less successful owners and trainers out of business.

Frankel was a master of the claiming race. He always entered his horses in contests he felt they could win; he could spot a good claim from someone else when he saw one; and best of all, he was wonderfully adept at unloading bad or ailing horses on other people. He was so skillful at that game, in fact, that for a long time few other trainers dared to take his horses, and Bobby profited from their timidity by being able to put some animals into races they could win easily at levels well below their actual ability. Basically, the claiming race is like a high-stakes poker game, in which bluff plays a major role, winners take all, and the bad players go broke very quickly.

When I was hanging around Frankel's barn that summer, he was in charge of about three dozen horses owned by fifteen different interests. If he had his way, every one of those animals was going to win at least once for him. Either that or out they'd go, back to the farm or down the claiming ladder. Frankel likes horses, but he's unsentimental about them and he hates the ones that don't put out for him. For the past few years he'd been the leading trainer on the southern California circuit, and he was planning to defend his title. But after winning both Santa Anita and Hollywood Park, he was having trouble getting going at Del Mar, and he wasn't happy about it. I suggested things would obviously get better and he nodded gloomily. "Yeah," he said, "in my life everything usually works out for me."

I enjoyed hanging around with him that early summer morning. In the dim, misty light, against a background of empty stands, about forty horses and riders were out on the track, just galloping or working hard and fast along the inner rail, the riders hunched over their mounts, blending into them and clucking encouragement. Up the track from us, high in the wooden guinea stands, trainers and assorted onlookers were clocking the works or just watching the way their animals moved over the chocolate-brown surface of the main strip. Frankel picked out his own and other people's horses for me as they came past. He didn't look or act like a horseman, but I realized then that he was one. "Most people can't tell one horse from another," he said. "To me they're just like people. This one here is Too Commercial."

The big rangy exercise boy up on the horse nodded to Frankel as he rode by. "He dug in real good," he called out. The trainer looked glum. "He's very sore," he said, "real stiff. But he's willing. Just point him toward the pole and he'll run your eyeballs out." A winner with no class but lots of heart, just the kind of horse Frankel thrived on. "He's the best trainer of twenty-thousand-dollar horses there is," a rich fancier of the sport had told me in the Turf Club the day before, the implication being that that was the only kind of horse Frankel could train.

I realized later, as I watched Frankel direct the work of his two dozen stablehands around his barn, that this estimate of his abilities was the one held by the racing establishment, all those people who simply wanted him to disappear. Frankel's success made a mockery of their traditions and their inherited expertise. But as I watched him walk from stall to stall, checking a quarter crack in a hoof, feeling for heat in an ankle, ordering butazolidin or other medications for a sore horse, suggesting a "scope" for another animal's throat to see if it was bleeding in the lungs (a common ailment), worrying in detail about every single one of his charges, I was impressed. The man obviously cared for these big dumb beasts, a caring that went beyond just winning races. Frankel's shedrow, unlike many others, was clean, with fresh straw in every stall, and there was an atmosphere of order and calm. "It's not so much work, but it's every day," he explained. "I look at it this way: if you're doing something you love, it seems easy."

The important horses in Frankel's barn those days were few—Impressive Luck, Yu Wipi, No Turning, one or two others—and all but Yu Wipi had been bought or claimed on the cheap. Frankel had improved every one of them. In the past he'd had two top stakes horses, Linda's Chief and Native Guest, but both had broken down in midcareer, further contributing to the myth of Frankel's inability to care for a really good horse. I once asked a leading turf writer from the East about that, and he began his answer by telling me what a louse Frankel was. "Personally, I find him sickening," he said, "but he's a hell of a trainer. He kept Linda's Chief sound when nobody else could. Native Guest was a complete cripple to begin with. Frankel knows horses. What he doesn't know is people."

Frankel began as a bettor at the New York tracks. His parents were caterers and he and his brother grew up in Far Rockaway. The whole family would go to the harness races every couple of weeks, to either Roosevelt or Yonkers, and they were strictly two-dollar bettors. Then one day Bobby's father took him to see the Thoroughbreds run at Belmont Park and turned his life around. By the time he was sixteen, Bobby was going to the races every afternoon with a group of friends, most of them considerably older than he. He dumped school and caddied in the mornings to finance his outings, but never took more than ten or twenty dollars to the track. He became an expert handicapper and picked winners for his pals. "I made some good scores out there," he recalls. "I had days when I'd run five dollars into thousands. One time I was broke by the fourth, but I borrowed five dollars and walked out with five thousand. Another time I ran forty dollars up to twenty-three thousand in two days. I picked fourteen winners in eighteen races."

He wasn't a spot bettor either, but a plunger who'd try to run the card and have fun doing it. "I looked for speed, man, and I loved that Bobby Ussery. What a rider, a lot like Sandy Hawley." Frankel once bet a hundred dollars in a stakes race on a cheap speed horse ridden by Ussery that went wire to wire and came in, paying $67 for every two-dollar ticket. "I was a player, man, and I had a real good time."

In 1964, a friend took Frankel to the backside and Bobby was fascinated. He began going out in the early mornings and hung around, meeting people. He attached himself to a trainer named Bill Corbellini and went south with him to Florida for the winter season. He bought a quarter interest in a cheap plater, won two races with him, lost him, made money gambling, took another horse on his own for five thousand dollars that had never won a race, put him in against winners one day, bet a hundred dollars on him and scored, at odds of twenty-one to one. "I don't know what happened," he says of that time. "I didn't know nothing, man. Miracles happen, that's all."

Back in New York, he went to work as a hot-walker, the most menial job at the track, for two hundred dollars a month with another trainer, L. V. Bellew. "He was a good trainer and I cashed some bets with him. One day I bet on a horse that paid eighty dollars and I showed up for work the next day in a brand new car." He also got careless about coming to work on time and Bellew fired him.

Frankel got friendly with Johnny Campo, then an assistant trainer who was working for Eddie Neloy, a top conditioner with a barn full of good horses. Neloy gave Frankel a little filly to train and coached him through it. The filly bowed tendons twice and never got to the races, but Bobby learned his business and got his trainer's license. "I was with her morning, noon and night," he remembers. "I still didn't know what the fuck I was doing. I knew nothing about legs and shoes."

He picked up a couple of untalented horses here and there and then, in 1966, a real sore one named Double Dash from an owner stabled at Finger Lakes, a bush league track in the northern part of the state. Double Dash won his first start there, Frankel's maiden win as a trainer, then four more races in a row. Back in New York, Frankel latched on with trainer Buddy Jacobson, another outcast from the establishment. "We had such cripples and we were winning, winning, winning," Frankel recalls.

Jacobson, however, was brash and loud and outspoken. He became so unpopular with the authorities that suddenly for a while he couldn't get stall space and Frankel was out of work. Somehow, though, he picked up a few horses here and there and won with them. Jacobson then put him together with Willie Frankel (no relation), a rich businessman who wanted to go into racing in a major way and was smart enough to give his trainer a free hand.

Bobby claimed horses right and left and began winning a lot of races. He soon became the leading trainer at Aqueduct, beating out his mentor, Jacobson. "I never had a lot of horses," he once said of that period, "but I always won more than my share. Everything was cool." Including his mouth. Willie Frankel was the only owner Bobby had (or needed) at the time, and Bobby knew how to keep him happy. To this day the trainer always refers to Willie as Mr. Frankel, the only show of respect he's ever demonstrated for anyone, at the track or anywhere else.

The Frankels moved their operation west during the 1972 Hollywood Park meeting, and Bobby immediately established himself as a wonder boy. He won fifty-five races his first full season at the Inglewood emporium, then set a record the following year with sixty wins out of a hundred and eighty starts, "plus about a million seconds and thirds." He was almost equally successful at the other major tracks in the area and became the darling of the two-dollar players, who began betting on every one of his horses. Marty Ritt, whose string Frankel trained, once summed up his phenomenal early California successes thus: "Bobby came out here and didn't know anybody. He claimed horses off everyone and nobody knew his style. He'd take horses for twenty thousand dollars, drop them down in class a notch or two and win with them. Everybody was scared of him, so nobody took *his* horses."

A few years later, however, a multimillionaire owner-trainer named Tommy Heard became annoyed by Bobby's brash style and by some disparaging remarks Bobby had allegedly made about Heard's training methods. He began taking every horse Bobby entered in claiming races. "Well, you know, a guy like Heard has got to get killed going up against Frankel," Ritt observed. "Bobby must have unloaded three hundred thousand dollars' worth of junk on him." But Heard, who seemed to have limitless funds, persisted and eventually the feud hurt Bobby, too, because his barn was being stripped and he was losing good horses as well. It was eventually reportedly ended by the intervention of Charlie Whittingham, with some mildly apologetic mumblings from Frankel himself.

When Willie Frankel began to curtail his involvement in racing, Bobby opened a public stable and continued to win more races than almost anyone else at every meet. The competition, however, was becoming stiffer. A lot of other sharp young trainers had begun to operate successful public stables, and Frankel had to work hard to stay on top. "Bobby's great contribution to racing out here has been the attention he pays to a horse's feet," another trainer told me. "He shaves the hoof down and he brought his own blacksmith out from New York to shoe his stock. Now everybody is doing it his way, so he's lost that advantage, too." His style in claiming races was also no longer such an enigma to his colleagues, and he began to lose almost as many horses as he acquired through the claiming box.

It was then that Frankel began seriously to consider getting out of that aspect of the game entirely, and by the time I met him he had already begun to make his escape. Luckily for him, he had the credentials to do it. His social liabilities had begun to matter a lot less in a world that was no longer dominated by the East Coast racing establishment and its snobbish power brokers in New York and Kentucky. In southern California nobody cares where you came from or what you accomplished in a past life; what everybody wants to know is what you're doing now and nobody could fault Frankel on that score. He was a proven winner and in the nineteen-eighties that attracted the entrepreneurial money to him. He bought good horses and he was on his way.

The point about Frankel is that, even when he's playing, he always keeps his mind on business. "Look, I got a job where I can't go out much at night," he once explained. "I got one thing I got to do every day, man, and that's keeping these fucking horses as sound as possible. Winning is what this is all about. I don't romance owners, go out to dinner with them, shit like that. But if anybody wants to win a race, they ought to come to me."

On my last day hanging around with him that summer I found myself in the paddock at Del Mar before the feature race. Dressed only in jeans, a white tennis shirt and deckers, Frankel looked as if he'd come straight from the beach and seemed about as concerned as a poker player holding four aces in a nickel-ante game. The occasion was the twelfth running of the Cabrillo Handicap, in which seven older horses had been entered to run for a total purse of about twenty-five thousand dollars. Frankel's contender was Yu Wipi, a five-year-old brown horse owned by Marty Ritt, actor John Forsythe, show-biz lawyer Jack Schwartzman and several others. The partners had paid a hundred and forty thousand dollars for the horse, a nice animal, but no Secretariat.

Yu Wipi was basically a sprinter who had never run, much less won, at any distance over a mile, and I had conveyed my doubts about his chances to Frankel earlier in the day. "You see any other speed in there?" he had answered. "This horse should open up three, four lengths on this field." Presumably he'd then get a breather and have plenty left to hold off the others at the finish. Del Mar is a track with a very short stretch that favors speed horses, and I knew, too, that Ritt, the shrewdest of bettors, thought Yu Wipi would win. I listened to Frankel instruct his rider, the veteran Fernando Toro, to hustle his mount out of the gate, then I watched him boost the rider into the saddle before heading upstairs to the grandstand.

I still wasn't at all keen about Yu Wipi's chances, but what did I know? When the crowd knocked him down to two to one from his morning line of nine to two, the enthusiasm became contagious and I put twenty dollars on his nose, then joined Ritt and some other racing cronies of mine in a box over the finish line to watch the race. Yu Wipi broke poorly out of the gate, never got the lead and finished next to last, a result that spread a smog bank of gloom over our formerly merry crowd. "I hate that goddamn Toro," the guy next to me said. "Why don't he get the horse out of the gate? He should have opened up five on these plodders."

Frankel had a horse called Cam Bay entered in the ninth race, this one a mile gallop for cheap claimers, and I went down to the paddock again. The trainer was still fuming over Yu Wipi. "These jocks never do what you tell them," were his opening words to me. But when Toro, who also had the mount on Cam Bay, reappeared, the jockey told Frankel that Yu Wipi had been "real rough in the gate," meaning fractious, and had tired himself out early. Frankel didn't answer and said nothing to Toro about how to ride Cam Bay.

On our way back to the stands, Bobby snatched the program

out of my hand and with his finger crossed off five of the eight horses in the race. "Cam Bay and these two here," he said. "There's your exacta." I asked him what his plans were for Yu Wipi. "You go day to day," he answered. "You get a horse ready for a race and they start coughing, they bleed, they lose a shoe. The public don't know that. They only lose their money, not their minds." And he slouched away, scowling.

I bet ten dollars to win on Cam Bay, at five to one, and I also bought exactas from him to the other two horses Frankel had indicated. Cam Bay, perfectly ridden by Toro, won and I also cashed an exacta ticket for a net profit on the race of one hundred and thirty-four dollars. Frankel can make a winner out of anyone, on four legs or two.

14

DAMON SCREWS PYTHIAS

"Nothing brings out the prick in a man faster than his first good horse."
—Francis P. Dunne, a New York steward

Over the past decade horse racing, even more than other professional sports, has become a game in which a vast expenditure of money would seem to generate success, if success is to be measured solely by winning. What is required of an owner now is nothing more than a willingness to lay out huge sums for the top athletes, the well-bred yearlings and two-year-olds who will soon propel him to the top and enshrine him, in his own eyes at least, as a true sportsman. The long-range goal, which used to be loosely defined as "the improvement of the breed," essentially the slow, careful development of a sound, ever-improving, superior sort of animal, has been replaced by a short-range one, in which little matters but the instant glory to be achieved by winning the most prestigious contests, such as the Kentucky Derby and the Breeders' Cup Classic, at no matter what cost—not only in money, but in the blood, sweat, bowed tendons, and broken bones of the contestants themselves.

The reasons for this change should be obvious, dictated as they have been by the proliferation of many forms of off-track wagering and the concomitant exposure of the sport on network TV. An owner with a champion horse can become an overnight celebrity, with all the ego-massaging perks that accompany that exalted position. Best of all, horses, unlike human athletes, do not belong to labor unions, do not have agents and can't talk back, so there is no one to contradict the great man when he spouts nonsense about his charges at his moments of triumph or informs the world at large that he and his trainer are paragons of virtue and good taste. No wonder George Steinbrenner found release in his racing stable from his travails as owner of the New York Yankees, most of whom he seemed to regard as a bunch of overpaid, malingering crybabies; horses do what they are told and shut up about it.

The late Eugene Klein, who died of a heart attack on March 12, 1990, at the age of sixty-nine, had a clearer fix on reality than most of his fellow sports tycoons. Having failed to buy and bully his way into a Super Bowl as the owner of the San Diego Chargers, Klein abandoned football, firing off in his wake a book that was little more than an acrimonious, self-serving account of his turbulent tenure in the National Football League, and began buying expensive Thoroughbreds. Freed at last from the nuisance of being contradicted and second-guessed by his hired hands, Klein almost immediately achieved in racing the renown that had eluded him in football. Between 1983 and 1988, he won more races, including a Kentucky Derby and seven Breeders' Cup contests, and more money, about twenty-five million dollars, than any other owner. His horses won eleven national championships in various categories, and he and his wife were voted Eclipse Awards by the racing fraternity as outstanding owners in 1985, 1986, and 1987.

Klein was no genius, but he was a smart, tough-minded businessman who found in D. Wayne Lukas exactly the sort of trainer who could instantly catapult him to stardom. Lukas, who began his professional life in sports as an unsuccessful high-school basketball coach before becoming involved with horses, is by far the greatest promoter in the game. Alone among the career horsemen, most of whom tend to be conservative, cautious, suspicious of outsiders and mired in tradition, he understood that this new breed of sports owners was not interested in sport per se, but in self-aggrandizement. Accustomed to wielding absolute power and making decisions affecting the lives and welfare of thousands of employees, while enriching themselves in the process, they were exasperated to find themselves suddenly thrust into a world in which their money couldn't buy them instant success, and they were often pilloried in the media for their indifference or outright hostility to long-established rules of conduct.

Lukas changed all that. A tall, permanently tanned, expensively dressed, supremely personable man with a sculpted hairdo, a gleaming smile, and eyes hidden most of the time behind designer shades, he projected precisely the corporate aura of success calculated to reassure the Kleins of this planet. He understood, first of all, that a businessman visiting the backstretch for the first time would not expect to be led to a scuffed barn badly in need of paint and flaunting used rub rags hanging from sagging clotheslines, a shedrow with piles of dirty straw at each end, overflowing trash bins, and staffed by lackadaisically attired migrants shuffling from task to task in time to a salsa beat from a nearby portable radio. And why would any big-time investor entrust expensive property to a cracker-barrel type who presides over such a dismal scene from an unswept and fly-infested office on the premises that he calls a tack room and that is usually furnished with a secondhand couch, a couple of metal or wooden chairs, and a battered-looking desk haphazardly strewn with charts, old programs, racing forms, and bits of odd-looking equipment. Who could be expected to risk big sums of money in such a venture? Why not just toss the folding green out the window to the homeless?

From the first, Lukas's operation was structured in the corporate style, with branch offices all over the country, immaculate shedrows, and employees at all levels, from the humblest hot-walker to the assistants in charge of his various strings, properly attired and indoctrinated to fit into the image he wished to project. His product was winning horses and he made it clear that, to achieve success, only the best would do. You couldn't make omelets without breaking eggs, and he was in an arena in which the rich were being asked to compete with each other. Once he had carte blanche, Lukas didn't care what he spent of his owners' money. Almost single-handedly, during the late nineteen-seventies and early eighties, he kept American buyers and breeders in competition with the Arabs and the Japanese, who had begun to frequent the Kentucky and Florida yearling sales and sent prices booming. In less than a decade, he established himself as the winner par excellence, alone at the top of his peculiar profession.

Lukas's horses won more races and more money than anyone else's. He ran them early and kept on running them until they dropped or fell apart on him, and he never backed off anything on four legs that could still stand up. He loaded animals onto airplanes and flew them all over the country to knock off big purses everywhere. When his champions broke down or died on him, it didn't matter, because there were always other ones coming up to take their place. ("What's the rarest thing at the racetrack?" a press-box joke began. Answer: "A four-year-old trained by Wayne Lukas.") When expensive yearlings turned out to be not worth the huge sums he had paid for them, it also didn't matter, because all the public and the press cared about were the ones who did achieve glory—Terlingua, Landaluce, Lady's Secret, Winning Colors, Steinlen, Grand Canyon, Criminal Type, a host of others. When Lukas and Klein hooked up, it was Damon finding Pythias, an encounter of mythological proportions.

It came as a shock to many, therefore, when Klein suddenly announced in June of 1989 that he was getting out of racing, selling everything in order to "take it easy," presumably because he wanted to spend time with his family and travel. Immediately, the rumor mills pronounced that he had decided to get out because he had lost too much money. Racing is such a risky and expensive game that only an estimated five percent of owners manage to show a yearly profit. Klein's horses had won a ton of races and big purses, but no one had ever mentioned the losses and the operating costs—all the expensive yearlings who turned out to be busts, the vet bills, feeding and training fees, salaries, and the like. Klein, so the theory went, had achieved what he'd set out to do. He had won everything in sight, except the Belmont and a Triple Crown, so why linger on and absorb any more red ink? He was a supreme egotist, yes, but not an idiot. And there were also rumors from various sources that he had accused Lukas of cheating him and that he and the trainer had had a very public falling out in a posh restaurant near San Diego from which Klein had stormed away visibly upset.

Not so, both Lukas and Klein maintained when the story surfaced and the speculation continued. The trainer also declared that at the dispersal sale in Lexington, Kentucky, in November, during which about a hundred and fifty of Klein's horses were auctioned, the owner would emerge with a healthy net profit. The animals and breeding shares in various stallions reportedly brought in over thirty million dollars, a figure that, according to Lukas, made Klein a winner at the bank as well as on the track.

The truth will probably never be known, because horse racing, like the movie business, is a field dedicated to what author Mario Puzo used to call kamikaze accounting procedures. Lukas obviously has a vested interest in maintaining that Klein made money, and Klein's heirs have nothing to gain by admitting that he might have been taken to the cleaners in order to gratify his lust for public eminence. But the rumors inside the industry have persisted, and the figure most often heard is that Klein lost in the neighborhood of about fifteen million dollars, which would certainly account for his precipitous exit from stage center.

As for Lukas, he is still at the top of the game and may even succeed in remaining there. Once again, during 1991, he showed more wins and more purse money earned by his charges than anyone else. But his golden time was the nineteen-eighties, the Reagan era of unbridled speculation, easy credit, overspending, and quick returns, with little thought wasted on the welfare of the participants and the future health of the operation as a whole. There have been signs of stress and fraying at the edges, too, with recurring but unconfirmed reports that all is not fiscally sound inside the Lukas empire. Furthermore, none of his horses won either a Triple Crown or a Breeders' Cup race in 1991, and it has become clear that he will no longer dominate the American racing scene as he has during most of the past decade.

People like Lukas, however, should never be underrated. Like Donald Trump, he's a master showman, one of the great entrepreneurs of recent history. Professing himself undaunted by the loss of Klein's seemingly bottomless wallet, Lukas has continued to promote himself and his operation as the only way to achieve quick success in the sport, and he is still a formidable presence at the major horse auctions, where the best-bred yearlings and two-year-olds pass under the gavel. He has also successfully established himself as the sport's most articulate spokesman. During the Klein years, Lukas was often openly contemptuous of the press and had been known to publicly savage reporters who had the temerity to express even the smallest reservations about his modus operandi, especially in regard to the horses themselves. No longer. Now Lukas will talk to anyone and everyone, and he has even shed his dark glasses to appear, in press conferences and on TV, as a passionate advocate of the game in all its facets, from breeding and racing to the gambling that fuels the whole enterprise. In that respect, at least, he's horse racing's greatest public asset. In this country, it's not substance that the society rewards, but the image of success projected by the spin doctors who manipulate public opinion.

15

HOOKED

"Yeah? Who do you like in the fourth?"
—Horseplayer at Caliente, after hearing
that the Japanese had just bombed Pearl
Harbor

I DON'T remember the exact year, but I do recall vividly the moment I knew I was hooked forever on the races. Back in the nineteen-fifties and early sixties, when I lived in New York and could only get to the track on weekends and holidays, the horses and their entourages would head south for the winter, mainly to Florida. I'd always try to make a point of going out to Aqueduct for getaway day in late November, when I'd huddle between races under the blowers with my fellow degenerates, trying to keep warm until we'd have to go out to the open stands again at post time.

Usually there would be a wind blowing in from the east, turning our fingers blue as we gripped our binoculars, our eyes tearing in the cold, our only hope for warmth the surge of blood in our veins caused by the prospect of a winner. Even on warm days, losers tend to freeze the marrow in one's bones, while a winner at good odds generates enough heat to fuel an expedition through the Arctic tundra. And then, during that same period, there were those wonderful Thanksgivings at the track, when we could retreat into the heated inner sanctum of the grandstand cafeteria to munch on dry turkey and canned cranberry sauce while scanning the *Morning Telegraph* past performances for winners.

Fond memories these, of a time when playing the horses in New York involved not only risk, but stamina and conditioning. No one who hasn't battled the Long Island Railroad, the New York subway system and the boulevards or sat in an open grandstand when a northeaster is blowing can possibly appreciate the game as it was then conducted. I'd come home from these outings to my bemused family, feeling as if I'd proved myself, accomplished something memorable, like scaling a rock cliff or competing in a marathon. My wife, a tolerant and loving woman, regarded me as eccentric, while my oldest daughter Natalia had been heard to boast to casual acquaintances that I was her Dad and that I went to the racetrack every day. Hyperbole was in vogue during her kindergarten years.

After getaway day, there would be a period of respite, four months during which the horses would be far away, out of reach at Hialeah and Tropical Park or elsewhere under warm skies. A number of truly dedicated fans would head south with them, swarming into Miami like a rabble of camp followers in the wake of a crusade in order not to allow the elements to separate them from their cause. Like most ordinary citizens, however, I'd remain behind, bound sweetly by family and career ties to my other life as an editor, writer, husband and father. I'd casually follow the fortunes of the animals and their keepers in the sports sections of the newspapers, but largely banish the game from my immediate consciousness during the long winter hiatus. But after the first March thaw, I'd begin thinking about the horses again, anticipating their return, once more to Aqueduct, in the early days of April. For me the spring began not with the first green leaves in Central Park or the reappearance of birds at ancient nesting sites, but with the first horse vans turning into the stable gates at Aqueduct and Belmont Park.

I never missed an opening day either, and it was on one of these occasions, sometime in the mid-fifties, that I got the message as to my relative standing in that great secret confraternity that is the world of the horseplayer. I had just emerged from a crowded subway car and was on my way down the ramp toward the clubhouse turnstiles when I found myself hurrying along beside an elderly citizen I had seen around the track for years and with whom I'd occasionally exchanged opinions regarding the merits of various animals we were considering making a bet on. "Hey, how ya doin'?" he said, as we rushed along, anxious not to miss the double. "Where was ya? I didn't see ya in Florida."

Useless to explain to him that my entire life did not revolve around the ponies. This was the same old codger who had once informed me, during a philosophical discussion between races on the disciplines of betting strategies, that he had stripped his life down to the essentials in order to survive in his chosen milieu. He lived year-around in cheap, furnished lodgings, usually motels, within an easy ride of whatever track was open. His basic living expenses were taken care of by his monthly Social Security check, leaving him unencumbered by other obligations to pursue his chosen vocation, which he identified as finding enough fast horses at good odds to bet money on, mainly across the board. He stuck to this regimen with the single-minded dedication of a Trappist monk and claimed that he was able to live comfortably and tax-free on his winnings. How comfortably, I couldn't imagine, since he was not sartorially resplendent; I had never seen him in anything but the same brown-and-black checked sports jacket and baggy gray slacks. But then, I reasoned, new clothes would naturally fall into that area of useless expenditure that he considered detrimental to his health. As for women and family, he had declared that aspect of the social compact to be an insurmountable handicap. "A woman is like a hundred and forty pounds on your back," is the way he put it. "You could stop Citation with weight like that." The fact that I had been recognized as a fellow disciple by this sage meant that I had arrived; it was as if, after years of toil and trouble in the service of a sometimes cruel god, I had been recognized and anointed by one of the elect. It didn't entirely elate me, since I was all too aware of the perils of becoming an addicted gambler, but it did reassure me. I was no longer a dilettante, but a regular, and I would have to behave as such.

. . .

Much nonsense has been written about gambling as an addiction, especially in regard to horse racing. Unquestionably, there are people at the racetrack every day who shouldn't be there, mainly because they are gambling money they can't afford to lose and they are incapable of self-discipline in regard to betting, not only on horse races but on everything. I once attended a meeting of Gamblers Anonymous in the L.A. area in connection with an article I was writing on a professional horseplayer, and I sat there as one person after another got to his feet to recount horrifying tales of destitution, misery, broken homes, and crime, lives shattered by an inability to resist risking money at tracks, with bookies and in casinos. All the speakers, women as well as men, declared themselves compulsively incapable of controlling the urge to wager and spoke glowingly of how they had turned their lives around by joining GA and embarking on a program of total abstinence. They had found peace and satisfaction while rebuilding their lives as solid middle-class citizens engaged in the pursuit of happiness. To achieve it, they were once again working hard at their chosen professions; but instead of gambling, they were putting their money into banks, savings and loans, bonds, stocks and real estate. This was called investing in the American Dream. They now viewed themselves as solid pillars of the community, not hooked gamblers.

I thought it was largely a question of semantics. They had achieved peace and a degree of control over their lives, which was unquestionably admirable and fine, but they were deluding themselves by maintaining that they had ceased to be gamblers. They were merely operating in a different arena, entrusting the fruits of their labors to banks, insurance companies, the stockmarket, venture capitalists, developers, and land speculators. In what way was owning junk bonds or purchasing shares in wildcat oil exploration any less of a gamble than a couple of hundred dollars on the nose of a maiden two-year-old with fast works? In life you pick your game, weigh the odds and take your chances. Howard Sartin, a psychologist who counsels horseplayers and has devised a fascinating methodology for picking winners, often likes to point out that the problem is not gambling, but losing. Even as casual

horseplayers, it behooves us to make ourselves into at least occasional winners or choose some other, less expensive form of entertainment.

Without gambling there would be no horse racing. This would
seem to be such an obvious fact that it hardly needs to be stated,
but astonishingly this aspect of the sport is regarded with distaste
not only by America's legions of bluenoses and the ignorant
general public, which regards all horseplayers as the comical,
slightly sinister clowns immortalized by Damon Runyon, but also
by segments of the racing establishment itself. This is probably
because historically only people rich enough to own horses could
afford to race them and they mostly confined themselves to betting with each other. By the time the fans got into the act, the
aristocratic owners and breeders, who didn't need the money, had
convinced themselves that they were above the herd. As the
exalted heirs of a great sporting tradition, they imagined themselves to be practitioners of what they called the sport of kings and
"improvers of the breed," quite forgetting the fact that they and
their ancestors had achieved wealth and public eminence mainly
by enslaving foreign populations, exploiting their own people and
plundering the environment. They removed themselves from association with the humbler folk at the race meets by withdrawing
into royal enclosures, jockey clubs, turf clubs, and other private
membership facilities, and to this day they have continued to
propagate the illusion that, if it weren't for their selfless patronage,
the game would die.

This may have been true in the old days and may still be true
in Europe, where in some countries public funds are devoted to
keeping the sport alive as private resources dry up. In this country,
however, the whole enterprise rests firmly on the back of the
wagering public, a fact largely ignored by a good many racing
associations, especially those dominated by the heirs and worship-
pers of the Anglo-Saxon tradition. A few years ago, the art director of a magazine that was about to publish my piece on the
professional horseplayer decided it would be nice to frame the
cover illustration with the logos of all the West Coast tracks. I told
her I thought it would be a charming and effective visual coup, so

she contacted the racing associations and acquired permission from all but one. Santa Anita, she was informed by the track's marketing director, did not wish to be associated with an article about gambling. The next time I went out to Santa Anita, I looked up this bubblehead and informed him that he could save himself and his employers a lot of expense and anguish by shutting down the parimutuel machines and firing all the clerks, parking attendants, ushers and other redundant employees. The two or three hundred of us who might still show up to see the horses run could simply mill around the infield, betting sportingly, as in good King Charles's golden days, with each other. He wasn't amused.

What makes it so difficult to win money at the races is the cost of making a bet. The tracks and politicians cut between fifteen and twenty-five percent out of the wagering pools in order to finance the operation and grease the wheels of government, which means, in effect, that every time we make a bet we are paying what gamblers call heavy vigorish for the privilege of doing so. There is also what is known as breakage, a method of calculating payoffs in most cases back to the nearest twenty cents. The convenient theory is that no one wants to bother with pennies, nickels and dimes. If a horse should actually pay $2.59 to show, for example, the track will return $2.40 to the winning bettor, thus pocketing the extra nineteen cents. It's a sinister little financial gimmick that imposes what amounts to an added tax of slightly over two percent on the public. In addition these days, if a bettor should happen to hit a big Pick Six or some other wager paying off at odds of three hundred to one or better, he will be compelled to sign an IRS tax form and endure having twenty percent of his payoff withheld on the spot, after which he will be expected to include his earnings as part of his overall income-tax return and possibly have to pay out additional money to the Feds and the state. No wonder John Scarne, in his classic, *Complete Guide to Gambling*, said of horse racing that it was impossible to beat the game in the long run. He recommended that we should take to the track every day only what we can afford to lose, consider it pure entertainment, and bet the favorite to show in every race. "I don't say that this advice will win you any money," he wrote, "but it will cut down your losses."

Betting strategies at the racetrack have undergone a revolution since Scarne made that recommendation, thirty years ago. The development of the computer has ushered in an era of high-tech handicapping strategies that have greatly helped not only the pros but the casual horseplayer as well. In the endless and unequal struggle with the parimutuel machines, smart bettors have turned to such seminal tomes as Andrew Beyer's *Picking Winners* and the works of Tom Ainslie, whose *Complete Guide to Thoroughbred Racing*, first published in 1968 and revised and updated several times since, is still the basic tool for understanding and wagering on horse races. The fundamental point about Thoroughbred racing is that speed and pace are the main factors to consider before making a bet, and it is now possible, thanks to the wealth of data available on the market, for people to acquire essential accurate information before risking their money.

Somebody, of course, has to lose. Unlike casino gambling, the players are not going up against the house but each other, once the vigorish has been cut out of the pool, and the tracks are indifferent to the outcome. This means that only the most sophisticated, hard-nosed gamblers are going to walk away with most of the money. It has been estimated, probably accurately, that only about two percent of the people who go regularly to the races come away as winners at the end of the year. And with all that information out there, not only in print but in the form of daily seminars conducted by experts every racing day all over the country, how can even the best-informed horseplayers hope to survive?

The answer, of course, dear Brutus, lies not in our handicapping stars but in ourselves. Three of the most successful bettors I know are James Quinn, Tom Brohamer and Gerry Okuneff. Quinn and Brohamer have written exhaustive treatises on handicapping and betting strategies, while Okuneff is mainly a small bettor who rarely risks more than a couple of hundred dollars of his own on any racing day, takes small percentages of the winnings he makes for various friends and clients, and shows a consistent profit on his own action at meet after meet. Furthermore, they are all three generous in sharing their knowledge and opinions with anyone who asks them, even a heavy player whose action might affect the odds. They all know a terrible secret about the human race, which is that the average person, at the track, as in every other human endeavor, is too lazy, too stupid, too undisciplined and too timid to benefit from their expertise. They can go on lecturing, counseling and instructing forever and they will still be able to go to the track and come away with their clients' money.

The average horseplayer, even the veteran of decades of losing days, is a dreamer. He believes in his heart that he knows at least as much as anyone else and that someday he's going to devise a perfect system that will assure him of steady profits without having to do any real work. Occasionally, he *will* have a big winning day and it will make him forget all of his losses. His testicles will swell with pride; he will feel himself invincible and will bestride his world like a colossus. (It's no accident that most big gamblers are men, whose masculine self-esteem seems to derive directly from the degree of power and dominance money provides.) When, inevitably, he begins to lose again, he will not look into himself for answers, but begin to blame everyone and everything else.

The track and the off-track betting facilities are cesspools of paranoia. The races are fixed, the trainers and jockeys are crooked, the stewards are blind and incompetent, the racing authorities thieves. After every contest the voices of discontent and outrage will be heard, sometimes in lightly cynical observations concerning the Shakespearean acting talents of the riders or the manipulative dishonesty of the trainers who are "giving their horse a race." Often the animals themselves will be blamed, castigated as "hanging dogs" or "fainthearted speedballs" or, in horseman's lingo, as "common sonsabitches." In some cases, the losers' foulmouthed rage will be so prolonged and vituperative that they will have to be escorted out and occasionally banned from the premises for varying periods of time.

My favorite terminal loser is a portly, middle-aged citizen known to the regulars in L.A. as the Desperado, Desi for short. He's so loud and scatological in his objections that he often finds himself banished, occasionally for weeks at a time. During one such period of exile at Santa Anita, he still managed to remain in action. He would drive to the track, park in the main lot and arrange for acquaintances ("Desi doesn't have any friends," Okuneff says) to run his bets for him. By the middle of one afternoon, after a customary run of disastrous losing wagers, he was observed clutching the iron railings of the fence between the lot and the paddock area, shaking it and shouting. "I hate this fuckin' place, I hate this fuckin' place," he screamed, "and when they let me back in, I'm not coming!"

It took me quite a while to figure out that not only is there no sure system for beating the races but also there's no sure way to guarantee a win on any one race. No matter what the figures say or what the conditions of a race, no matter what a lock the animal may seem to be, horses can find hundreds of ways to lose, and every year they discover new ones. They stumble out of the gate, they rear up in the air, they get carried to the outer fences on the turns, they get shut off in the drive, they fall down, they jump shadows, they bolt into the infield and have even been known to drown in infield lakes. There is nothing that cannot happen to a horse to keep him from running his best race, and whatever can possibly go wrong at some point will. And then there are the days when even the greatest horses not only lose but run out of the money, often simply because they don't feel like extending themselves. Secretariat was beaten five times during his illustrious career and even Man o' War lost once.

This bitter lesson was driven home to me one day by an experience I had with Kelso, the great gelding I still consider the finest racehorse I ever saw. I had put aside seven hundred dollars, a not inconsiderable sum in those days, to bet on him in the Metropolitan Mile, a handicap run on May 30, 1962, at Aqueduct. Kelso was carrying a hundred and thirty-three pounds, ten more than his nearest rival, the four-year-old Carry Back, and he figured to go off at even money or less. I didn't care. He had won under this sort of crushing weight before, and he was by every standard so superior to his eight rivals in the race that I didn't see how he could possibly lose. So I drove out to Aqueduct and waited all afternoon to make my big bet on this sure thing in the seventh.

Here's how the chart of the race read the next day: "Kelso, away alertly, raced evenly to the stretch but failed to respond when set down for the drive." He finished sixth, with Shoemaker up, and beaten more than eight lengths by Carry Back, the winner of the 1961 Kentucky Derby. Kelso had been backed down to three to five at post time, which meant that I had risked my seven hundred dollars in order to make about four hundred. My recollection of the race is that he stumbled, going nearly to his knees, coming out of the gate, but there's no mention of such an incident in the chart, so perhaps my memory is playing me a merciful trick. Otherwise, how to account for such a poor effort from such a great athlete? Whatever the reason, I had lost my seven hundred and I was broke. On my way out of the track, I put my last quarter into a slot machine to buy a peanut bar. The machine kept my quarter and held on to its peanuts. I figured there was a message in there somewhere. And I have never since then risked more than a couple of hundred dollars on any horse and certainly not on one going off at less than even money.

It was also about this time that I decided to put my betting life in order. I have never, since that memorable loss, deluded myself that I could become a professional horseplayer; I don't have either the patience or the nerve for what it takes to become one. I do pride myself on being a good handicapper and I rejoice on my good winning days, while riding out the inevitable losing streaks with as much aplomb as I can muster. The beginning of wisdom in any form of gambling is the realization that betting on anything in order to make a living is essentially a mug's game. Not only are the odds stacked against you, but having to show enough of a profit to make the effort worthwhile takes all the pleasure out of it, for me at least. I don't know a single professional horseplayer who enjoys the sport for its own sake or feels any sense of identification with the animals and the riders who provide us with the thrills that keep us coming back again and again to hippodromes all over the world. And I also find it significant that almost all of the pros have something going for them besides their daily bets. Andy Beyer, the most fearless plunger of them all, also writes a witty racing column for the *Washington Post;* Quinn and Bro- hamer write books, conduct seminars and counsel clients; Gerry Okuneff works occasionally as a bit player and stunt man in TV and movies. It's too tough out there, entirely on your own, and not worth it either, if all it means is a buck. Why not just get a job?

My own approach to making the track a winning proposition has been to write about it, though it didn't take me long to discover that my reading public did not consist primarily of horseplayers, who are the sort of people who think nothing of wagering a couple of hundred dollars on some odds-on crippled plater with no more chance to win than Wiley E. Coyote, but are not going to shell out twenty bucks for a book.

I was at Santa Anita one day when a bust-out movie producer I know approached me in the grandstand and implored me to pick him a winning triple. He had lost his shirt, as usual, and he needed help. I hadn't even planned to play the triple, an exotic parlay wager (known in the East as a Pick Three) I consider a poor risk, but I obliged by coming up with a basic twelve-dollar wager for him—two horses in each of the first two races in the series and a single in the third. To my amazement, the combination hit, for a payoff of a hundred and seventy-six dollars for each twelve-dollar ticket. My movie producer is a big bettor and he must have had it at least several times. He was appropriately grateful and thanked me effusively, though I felt a bit chagrined, since I hadn't risked a dollar of my own on the bet.

Several weeks later, back at Santa Anita, I ran into my movie producer again. He came rushing excitedly up to me in the aisles. "Bill," he said, "I was in New York and I was walking down Fifth Avenue and I saw a copy of your new book in the window of the Doubleday bookshop there!" "That's wonderful," I said. "I'm pleased to hear it." "You know," he said thoughtfully, "I almost bought it."

Someday I'll get even with this guy. Maybe I'll base an evil character on him in one of my novels or use him as comedy relief. In the long run, like all the other characters—good, evil, wise, and foolish—I've met at the track, he'll enrich me by contributing to the world I've created that nourishes me.

"How have you done at the track over the years?" a newspaper interviewer asked me not long ago. "You've got to be a big loser overall, wouldn't you say?"

I thought about it for a few minutes before answering. What did I have to balance against my betting action? Lots of articles, all those books, and a lifetime of thrills, drama, heartbreak, friendships, and love for certain horses—Stymie, Kelso, Secretariat, so many others now long gone, and the ones I love today, especially a big black game filly named Ultra Sass, in which I have a small interest.

And then there was the day I went out to Santa Anita, on a fall afternoon in 1972. I had recently come back from fourteen months in Italy, working for *Playboy* and *The New Yorker*. My first marriage had ended, so had a second, stormy relationship with an actress, and I was living alone in an apartment on the beach in Santa Monica. Sitting in a box next to me that day was a pretty freckled blonde woman with a sweet Irish face, hazel eyes and long arms. I wanted to get to know her, but I couldn't think of a graceful way to introduce myself to her. Finally, with all the savoir faire for which I am world-famous, I leaned casually toward her and thrust my program at her. "Who do you like in this race?" I asked. She smiled and picked a winner, so what could I do but marry her?

I had my answer to the question. I'm a lifetime winner at the track.

16

TRIPLE CROWN FOLLIES

"I wouldn't invite anyone I love to Louisville."
—Andrew Beyer, in conversation

RELATIVELY FEW people ever get to attend a Triple Crown race. We watch them on TV and read about them in our sports sections, but we're reluctant to undergo all the expense and trouble of actually being present at one. I had been to a number of Belmonts over the years, but never to the Kentucky Derby or the Preakness, the first two races in the series. It seems a long way to go from California just to see a horse race, but during the past few years the conviction had grown in me that I *had* to go. How could I call myself a true racetracker? Could one be a lifelong baseball fan and never attend at least one game of a World Series? Or major in art and never visit the Louvre? Obviously not. So, a couple of years ago, I made arrangements to go to Churchill Downs for the running of the one hundred and sixteenth Derby, then move on to Baltimore for the Preakness two weeks later. I intended to drive to Louisville in a friend's car from Washington, D.C., but I'd spend a week first around Lexington, going to the races at Keeneland and having a look at some of the horse farms I had heard about all my life. Usually, in the spring, I'd head for Italy, but not this year.

"You're going to the Kentucky Derby? What for? How can you put up with all that aggravation?" a friend of mine asked me a couple of weeks before my departure. We had bumped into each other at the betting satellite in Del Mar and had been discussing the year's crop of three-year-olds, strictly as a betting proposition. Wagering on racehorses was the only thing in life that interested my buddy, who, like many of my fellow horseplayers, seemed to have no visible source of income but somehow managed to stay in action. When I revealed to him that I was on my way to Kentucky to see for myself about the three-year-olds, he was appalled. Why would I get up from my comfortable table facing a large TV screen, only a short stroll from a parimutuel window, to subject myself to the expense and horrors of modern travel simply in order to be part of the huge crowd flocking into Church-ill Downs on the first Saturday in May? "You ain't even gonna see the race that good," was his parting shot.

He was probably right, I realized, but it didn't matter. If you love any sport, then occasionally you have to subject yourself to its realities. In racing you had to be there, with the horses and the people they represent, see all the sights, smell the smells, mingle, become a part of it. The economic future of horse racing, which is under increasing pressure from having to compete with state lotteries (even Kentucky has one) and other forms of legalized sports betting, undoubtedly depends on the spread of the off-track facilities, exotic wagering and the huge betting pools they generate, but they are not what the sport is essentially about. Its soul is still the animal itself, as those of us can testify who have fallen in love with various great horses over the years, and often it's the Kentucky Derby that establishes the true quality of a contender. In every sport certain events transcend the hype that engulfs them, though I knew I could never explain that to my friend.

By the time of the Derby the year before, I had already fallen in love—with trainer Charlie Whittingham's feisty black colt, Sunday Silence. Most of my friends in the East had committed their hearts to his chief rival, Easy Goer, owned by Ogden Mills Phipps, and much had been made of the East-West rivalry that had domi-nated the sports pages for months. I never took that aspect seri-ously, because, after all, both horses had been bred in Kentucky, but the publicity generated tremendous excitement. Even after

Sunday Silence's Derby victory, the controversy raged, all through the Triple Crown contests (Sunday Silence won the Preakness, too; Easy Goer the Belmont), until the two horses met for the last climactic confrontation at the Breeders' Cup Classic in Miami that fall. Good for the game, as they say.

There have been other great rivalries that have distinguished various Derbies, such as the outstanding one between Affirmed and Alydar in 1978, but a great rivalry doesn't seem to be essential to public interest in the race. Often it's simply the presence in it of a horse that has captured the public's fancy. Secretariat went into the 1973 Derby as an odds-on favorite and demolished his rivals, but was so beloved that he continued to receive correspondence from admirers until his death.

We all retain certain firmly rooted images from every Kentucky Derby, more than from any other Triple Crown race. From recent ones I recall, for instance, the way Bill Shoemaker rode Ferdinand like a cowboy in 1986, weaving recklessly through horses down the stretch to bring Whittingham his first Derby victory; the way a plodding outsider, Gato Del Sol, suddenly exploded out of the pack in 1982 to claim his moment of glory with an effort he was never able to repeat; and the way the big roan filly, Winning Colors, humbled her field in 1988, leading every step of the way over Churchill Downs's deep, tiring course, a performance that capped her career and that she, too, was never able to duplicate. An equine athlete, like a human one, will sometimes rise to a great occasion and accomplish feats quite beyond himself, like a chorister at the Met suddenly taking center stage to sound like Domingo. Nothing seems to bring this quality out in an animal like the Kentucky Derby.

The year I decided to go the race had acquired a flavor all its own. Most of the best horses seemed to be in the East, but there was no outstanding athlete, and the contest was coming up as a typical scramble, with half a dozen major contenders on the boards and a host of obscure candidates poised to swoop out of the wings. But over the past couple of months, the field seemed to have shaken itself down to two major competitors, Summer Squall and Mister Frisky.

At first glance it looked like a rerun of the previous year. Summer Squall was royally bred, cost three hundred thousand dollars as a yearling and had done all of his racing in the East, having lost only once, in a sprint to a top speed horse and after a long layoff. Mister Frisky cost only fifteen thousand dollars, had been sired by a cheap stallion, was undefeated and had been running in California.

There, however, the similarities ended. Summer Squall was a small colt who had been delayed getting to the track that year by a bleeding episode and had been raced hard to get into condition. Mister Frisky had also been raced hard, a total of sixteen times in his brief career, and had "beaten no one," as horseplayers put it. Thirteen of his victories had been registered in Puerto Rico, and his wins at Santa Anita had been over second-raters in unimpressive times. So although they had lost only one race between them, they were still not considered dominant by the horsemen and there would be at least several other animals in the field whose connections felt had a legitimate chance to win.

Among them would be a maiden named Pendleton Ridge, who had run a closing fourth in the Wood Memorial at Aqueduct a few weeks earlier and whose trainer, Bobby Frankel, ought to have known better. The last maiden to run in a Derby had been a nonentity named Great Redeemer, who finished a distant last in 1979. Still, you never know. Broker's Tip was a maiden when he won in 1933, and before him two other maidens had found themselves draped in roses in the winner's circle, Buchanan in 1884 and Sir Barton in 1919. That was the beauty of the Derby and it was the main reason I planned to be there that year, with a parimutuel ticket in my pocket and a possible dawning love affair in my heart.

I flew east to New York and Washington, then drove down by car through the lush Shenandoah Valley and across the rocky, wooded ridges of West Virginia. The trip was a scenic delight, even though I covered the roughly six hundred miles quickly, with only one overnight stop. When I arrived in the countryside around Lexington, however, I realized that nothing had prepared me for the beauties of the horse country, with its rolling meadows, barns, palatial dwellings, endless dark wooden fences, tobacco fields, cattle pastures, and narrow country roads weaving through it like the strands of a huge spider web. After turning off the main highway to get a better look at it, I suddenly topped a low rise and found myself cruising along beside a herd of mares with new foals by their sides. It was a sight most horseplayers never see, mainly because it is not a betting proposition.

I spent the next few days as a guest at a horse farm named Jonabel, a 760-acre spread a few miles west of Lexington that is home to several hundred broodmares, their new foals and yearlings, and eight or nine stallions whose progeny keep the racing industry supplied with competitors year after year. The horses receive better care than most human beings. I watched a mare give birth late one afternoon on a patch of lawn outside her stable, with three expert hands in attendance to help her along. It was an easy birth, I was told, with the foal emerging as it is supposed to, front feet first with its head tucked in between its legs. An hour and twenty minutes later, it was up on its feet, already nestling close to its mother. In the breeding shed, I observed a Jonabel stallion named Slewpy being mated to a panicky three-year-old filly in a ceremony devoid of ritual and delicacy, but astonishing for the meticulous care with which the human attendants made sure the premises were spotlessly clean and the act fully consummated. One man even helped the stallion achieve penetration, while two others held the filly still for him by lifting one of her forelegs off the ground and holding her head in place with a strap tied around her upper lip. Not the sort of wedding night any bride would remember with fondness.

Though casual visitors are not allowed simply to drop in at most of the horse farms, I made provision to tour a couple of the larger ones, Claiborne and Land's End, where I discovered that a five-dollar tip to any attendant will almost always get you in to see everything. Kentucky teems with good old boys who tend to burst into bloom if you mention the word "horses" and who are not only accommodating but full of good stories about their fabled charges.

On my second day in the area I went out to the Kentucky Horse Park to see two of the greatest racehorses who ever lived, John Henry and Forego. The park is a thousand-acre public facility that includes a half-mile exercise track, dressage arenas, and several collections and museums, one devoted to the horse in general and others to specialized breeds and activities. Several times a year the park is the site of equestrian competitions, including one that is used to choose horses and riders for international events, including the Olympics. But the most popular attraction at the park is grumpy old John Henry, the fabulous old competitor who was still winning important races at the advanced age of nine and who earned more money in his lifetime than any horse before him. The reason that he and Forego, a huge animal whose fragile ankles made it impossible for him to run more than a few times a year but who could have probably beaten even John Henry on his best day, are at the park instead of on a breeding farm is that they are geldings. During a horse's racing career, a penchant for brawling and sulking or the sort of encounters encouraged in singles bars can only be cured by drastic surgery. "It's the only way you can get some studs to keep their minds on business," I remember Willis Reavis once telling me.

I don't really believe in a life after death, but if there is a heaven, I'd want it to be something like Keeneland, which I visited for the first time the day after my arrival in the area. I drove into the premises through groves of dogwoods and other flowering trees in whose shade I had no trouble finding a parking place. Then I walked into the grandstand, which looked more like an Ivy League football stadium than a betting emporium, and found a seat overlooking the main dirt oval, which is a mile and a sixteenth in circumference, and lush-looking inner turf course. Everywhere I gazed I saw trees, hedges, green fields, while the people around me had a cheerful country look, as if they had come to attend a county fair. It was a revelation to me, a pastoral celebration of sport totally removed from the racing atmosphere I had grown up in: a scene of incipient desolation and carnage populated in part by addicts about to blow their welfare checks on the daily double.

The track is open for racing only twice a year, for a couple of weeks in April and again in October. Conceived during the Depression by a celebrated local horseman named John Oliver (Jack) Keene, the facility exists mainly as the site of four annual yearling sales that are the most important in the nation, grossing hundreds of millions of dollars. The racing is strictly a secondary activity and largely divorced from the profit motive. Stockholders receive no dividends, and all net earnings are poured back into capital improvements and boosting the purses for the horsemen. Money is also donated to charities, to educational organizations and for equine research. The emphasis here is on the sport itself, which makes Keeneland unique in an era in which the nation's racetracks are regarded by politicians as machines for separating the betting public from its dollars.

I almost missed getting a bet down on the first race because I became so immersed in my handicapping that I didn't hear the announcer inform the public that the horses were nearing the starting gate. Then I remembered that Keeneland has no public announcer; the horses simply appear on the track for their race and the field goes off in silence. The assumption at Keeneland is that if you need to be told what is happening at a racetrack, you shouldn't be there.

After making my wager, I rushed back to my seat just in time to see the horses burst out of the starting gate. As they turned for home, the crowd began to root and the race ended as they all do, with people shouting and clapping or tearing up tickets in disappointment. The absence of a race caller struck me as a blessing, since a major affliction at this country's sporting events, especially on TV, has always been an excess of verbiage, with announcers and pundits chattering idiotically away as they proceed to belabor the obvious to the initiated.

I didn't cash a ticket that first day, but somehow it didn't seem to matter. I spent some of the time between races watching the horses being saddled under the trees, then paraded around the grassy walking ring before filing out through a tunnel under the stands toward the track. Everyone in the paddock seemed to be well heeled, with the men wearing coats and ties and the women mostly in dresses or elegant pants suits. I began to imagine myself a member in good standing of an elite cadre of sportsmen for whom the Thoroughbred symbolized class and grace and consummate style. I walked out of the track that afternoon entirely at peace with myself, indifferent to my dismal handicapping and empty wallet.

It was a terrific week, but not just because of the ambience and the horses. For one thing, I rediscovered bourbon whiskey and was introduced to Kentucky cooking, which, thank God, has nothing to do with health food. Nobody on the backside jogs, and people in Kentucky think the cholesterol count has something to do with the space program. For a little over two dollars in the track kitchen I bought myself a light local breakfast of eggs, bacon, biscuits, gravy, grits, butter, jam and coffee, which cost twenty-seven cents a cup and was actually drinkable. In the grandstand, I loaded up on gumbo and burgoo, a tasty local dish as feathery as hot lead, and also aspirin. Kentuckians will eat almost anything. I met a man named Mike Shannon, who owned a top grass horse named Manila and travels frequently to the Philippines, and he told me that he had once eaten dog meat, which turned out to be like chewing a tennis ball, but had found the snake soup not too bad.

In downtown Lexington I discovered a bistro called Buffalo and Dad's, which consisted of three dimly lit rooms, a couple of bars, a jukebox and walls decorated with old racing pictures and track paraphernalia. There I ate something called a hot brown, which consisted of turkey slices buried under a delicious cream sauce. I also enjoyed the clientele, which was mostly male and dedicated to sporting activities, not all of them entirely legitimate. The Feds had staged a drug bust involving an out-of-town horse trainer in the place a few weeks earlier, and when the agents stood up, guns drawn, to arrest the suspect, the premises emptied, with customers diving under tables and going out the windows and doors.

I didn't miss a day at Keeneland that week, not only because of the good racing, with a bunch of promising two-year-olds on the grounds, but mainly because I found it aesthetically satisfying to be there. Not the least of the track's charms are such eccentricities as a grandstand facing into the afternoon sun, a clubhouse not on the clubhouse turn, and the so-called Beard Course. The latter, named after one Major Louie A. Beard, is for races on the dirt at a distance of seven furlongs and one hundred and eighty-four feet. The horses break from the very end of the chute across the infield. Why did they bother building it? "They had all this extra dirt when they made renovations in 1953," I was told by a man I met in a betting line, "so they decided to use it." Of course.

Despite its many charms, I found Keeneland a tough place to pick winners. Horses come in from all over—Oaklawn, the Fair Grounds in Louisiana, Chicago, the Ohio circuit and the bush tracks, as well as from both coasts. A vast knowledge of racing across the country is required, as well as caution. The local clockers almost never report an accurate workout and sometimes no work- outs at all. Maiden two-year-olds show up on the program at long morning-line odds, go off at even money and win easily.

The betting action is best understood by hanging around the sharpies who mill about under the odds board by the gap near the walking ring. I usually ignore tips of any kind, but at Keeneland it can pay to keep your ears open. One of my new acquaintances, an affable young man nicknamed Hog whose real name is Harold Black and who has the pink, cheerful countenance of a Scout leader, came up during my visit with a Pick Six and a ninety-nine-to-one shot that he bet to win and place and in exactas for a twenty-five- hundred-dollar hit. The point about the horse business in Kentucky is that the locals invented the game, and they're not about to let it get away from them, either at the track or in the sales ring.

After the delights of Lexington and Keeneland, Louisville turned out to be a purgatory. "It is a city without a single redeeming virtue," Andy Beyer had pronounced, when I first asked him about the place. He went on to point out that for one week every year it also became a bazaar in which all of the citizens were magically transformed into thieves. Prices for everything having to do with the Derby tend to quintuple, and no outsider or humble member of the betting public gets a good seat without having to shell out a minimum of five hundred dollars for it.

I found this financial assessment to be fairly accurate. I had reserved accommodations in a pretentious motel near the airport that gouged several hundred dollars a night from me for a dark, dingy room with whorehouse decor through which airplanes roared every twenty minutes around the clock. During the day, as I wandered around, I found the locals hustling the arriving suckers for everything having to do with the Derby, from parking spaces on people's front lawns to tacky souvenirs and appalling haberdashery. The town itself was ugly, a prime example of an inner-city wasteland caused by reckless redevelopment and the flight of the middle class to the suburbs. Downtown consisted of a handful of isolated luxury hotels and modern office buildings surrounded mainly by slums and parking lots. Freeways debouched directly into it, and other roads cut off the citizenry from access to most of the waterfront along the Ohio River. There were a few decent restaurants and a couple of older residential enclaves of elegant mansions, as well as two or three avenues of once-grand old houses now chopped into apartments and offices and rapidly decaying. The racetrack itself, with its familiar twin towers and gracious old grandstand, was surrounded by a sea of tacky-looking bungalows of the sort Archie Bunker would have felt at home in. After my first couple of days, I spent most of my time inside the track and in the stable area, venturing into Louisville itself only at night in order to eat.

Not even the race itself quite justified the whole week I had to spend there. Admittedly, it was exciting seeing fifteen of the best three-year-olds in the world out on the track and moving about the backside every day, and then, too, there was the racing in the afternoon, during which I could also wander about the premises, absorbing atmosphere and color. I spent a magical two hours one morning inside the Kentucky Derby Museum, immersing myself in history and horse lore, as dazzled by the experience as I had been years before during my first tour of La Scala in Milan, the birthplace of grand opera. The situation of Churchill Downs, in fact, is not unlike that of La Scala; both are major cultural oases flourishing in urban industrial wastelands.

I never did fall in love that week. I wanted Mister Frisky to win, mainly because I always root for the commoners over the plutocrats, and I also admired Summer Squall for having overcome so many physical adversities during his brief career, but my heart, I discovered, was still uncommitted or, perhaps, still with Sunday Silence. From the roof of the grandstand, the only place I'd been able to commandeer to see the race, hemmed in by photographers, buffeted by an icy wind and out of range of the public-address system, I found myself gazing down on an ocean of people, over a hundred and twenty-eight thousand of them packed into quarters that could comfortably accommodate a third of that number. The best moments were the arrival of the horses, making the long walk, accompanied by their handlers, around the clubhouse turn from the stables to the paddock, and the singing of "My Old Kentucky Home" by the huge throng as the animals paraded to the post, and, finally, Unbridled's electrifying surge from twelfth at the half to win going away by three and a half lengths over Summer Squall, at odds of nearly eleven to one.

At the end of that exhausting day, I told myself that I was glad that I had come, but it wasn't until I saw the race replayed on the TV screens down below that I could say I had really seen and understood the race itself. I had participated in the event, but been unable to appreciate its nuances, much as if I had been compelled to listen to a favorite opera from the theatre lobby.

After Louisville, Baltimore was a revelation. I don't know whether the late H. L. Mencken, our most famous social critic and professional curmudgeon, ever attended a horse race, but it can't be any accident that he was born and lived all of his life in this city. He loved women, tasty food and good beer, not necessarily in that order, and he regarded competence in any field as a rare and admirable quality. I like to imagine that, if he were living today, he'd still have a few kind words not only for his hometown but for Pimlico as well. In the vast sea of incompetence and self-serving shortsightedness that characterizes much of the American racing scene, Baltimore and the Maryland Jockey Club emerge, at least during Preakness week, as islands of sanity and good cheer uncorrupted by excessive venality. I had such a good time at my first

Preakness, in fact, that I attended again the following year. When someone suggested I might want to move on from there to the Belmont in New York, too, I was able to decline by quoting Mencken. "A third-rate Babylon," he called the city.

The Preakness, named after Pimlico's first stakes winner back in 1870, lacks the glamour of the Derby and the Belmont, but makes up for it by involving the whole city in a celebration that begins with a wonderful parade the week before. No stuffy pomp and pageantry here, but dozens of cacophonous bands and hundreds of leggy high-school kids and colorfully attired representatives of the city's many ethnic groups, all marching out of step, waving to friends lining the sidewalks, dropping batons, and generally disporting themselves as if convinced that the whole purpose of the exercise is to have a terrific time. It had been quite a while since I had attended a public event divorced from exploitation, in which tourists and horse people were regarded as welcome guests, not victims to be gouged.

The racing management made visiting owners feel at home, showered them with courtesies and gifts (the previous year's goodies had consisted of a large wicker basket stuffed with fruit, cheeses, cookies, glassware, liquor, and a bright yellow terrycloth robe embroidered with the Preakness logo), made seats to the races available to them and to the public at a reasonable cost, and waited on them as if they mattered. It also threw great parties, my first year a dinner in the marble atrium of the ornate Peabody Library and a dinner dance, with two bands, at the National Aquarium in the Inner Harbor; the following year, on a huge Norwegian cruise ship, with several bands, a night-club revue, and a smorgasbord copious enough to sate the appetite of a Roman emperor. Although these classy wingdings were not open to the general public, they were expressions of an attitude that most other managements don't share. In Maryland, incredible as it may seem, they actually want you to have a good time at the races.

I didn't know what to expect when I first saw Pimlico. The horses entered in the Preakness are all stabled in the so-called stakes barn, a shabby wooden structure in the old barn area behind the grandstand. From there the plant looks like a huge bakery or a failing steel mill. Even inside it doesn't have much to recommend it aesthetically. Painted mainly in battleship gray, with a red trim, the interior looks as sterile and devoid of charm as a warehouse. Much of the grandstand is sheltered behind glass and the seats are made of plastic. The paddock is indoors and as graceless as a men's room, while from the stands the view over the infield provides an uninspiring panorama of red-brick stables and decaying wooden-frame houses only partly redeemed by clumps of large trees. The general effect is one of functional dreariness.

From a practical standpoint, however, I noticed abundant seating everywhere, plenty of TV monitors and refreshment stands, an effective cooling system, clean restrooms, and lots of betting options and windows. Still, it wasn't until I visited the Sports Palace on the top floor that I began to appreciate this track as a haven for the pure horseplayer. Here was a spacious interior room bristling with TV screens, comfortable padded armchairs, a large circular bar, and banks of TV monitors at which bettors could summon up past races by telephone in order to aid their handicapping. The atmosphere was that of a luxurious gambling ship. I met people in there who hadn't seen a live horse race in years, including a middle-aged couple from Ohio who come to the Preakness every year, sink into their seats facing one of the giant screens, and never so much as stick their noses out into the fresh air. Not my idea of going racing, but clearly an inspired one, if the whole purpose was to make the experience a pleasant and comfortable one, easier even than sitting and watching it at home.

The race itself my first year there turned out to be as memorable as Preaknesses often are, with Summer Squall turning the tables on Unbridled and poor Mister Frisky (already ill with the as yet undiagnosed abscess that almost ended his life) tottering in a well-beaten third. The Preakness often turns out to be the most dramatic of the Triple Crown races, a fact noted by William Legget, one of the best of the racing writers, in his program article on the race, when he recalled the previous year's confrontation between Sunday Silence and Easy Goer. "There they were, two outstanding horses, Sunday Silence and Easy Goer," he wrote, "driving down the length of the Pimlico stretch to a desperate nose finish and underlining the genuine essence and splendor of horse racing."

The only hazard I found myself having to cope with in Baltimore during Preakness week was the Triple Crown Ball, which is usually held in one of the big waterfront hotels and features a series of stupefyingly dull speeches by establishment figures and local politicos, all grand masters of the platitude and the cliché. That year's edition, coming in the wake of our military victory in the Gulf War, propagated a patriotic motif that would have made Mencken roar with disapproval—too many patriotic songs, too much self-congratulatory back-patting, with one of the entertainers even stepping forward at one point to "thank all our men for a wonderful time in Desert Storm." "Nowhere in the world is superiority more easily attained, or more eagerly admitted," Mencken wrote. "The chief business of the nation, as a nation, is the setting up of heroes, mainly bogus."

The next time I'm in Baltimore for the Preakness, I may even get to visit Mencken's house, now a museum. He'd have made a great horseplayer.

17

A HELL OF A SHOW BET

"My daughter's got me on a new regime of bringing only two hundred dollars to the track. But after you put in your doubles, the Pick Six and the triple, a man hasn't got any money to bet."

—TRAINER MEL STUTE, at Del Mar

THE FIRST person I saw in the stable area at Gulfstream Park in Miami when I showed up there for the sixth edition of the Breeders' Cup in early November, 1989, was a friend of mine whom I'll call Mark. He wrote about racing for an important eastern daily and had a reputation as a fearless plunger, especially if he felt certain the animal he favored couldn't lose. "Well, what do you think of this East-West rivalry regarding Easy Goer and Sunday Silence?" he asked. "Who are you picking?"

I told him I thought all the stories I'd read seemed to have missed the point, mainly because both horses had been bred in Kentucky. What difference did it make where they raced? "But I'm picking Sunday Silence to win," I added, "mainly because I think you guys in the East tend to underrate this horse."

Mark thought my answer over for a few seconds, then grinned. "Yeah, he's a good horse," he said. "He might run third."

I had never been to a Breeders' Cup before or ever gone racing in Florida, so I was happy to be there. There's nothing quite like being at a racetrack in the early morning to look at seventy or eighty of the best racehorses in the world going through their paces, either walking or galloping or working under the supervision of some of the best horsemen in the game. The Triple Crown focuses public attention on horse racing every spring, but the Breeders' Cup had become the World Series of the sport, a media event patronized in part by the sort of fans who ordinarily don't go regularly to the races. "Until we had the Breeders' Cup, we'd see you guys at Kentucky Derby time in the spring and that's it," D. Wayne Lukas told a group of foreign reporters outside his tack room that morning. "Now it's November and here you all are again."

The concept of the Breeders' Cup was the creation of John R. Gaines, then a leading breeder and owner of Thoroughbreds, who first propounded it publicly on April 23, 1982, at an annual awards banquet in Louisville, Kentucky, a couple of weeks before the Derby. The entire program, as Gaines outlined it, was to be funded by annual nomination payments for stallions, as well as other one-time payments for their progeny, with all of that money to be placed in a special account to boost the purses of certain key races in various categories throughout the year and leading up to a culminating day on which the best horses would race against one another for the largest pots ever offered—a total of ten million dollars for a program of seven championship races, all to be contested on the same day.

The idea seemed such a natural that it received immediate backing from half a dozen of the most important breeding and racing establishments in Kentucky. An entity called the Breeders' Cup Limited opened permanent offices in Lexington and set about implementing a specific program that would "build positive public awareness for Thoroughbred racing, increase fan participation and further develop and expand opportunities in the Thoroughbred industry." By late July, a newly appointed board of directors that included Gaines had outlined the one-day program of seven races that has become the basic format for the event, and by early September had selected Hollywood Park as the site for the inaugural, to be held on November 10, 1984.

By mid-April of 1983, the special account had accumulated

nearly eleven million dollars in nominating fees for one thousand eighty-three stallions, more than enough to guarantee the first year's program, and by mid-September a major television network, NBC Sports, had contracted to broadcast all seven races in a four-hour special to racing fans all over the world. There was to be more than enough loot to fund not only the day itself but a so-called awards program to swell purses at ninety race meets here and in Canada. By the time over sixty-four thousand people showed up at Hollywood Park the following year, the Breeders' Cup festivities seemed certain to eclipse even the hoopla associated with the running of the Triple Crown races, which until then had been the only American races to qualify as media circuses, the sole standard of success by which public occasions seem to be measured in our time.

Every year since then the Breeders' Cup has grown in importance, both as a monetarily rewarding day for the owners, trainers and breeders, but also as a joyous manifestation of the American genius for hype. Practically overnight a yearly occasion had been created that has definitively altered the nature of American racing, which until then had been content to bumble along from year to year with the individual racing organizations devising seasons around their own traditional events. The New York Racing Association, for instance, has always structured its programs around long-established series of races such as the Woodward, the Metropolitan Mile, the Travers, the Champagne, and the Jockey Club Gold Cup, all stakes and handicaps intended to establish the best horses in each division.

Some of these events, such as the Champagne and the Jockey Club Gold Cup, which occur in the fall, have been greatly diminished in prestige, mainly because trainers pointing their horses for the Breeders' Cup have been reluctant to run their charges in races scheduled only a few weeks before what they now obviously consider the main event on the calendar. Other important races have had to be rescheduled to survive, such as the Washington, D.C., International at Laurel, in Maryland, which used to be held in early November and is now run in late October, and the Norfolk Stakes and the Oak Tree Invitational at Santa Anita, which have been moved up to early October, during the first two weeks of the southern California fall racing season.

Even such midsummer events as the Travers, Saratoga's most prestigious race for three-year-olds, have been affected. After the grueling ordeal of the Triple Crown, most owners would have preferred to rest their charges and freshen them for the Breeders' Cup. To lure contestants, the purse for the Travers has had to be kicked up to a cool million dollars, but even so the fields have been disappointing. In 1989, Easy Goer annihilated a mediocre group of contestants, while the best horses from the rest of the country stayed home.

By the time Gaines came up with his concept, the racing industry was in considerable trouble. Prices at the yearling sales in the early eighties had first flattened out, then tumbled. Many of the speculators and breeders who had indebted themselves to the banks on the assumption that prices could only go up found themselves unable to pay off their loans. A number of them have since declared bankruptcy, including Calumet, one of the biggest and most famous, and there are currently plenty of farms for sale in Kentucky at very reasonable prices.

The end of the boom compelled the horsemen to focus their attention on the racing itself, which is where the emphasis should have been all along. The public, from the hard-core horseplayer to the most casual fan, cares nothing about the arcane intricacies of breeding or the esoteric nuances of bloodlines. People mostly go to the races to gamble on favorite horses and periodically fall in love with their champions. There isn't a horseplayer alive who doesn't retain vivid memories of favorite horses and great races, and it's no accident that in the past public affection has tended to settle on the sport's great geldings—Armed, Kelso, John Henry, Forego—who had long careers and built up fanatically loyal followings. If the Breeders' Cup has done nothing else, it has at least given racing back to its fans.

The best horse in each of ten categories is selected each year by industry representatives and the turf writers, who in the past have often had to make their selections based on their own estimates of an animal's skill, mainly because the leading contenders for these

Eclipse Awards (named after the legendary English racehorse and stallion) may never have had a chance to run against each other. In February, 1985, seven of the ten horses picked had participated in the first Breeders' Cup day, and since then most of the Eclipse winners have been participants. The voters, a majority of whom represent eastern racing interests or work for the East Coast media, have often been accused of regional prejudice, but less so since the winners have had to prove themselves before the eyes of a TV audience that has grown to over twenty million all over the world. The Breeders' Cup now provides what it defines as "the single richest day in sports," which is one way of banishing apathy.

What no one could have predicted from the start was whether the actual racing on Breeders' Cup day would justify the hype. Luckily, every contest on that opening card at Hollywood Park provided some drama, even an easy win in the million-dollar Distaff by Princess Rooney, a four-year-old gray filly whose seven-length margin of victory was so outstanding that her race is still regarded by many as the most impressive single performance by an animal in the history of the cup. All of the other races on the card were hotly disputed, and the Classic, in which the best handicap horses in the nation are asked to compete on the dirt at a mile and a quarter for a huge purse of three million dollars, produced a thrilling three-horse finish won by Wild Again, a thirty-one-to-one shot who survived a dramatic bumping duel down the stretch to score by the margin of a head.

That opening card established a number of precedents that have been repeated in every Breeders' Cup since. Most of the races every year have been highly competitive, with national championships at stake as well as money. To keep the two-dollar bettors interested, longshots have persistently popped up from time to time. That first year, Lashkari, an English-bred three-year-old colt trained by Alain de Royer-Dupré, a Frenchman saddling his first horse in North America, won the two-million-dollar Turf, at a mile and a half on the grass course, paying $108.80 for every two-dollar ticket. Eight of the eleven contestants in the race came from

Europe, where most of the running is conducted on grass, and foreign horses have continued to show up every year since, mainly to compete in the Turf and the Mile, the only other event run on the grass. They have won a number of these competitions, and their presence has ensured the continuing interest of the racing public abroad.

Inevitably, the focus of every Breeders' Cup day has been on the Classic, for the same reason that on any boxing card it is the heavyweight match that attracts the most public attention. Since its first running, only once has the Classic failed to provide an exciting race. That was the third edition of the event, at Santa Anita, when a ten-to-one shot named Skywalker led practically all the way to easily defeat a mediocre field. In 1988, a tough four-year-old named Alysheba, who had done most of his racing in the West, defeated in a hard-fought stretch duel a good-looking colt named Seeking the Gold, trained by Claude (Shug) McGaughey III and owned by Ogden Phipps. It reversed a disappointment suffered the year before, when Alysheba had lost by a nose to another West Coast horse, Ferdinand, trained by Charlie Whittingham. Those two races set the tone for the confrontation in 1989 that reflected the entire structure of the American racing scene and vividly dramatized some of its public and private conflicts.

The story of American racing over the past two decades has largely been one of a gradual shift in power from East to West. Traditionally, the sport has always been dominated by the New York Jockey Club and its creature, the New York Racing Association. The biggest purses and the most prestigious races were run in the East, most of them at New York tracks or during the winter months in Florida. The rapid burgeoning of the sport in California, beginning in the nineteen-thirties with the legalization of parimutuel wagering and the opening of Santa Anita, did not affect the East. Even when the purses on the West Coast became large enough to lure good horses out to compete for them, the eastern trainers kept most of their better charges home. California racing, with its hard, fast surfaces and tight mile tracks, was regarded as inferior and not worth becoming involved with, even after jet travel made the shipment of horses from coast to coast a relatively easy matter.

The situation began to change in the late sixties, after the advent of off-track wagering and the proliferation of other forms of gambling began to make serious inroads on the financial operations of the eastern tracks. In New York, the industry bungled its lobbying efforts in Albany with the state legislature and declined to involve itself with the administration of off-track betting, thus leaving it to the state to manage it in blundering, bureaucratic fashion, while in Florida the tracks found themselves competing with a state lottery, jai alai and dog racing. California's relative isolation from the main scene became its salvation. When off-track betting came in a few years ago, the tracks banded together to oversee the process, and the industry fought successfully to keep dog racing and other new forms of legalized gambling, except for a state lottery, out.

The financial soundness of California racing and the size of the purses began attracting more and more horsemen from the East, many of whom transferred their activities permanently there. The average daily handles at Santa Anita and Del Mar are larger than all but the biggest days at Belmont and Saratoga. And with the money has come prestige, since California-based horses now not only win at home but have successfully invaded the East to capture far more than their share of the major traditional races, as well as the Breeders' Cup events.

The relative superiority of California racing has not been readily accepted in the East, and cries of foul inevitably emanate from the West every time an eastern horse wins an Eclipse Award in a close contest, as was the case in 1988 when a three-year-old colt named Sunshine Forever was selected over Great Communicator, the five-year-old who had beaten him in the Breeders' Cup Turf at Churchill Downs. A year later, the situation came into full focus when the two favorites for the Classic turned out to symbolize the points of view of the opposing camps.

Easy Goer was a royally bred three-year-old by a top sire named Alydar, out of Relaxing, an expensive broodmare. He was owned by Ogden Phipps and trained by Shug McGaughey. Despite the fact that he had been upset in the mud the previous year in the Juvenile by a Lukas-trained longshot, he was overwhelmingly voted the best two-year-old colt of the year, and in the spring had been heavily favored to sweep the Triple Crown races.

Sunday Silence, on the other hand, was a colt nobody really wanted. Also a Kentucky-bred, though by a less glamorous stud named Halo, he was deemed to have poor conformation and wound up being owned partly by his breeder, Arthur Hancock, who had tried vainly to sell him, and Whittingham, who sold off half of his fifty percent to a friend, Dr. Ernest Gaillard. He was sent to southern California, where he soon proved himself to be a runner, even though his achievements and ability failed to impress anyone in the East. Whittingham, a conservative trainer who doesn't believe in rushing young horses, did not begin to race him until late in the year and did not enter him in the Breeders' Cup.

By the following spring, however, Sunday Silence had established his credentials as the best three-year-old in the West. He had won four of his first six races, including the Santa Anita Derby by a margin of eleven lengths. When he showed up in Louisville for the Kentucky Derby on May 6, he was being taken seriously, even though few of the experts in the East thought he had much of a chance against Easy Goer, who had breezed to consecutive victories in three of the traditional races used as preps for the Derby. He was made the favorite at odds of four to five, while Sunday Silence was established by the bettors as the second choice in the field of fifteen, at three to one.

Sunday Silence horrified Easy Goer, defeating him easily by two and a half lengths despite having been forced to steady at the start of the race and weaving erratically down the stretch. The partisans of Easy Goer, however, largely dismissed their colt's defeat, attributing it to the muddy condition of the track after several days of heavy rain, even though great horses are supposed to be able to run well on any kind of surface. The eastern turf writers overwhelmingly picked Easy Goer to reverse his loss in the Derby at the Preakness in Baltimore, two weeks later. The horse was again established as the odds-on favorite, this time at three to five, with Sunday Silence going off at two to one in a field of eight.

The race was a thriller. This time it was Easy Goer who broke poorly, though he soon rushed up along the rail and took the lead after three-quarters of a mile, with Sunday Silence two lengths behind him. When the latter's jockey, Patrick Valenzuela, asked his colt for speed on the turn for home, however, the California champion charged up to Easy Goer and stuck his head in front at the beginning of the stretch. From there the two horses staged one of those epic duels that horseplayers go to their graves remembering. Sunday Silence won by a nose and once again Easy Goer's defeat was blamed on an outside circumstance, this time a poorly judged ride by the horse's jockey, the supremely talented Pat Day, who was blamed for his mount's sluggish start and for having allowed himself to be trapped in tight quarters along the rail during the stretch drive.

By then the public, if not the writers, had seen enough to convince itself that Sunday Silence would win the Triple Crown. At Belmont Park, three weeks later, the California horse was established as a slight favorite, at just under even money, with Easy Goer at eight to five. The distance of the Belmont is a mile and a half, which abroad is considered the true classic distance for a horse of quality, whereas in this country a mile and a quarter is the standard by which we measure talent. Easy Goer turned out to be much the best horse at the longer distance. He broke fifth in the field of ten, then swept to the lead at the six-furlong mark. Sunday Silence moved at him on the final turn and even managed to stick his head in front briefly, but Day immediately asked Easy Goer for his best and the big chestnut colt moved steadily away from his rival to win by a very convincing margin of eight lengths, with Sunday Silence a tiring second.

The win in the Belmont was regarded in the East as a vindication, and it wasn't long before the local experts had convinced themselves that Easy Goer should have won all three previous encounters. Sunday Silence went back to California, where he managed to lose his next effort, the Swaps Stakes at Hollywood Park on July 23, five weeks after the Belmont. Whittingham uncharacteristically blamed his defeat on a misjudged ride by Valenzuela, though most knowledgeable observers felt that he had rushed his colt back into competition too soon after the grind of the Triple Crown races and had tried, as the saying goes, to steal a purse with a horse not quite ready to run a mile and a quarter. Sunday Silence had a four-length lead an eighth of a mile from the finish line, only to be caught in the last few yards by a closer named Prized.

Easy Goer, meanwhile, did not come back to the races until August 5, when he overwhelmed a field of five older contenders in the Whitney, a mile and an eighth contest at Saratoga. He ran three more times before the Breeders' Cup, in the aforementioned Travers and in the Woodward and the Jockey Club Gold Cup at Belmont, winning all the races easily, the latter again at a mile and a half. Despite the fact that Sunday Silence had come back two months after his defeat at Hollywood to trounce a field of eight by six lengths in the Louisiana Super Derby at Louisiana Downs, the eastern racing press dismissed the feat as the victory of a good horse over a field of nonentities. They largely ignored the fact that Easy Goer's own recent wins had come over what racetrackers call useful horses, essentially established second-raters, who win their share of contests but never the important ones. Easy Goer, according to his devotees, was a great horse, the victim against Sunday Silence of a couple of bad breaks, but clearly the superior animal.

In the past, the two horses would probably never have competed against each other again. Easy Goer's connections would have had nothing to gain by seeking out Sunday Silence for a climactic confrontation, and the latter's entourage would probably not have risked coming into New York to challenge Easy Goer on his home grounds, where he had been invincible. Easy Goer would have been voted an Eclipse Award, after which he would almost certainly have been retired to stud, while Sunday Silence would have continued to gobble up the opposition in the West and fatten his owners' bank accounts. The existence of the Breeders' Cup ensured that the championship would be decided on a racetrack rather than on a ballot, and it promised to provide the most dramatic face-off in the history of the Classic, with the prestige and reputation of both the human and equine contenders at stake.

So thoroughly did the Classic dominate that year's cup program that during my whole stay in Miami I heard talk about little else. Gulfstream Park is an attractive facility that sits on flat land about a mile from the beach in Hallandale, a middle-class suburb north of the city. Recently refurbished, it has a slick contemporary look, with a two-tiered grandstand, a dining terrace and a rooftop bar and grill overlooking the racing surfaces, both a mile in circumference, and a large infield lake framed by palm trees. The stable area contains parallel rows of low, airy barns with slanted green roofs and is the most meticulously groomed backside of any track I've ever visited. It was here in the early mornings, where the animals were stabled, that the horsemen and media representatives gathered to oversee the workouts and other preparations, as well as to pick each other's brains about the goings-on.

Everyone I talked to sooner or later wanted to know my opinion on the Classic and made his own views felt. And without exception, no one not from California thought Sunday Silence had a chance. Whittingham rather testily pointed out in an interview that his horse held a two to one edge in the series and was coming up to the race in great form, but his opinion was mostly dismissed as that of a man with a small ax to grind. Some of the eastern trainers were comparing Easy Goer with Secretariat, while others pointed out that he couldn't be considered that good because, after all, he had only beaten mediocrities like Sunday Silence. "I've never seen anything like it," a young sportswriter from Los Angeles informed me. "It's the greatest brainwash in sports history."

The publicity about the race completely overshadowed the rest of the card, which was shaping up to be an interesting and contentious one. The Sprint was considered a wide-open affair, with fourteen speedballs contending for the title, as were both the two-year-old races, the Juvenile and the Juvenile Fillies, and the Turf, all contests in which no dominant animal had yet been established. The Distaff featured Winning Colors, the big roan filly who had won the 1988 Kentucky Derby, a top three-year-old named Open Mind, and Bayakoa, a late-developing Argentine-bred mare with tremendous front-running speed. Zilzal, an undefeated English-bred three-year-old colt with a nervous disposition and a tendency to act up in the paddock, was the focus of attention in the Mile. And in addition to the seven championship contests, Gulfstream had designed a dazzling three-day cup program that included twenty-three other races, eight of them stakes events for purses of one hundred thousand dollars and one for a prize of two hundred thousand. The management of the track legitimately claimed to be putting on by far the most generous and ambitious racing program ever scheduled in this country.

Gulfstream can normally handle comfortably no more than thirty thousand customers, but was planning to accommodate about fifty thousand on cup day, with the addition of temporary bleachers and hundreds of portable toilets. Reporters for the *Miami Herald* and other local newspapers predicted massive traffic jams and intolerable crowding within, with one columnist even urging fans to stay home and watch the events on television. Not the least of Gulfstream's problems was having to take care of the more than eleven hundred media representatives on hand, "America's guests," as one California horseman defined them up in the guinea stand one morning.

As is customary at these shindigs, the press was wooed with gifts—sports bags, folding binoculars, digital stopwatches, commemorative drinking glasses, even chocolates—and thrown a party one night at a sprawling waterfront restaurant complex in Fort Lauderdale that cost well over a hundred thousand dollars, with bands, entertainers, food, drink, and a man wrestling an alligator. At the Diplomat Hotel in Hallandale, where most of the reporters were stabled, an abundantly staffed press headquarters supplied stacks of publicity releases, interviews, passes, and more free food and drink, as well as TV monitors showing videotapes of races run by the horses entered in the cup events. "I wonder why I'm even here," a bemused visitor from England said to me, as we watched reporters interview each other at the party. "We could simply have arranged to have all this stuff shipped to us and written about it from there."

All of these preliminary shenanigans could only have been justified by the racing itself, when it finally took place. Luckily, no one was disappointed, least of all me. My friend Brian Mayberry, who trains horses in California, showed up with four contenders for the smaller pots and won all four of his races, three of them on cup day. Mayberry is a third-generation horseman who not only knows his animals, but can actually read books without moving his lips, a talent that has established him as an intellectual on the backside. I had bet on all four of his horses and so, as the saying goes, I was holding by the time the Breeders' Cup events finally got under way. As a bettor, I could afford to sit out the earlier races and wait for the Classic.

The omens were not auspicious. A colt named Dancing Spree, owned by Phipps and trained by McGaughey, won the Sprint with a late charge down the stretch to catch Safely Kept, the only filly in the race, and beat her by a neck. Another McGaughey-trained entry, Rhythm, won the Juvenile, and Go For Wand, a beautifully balanced bay filly, easily took the Juvenile Fillies. Bayakoa proved herself to be a monster by laying off the pace in the Distaff to win handily, with Winning Colors, an overraced, pale gray shadow of herself, staggering in lengths behind. (A year later, on cup day at Belmont Park, Bayakoa and Go For Wand were to hook up in the Distaff in a memorable stretch duel that ended in tragedy, when Go For Wand's leg shattered as she drove for the wire and she went down, then had to be destroyed—one of the most horrifying examples of what can go wrong in a horse race. "These animals give their lives for our enjoyment," Ron McAnally, the trainer of Bayakoa, said afterward.) Steinlen, a tough six-year-old English-bred performer, captured the Mile, under a clever ground-saving ride by his jockey, José Santos. He was the only one of Lukas's eleven entries to run impressively, although his two-year-old colt, Grand Canyon, closed belatedly for second in the Juvenile. Prized, the conqueror of Sunday Silence, made a huge late run to capture the Turf in his first start ever on the grass. The major disappointment of the day was Zilzal, who went off at even money, behaved himself well in the paddock and the post parade, but broke poorly from his outside post position, ran wide around both turns and finished back in the pack. He was promptly retired to the breeding shed by his English owners.

By the time Easy Goer, Sunday Silence and the other six contenders in the Classic were led into the walking ring for what one local observer had dubbed "the race of the decade," an excited mob had gathered in the temporary stands erected around the paddock, and the tension was as palpable as the steamy tropical air of the late-fall Florida afternoon.

Easy Goer looked the part of a great champion. He was a big, powerful-looking chestnut colt who seemed always to be ready to explode but remained calm, "well within himself," as I noted in my pad. Sunday Silence, on the other hand, was a nervous, feisty animal, nearly black, with a white blaze on his face; he was on his toes, like a dancer in the wings waiting to make an entrance. In his stall, he tended to be sullen and would snap at anyone who came too close, but on the track he was an athlete, all business and concentration, who seemed to understand exactly what was expected of him. His coat gleamed with health and I thought he looked formidable, but a Kentucky horseman I know said to me, as we watched him being led around the ring by his groom, "He still doesn't look like much, more like a giraffe from the back than a horse."

I watched the race from the terrace upstairs outside the press box. The bettors, obviously influenced by the attitude of the local writers and handicappers, established Easy Goer as the one-to-two favorite, with Sunday Silence at two to one and all the other entries at long odds. I couldn't ignore the price and I made my biggest bet since Kelso—two hundred to win, on the nose. I didn't tell Mark, who had predicted in his column that day that Easy Goer would bury Sunday Silence.

In the starting gate, the two favorites sandwiched the field, with Easy Goer on the rail and Sunday Silence in the outside stall. At the start, which was greeted by a roar of excitement from the more than fifty-one thousand people present, a fast five-year-old named Slew City Slew, trained by Lukas, bolted to the lead, opening up two and a half lengths in the first quarter mile and then three at the half, with Blushing John, a four-year-old ridden by Angel Cordero, one of the cagiest riders in the game, in second as they swept past the stands and around the clubhouse turn.

Sunday Silence broke alertly and settled into third, while Easy Goer seemed a bit sluggish at the start, swerving slightly in as he found his stride. He was sixth at the half, six lengths back, but Pat Day then asked him to move and he immediately swept up alongside Sunday Silence as the field reached the six-furlong mark, with Slew City Slew and Blushing John still running one-two.

At that point in the race it looked as if Easy Goer could win whenever he chose to extend himself, so easily had he made up the ground separating him from his main rival. But on the turn for home, Chris McCarron on Sunday Silence clucked to his mount and asked him to move. With the agility of a ballet dancer, Sunday Silence seemed to leap away from Easy Goer, opening up two and a half lengths and closing to within a head of Blushing John. The latter had blown by the tiring Slew City Slew and was driving for home along the rail, with Cordero flat along his neck, pumping and slashing.

McCarron drove Sunday Silence past Blushing John, then glanced under his arm to see if Easy Goer was coming. He was indeed, making a tremendous run, with Day whipping hard, but McCarron knew about seventy yards from the wire that he had the race won. Without having to use his whip once, he brought Sunday Silence in first by the margin of a neck over Easy Goer, with the courageous Blushing John a length farther back. Sunday Silence could have won by more, and it was a splendid performance, even though it didn't impress everybody. "Day blew it again," an East Coast reporter standing next to me said in disgust as the race ended. Some illusions die hard, especially at the racetrack. I couldn't resist coming up behind Mark, who looked as if somebody had tapped him on the forehead with a small padded hammer. "Hell of a show bet," I said.

After the race, Charlie Whittingham pointedly reminded everyone that his horse had now won three of the four meetings between the two rivals, including "this Triple Crown thing." He quickly corrected the slip by explaining that "I was trying to get to three million dollars and it got mixed up in my chewing tobacco." Charlie was seventy-six years old, a tall, slightly stooped, lean man with a round, completely bald head and the canny look of an amiable card shark. For most of his career he had been a close-mouthed loner and not always easy to approach, but television seemed to have turned him, at least publicly, into a cracker-barrel comedian. He said he had told McCarron, one of the smartest jockeys in the business and a superb judge of pace, to hang on when he reached the turn because the horse might run out from under him. He smiled, then added, "We have tough horses in California."

Shug McGaughey was too upset by his champion's defeat to comment until the following morning, when he finally appeared at the entrance to his tack room to confront the crowd of reporters waiting to interview him. McGaughey is a stocky, round-faced Kentuckian, then thirty-eight, with curly black hair and round blue eyes. He reportedly has a formidable temper and a foulmouthed way of expressing his anger, but his public persona is that of an affable rube just down from the mountains. He answered even the inevitable silly questions graciously and refused to inculpate his jockey for the loss. "He just got beat," he said, confirming what Pat Day had declared after the race—that Easy Goer had "fired big, but Sunday Silence got away from us."

The two horses never ran against each other again. They came back to the races as four-year-olds, but were injured early in the season, never regained their best form and were retired. What they've left us is what most fans take away with them from all sporting events—memories, the images of great or terrible moments that remain vivid through the years, like scenes from old movies or snapshots in a family album. What I will never forget is the casual elegance of Easy Goer's first sweeping move, the way Sunday Silence spurted away from him on the turn, and McCarron's hasty backward glance as he neared the finish line, with the onrushing chestnut colt behind him eating up ground as he dug in. Who cares, in retrospect, which animal came from where? After all, whether they run in New York or California, one constant in the sport remains: the best ones still come out of the Kentucky Blue Grass.

18

BEAUTIFUL HEARTS

"That last one got me well."
—Man running out of the
track at Del Mar with a
crutch under his arm

I DROPPED in a while back on some old friends of mine, who are living in retirement on a small ranch in French Valley, a few miles northeast of Murietta Hot Springs, in southern California. I found them, as usual, almost entirely indifferent to my presence. They were having breakfast and had their heads mostly buried in it. "Hello, guys," I said, as I walked toward them, "where's all that money you owe me?" Only one of them looked up from his meal and then just long enough to shake his head at me before sticking his face back into his food. Oh, well, I thought, as I joined them, I guess they really don't owe me a thing. They almost always did their best, and it wasn't their fault they couldn't win every time out. God knows they tried hard enough.

These pals of mine, thirteen old geldings standing in two parallel rows of paddocks on the grounds of the California Equine Retirement Foundation (CERF), are known to horseplayers as hard knockers. They're the club fighters of the game, animals who, win or lose, always ran their hearts out. They had competed at the California tracks month after month, year after year, until compelled by old age and various infirmities to quit. Now they had a permanent home. In the three years since it was founded by a retired schoolteacher named Grace Belcuore, CERF not only had provided a haven for them but had managed to retrain and send out over fifty other horses for adoption, under an agreement giving the foundation the right to visit the animals placed with new owners and to reclaim those who didn't work out or weren't being properly cared for.

As for these old warriors, I had bet on every one of them at one time or another during their careers, and their names, listed over the chunks of past-performance statistics published in the racing forms, were as familiar to me as those of my own children. Like most horseplayers, however, I had seen them usually only from a distance and through binoculars, during the post parade or while running, so I now needed help in identifying each of them. They had only moved into their new outdoor pens about a week before my visit, and I had to depend on the kindness of a stranger, a young horseman named Sam Ownby, who was in charge of them.

We strolled in bright sunshine past the metal railings while Sam told me about each of them. Here, for instance, was Pettrax, now eleven years old, who went out a winner at Santa Anita in March, 1988, at odds of thirty-seven to one. He used to run at distances of a mile or more, usually on the front end, and he was always, as Sam now put it, "pure class." Next to him was Bedouin, a roguish roan who used to come charging down the stretch from way out of it and had once shown enough promise to compete in a Kentucky Derby. Here was Coyotero, a speedball, who won eleven of his forty-four lifetime starts and used to follow his trainer around his shedrow like a big dog. Also present were Goldy's Commander, One-Eyed Romeo, Plenty Conscious, Right on Red, W. C. Shecky, Father Mac, and Buen Chico, all winners of a hundred thousand dollars or more over their careers. Here, too, were Perry Cabin, a twelve-year-old bay who never missed a dance, having run a hundred and eleven times over seven seasons, while picking up about three hundred and fifty thousand dollars in purse money; Item Two, a big, rangy chestnut who won or placed forty-five times in seventy-eight attempts and earned about three hundred and eighty thousand dollars for a series of owners; and last, but by no means least as far as I was concerned, Menswear, a tough old competitor whom I knew well from having hung around trainer Dick Mandella's barn during the early-morning workouts at Del Mar a few summers earlier. Menswear, a winner twelve times in a career of forty-two starts, had been Mandella's stable pet, the sort of hard knocker who never fails to arouse admiration among the horse people. "He's now the head honcho here," Sam said, "even if he is a mess."

The comment was apropos, because these veteran campaigners, like the old pugs with their cauliflower ears and flattened noses, carry visible scars from their racing wars. Menswear had a banged-up look about him and had metal screws in both knees; Perry Cabin had a right front ankle swollen from calcium deposits, the result of too many cortisone injections; Buen Chico, the most recent arrival at the ranch, had an injured left rear hock and was so nervous that he spooked at his own shadow. Worst-looking of all was Item Two, who had a lower left front leg that looked like a boomerang-shaped balloon. He shattered it during his last race at Fairplex Park, in the fall of 1987, so badly that the vets who first examined him urged that he be "put down," racing's euphemism for death by injection. "Nobody can tell me horses aren't smart," Sam Ownby said. "This one saved himself, because he had the sense to lie down." Old Item Two's brain, as the horsemen put it, was connected to his ears.

Nobody ever pretended that racing is an easy game and fun for the animals. Thoroughbreds are bred to run fast and most of them instinctively want to, but not necessarily with little men mounted on their backs, slashing at them with whips, and forced to go around in a circle under all sorts of conditions, on all kinds of surfaces, on days when, due to injury or illness, they just might not feel like it. Sooner or later, most racehorses sustain injuries that either shorten or end their careers. The good colts and the better mares lead lives of sybaritic luxury on breeding farms, where their sole task is to produce more winners. Only the old geldings have absolutely no place to go, and most of them, after their racing days are over, are sold to "the killer" and converted into pet food.

This is the brutal reality that the creation of this small equine retirement home in French Valley was designed to correct. Not one of these gallant old campaigners would have still been around if it hadn't been brought into being. And although its creator knew almost nothing about horses when she decided to found it, she knew about heart. "That's the only thing that kept these old horses running," she said. "They've earned the right to be alive. Why should they be stuck in a can just because they can't run anymore?"

Grace Belcuore is aptly named, because her last one means "beautiful heart" in Italian. She is a small but sturdily built woman, with close-cropped iron-gray curls, dark eyes, a quick smile and a forthright, no-nonsense manner. She moved to Los Angeles from her native Boston in 1956, taught in the public-school system and eventually became a clinical psychologist, working with juvenile delinquents. After her retirement in the late seventies, a friend took her to the races and she became a regular, though strictly a two-dollar bettor. "It was something to do," she recalls. Then, about five years ago, her attention was caught by an attempt to return old John Henry, who had been happily turned out to pasture, to the races. John Henry had been a great star and a public favorite, but he was nine years old and no longer in form; he would never have been able to compete again in top company. "That was the moment I decided I had to do something to keep this kind of thing from happening," she says. "But I didn't know anything about how things worked in racing."

She made friends with a veterinarian named Greg Ferraro, who introduced her to Ron McAnally, John Henry's trainer. McAnally allowed her to hang around his shedrow for about six months, while she fed carrots and other dainties to her favorites and learned about the horse business. She also began to notice that from time to time horses would quietly disappear. When she asked about them, she'd often be given evasive answers. But she persisted. "Trainers would tell owners about horses that had broken down or couldn't compete anymore, and the owners would tell the trainers to get rid of them," she explains. "There were always buyers around, guys who'd show up with their horse vans. They'd be dressed up in suits and pretending to be something they weren't. They'd pop up here, there and everywhere, and the trainers would sell them the animals. The owners wouldn't know, and wouldn't want to know, who was doing the buying. Then the vans would cart the horses away to the slaughterhouses. You couldn't tell who 'the killer' was back there, but he was always an invisible presence. And one day the reality of what was actually happening just hit me."

By the time McAnally, one of the best and most humane trainers in the sport, had persuaded John Henry's owner that the old boy wouldn't be able to make a comeback and shipped him back to the Kentucky Horse Park in Lexington, Grace knew what she had to do. "Somebody here had to speak up for these old horses," she says, "even though a lot of people told me not to bother, that nobody cares."

She discovered immediately that quite a few people did care. She incorporated CERF as a nonprofit foundation and made her first pitch for funds to the six thousand names on a mailing list provided by the California Thoroughbred Breeders Association. Soon helpful strangers began popping up everywhere. Within a matter of weeks she acquired her first retiree, an unraced gelding named Pecos Pippin, and soon found herself in charge of a string of animals then being boarded temporarily in loaned facilities. The costs, including insurance, mounted daily and money was in short supply, but Grace never wavered in her commitment. "I listened and I asked questions and I accused no one," she recalls. "All I cared about was the horses."

Not everyone in the racing industry responded positively, partly because a good many owners and trainers still don't see the necessity of donating money just to keep a bunch of broken-down old nags alive and partly because some people in the game feel uncomfortable about sponsoring an undertaking that might focus public attention on the seamier aspects of the sport. Grace has sat through meetings during which she has heard all sorts of exculpatory and self-serving objections from people who have made fortunes out of the animals they exploit, but she has never lost her cool or become accusatory. "They're all going to have to come around sooner or later," she says, "because I'm very persistent and I'm not going to go away." Besides, she likes to point out, it only costs about seven dollars a day to keep a horse at CERF, a little more than that if there are vet bills.

When the free land that was promised her from various sources failed to materialize, she dug into her own savings and borrowed from a bank to buy and equip the ranch, which consisted originally simply of a modest house on five acres of flat, treeless land. Since then, she has added five more acres, a barn, sixteen paddocks (ten of them donated) and has planted a couple of dozen trees on the otherwise barren property. She plans to put in a three-eighths of a mile track to exercise the old horses and keep them in good shape, then to divide the rest of the land into fenced pastures where the animals can be turned out on their own. The new barn, which was being finished the day I showed up, contains four stalls, in which the more fragile tenants, like Perry Cabin and Item Two, can be housed during the winter months. Eventually, she wants to add a museum and be able to take care of fifty or so horses, and her dream is to acquire a star like John Henry in order to attract paying visitors to the facility. "Of course they're all stars to me," she says, waving her arm toward her charges, "but you know what I mean."

She envisions that it will take seven or eight more years to bring all these plans to fruition, and she estimates that expenses will then run to about five thousand dollars a month. So far she has spent about eighty thousand dollars of her own money and devotes all of her time away from the ranch to proselytizing and promoting events that will raise funds, an average of about eighty thousand dollars a year. She never fails to cite and to praise all of the people—trainers, owners, the racing associations, jockeys, and just plain fans—who have helped her and she never complains, but to an outsider it seems incredible that she should have to be working so hard to raise a relatively modest amount of money from an industry as rich as this one, in which millions of dollars pass through the betting windows every day.

Meanwhile, back at the ranch, the work goes on. The only paid employee on the premises the day I was there was Sam Ownby, who was twenty-eight years old, grew up around horses in Arizona, began riding when he was seven and worked for one of the better trainers in Phoenix. Bitten by the movie bug, Sam moved to L.A. to pursue an acting and writing career, which, like those of most newcomers to Hollywood, soon bogged down into a series of so-called background bits and rejections. He was living pretty much hand-to-mouth with friends in Venice when Grace met him and quickly realized that he might be the right person to run the day-to-day operation of her facility. By that time, after several years of battering at the doors, Sam had become disenchanted enough with the acting end of show business to accept, since living at the ranch would also enable him to go on writing (he was working on ten or twelve scripts at the time) and pursue a new passion for sculpting. Part Cherokee, with a copper-colored skin, high cheekbones and long brown hair, Sam, as Grace put it, "has an aura of horses" about him and rode with the casual elegance of his Indian forebears.

Just watching him with the animals was a revelation. He talked to them as he would to his friends, knew each one of them intimately and was totally accepted by all of them, even Bedouin, who had turned into a dangerous rogue by the time Grace got hold of him. But work around any ranch is mostly hard and dirty. "I guess I had to face the fact that I don't like doing a lot of this," Sam told me, as we headed toward the pens, "but Grace is right there with me, shovel for shovel, every morning."

They made an odd couple, I thought. Grace lived in the house, which was sparsely furnished with pieces donated by friends ("Everything is for the horses," she explained), while Sam occupied a trailer outside. They alternated the cooking and divided the chores, with Sam moving pretty much at his own pace. "I sit back and kind of ponder and then I get it done," he said. "Grace, she'll move a pile of rocks just to move them, where I'm liable to say, 'Okay, add it to the list.'"

The list has not grown shorter and several people, including Sam, have come and gone since I last visited CERF. Grace has also sold her Los Angeles-area house, and with the proceeds she purchased the additional five acres of pasture and moved permanently to the ranch. "It's got to expand, it's got to grow, and I dread the day we can't take any more," she says. "We need an endowment, a million dollars in the bank so we could live off the interest." But if that never happens, it's not going to stop her. "We can retrain and find homes for the younger horses," she explains, "animals who just won't run or didn't work out at the track for one reason or another."

As for the old hard knockers, "They're so ingrained they can't be changed. A bell goes off and they're ready to run." She likes to look down the paddock rows at her permanent guests. "They've got a free ticket," she says. "They've earned it."

19

THE WRONG HORSE

"It's not a beauty contest."
—Old racetrack maxim

WHEN YOU buy a racehorse, someone early on will warn you not to fall in love with it. The advice is practical, because Thoroughbreds are not household pets. They are big and powerful and dumb. They will disappoint you in a variety of ways. Most of them will turn out to be not talented enough to win anything but unimportant races for meager rewards. Many of them will never win anything at all. Some will have the talent but not the will or the courage to compete. They will come out on the track in the morning looking unbeatable and work like cheetahs, but in the afternoon, when it counts, they will plod along like burros or flash brief speed, only to fold when challenged. They will prove to be what the horsemen call "common," animals with ability but no heart, no competitive fire.

Even the good ones will almost always disappoint you in the end. They will run their great races, lift you toward heaven on their talent, then get sick or break down just as the pot of gold at the end of the rainbow becomes visible on the horizon. It is not their fault, because they are fragile, primitively constructed on the evolutionary scale, and they pay a physical price for it. The racetrack is not a kind environment, even though at the better facilities the animals are well cared for, if only because a mistreated athlete will not win, and winning is what the game is about.

The few who make it to the top—the Secretariats, the Affirmeds, the Bayakoas, the Sunday Silences—don't remain there very long. Their racing careers rarely last more than two or at most three years. They flash across your life like dazzling comets and disappear into the breeding sheds or destroy themselves on the track before your very eyes, leaving unbearable wounds in your memory. Even the great old geldings, who hang around a few years longer and capture the public fancy, don't satisfy your yearnings. (What are five or six years in the span of a human lifetime?) Then, too, most of the old pros are allowed to linger too long beyond their talent, and it is sadder to watch them fade away, unable to compete against horses they'd have humbled earlier, than to look up from a racing form one day to find them gone. The Thoroughbred will break your heart, if you let him.

So why do those of us who care keep coming back for more, keep trying, keep hoping? It's not the money. Only a fool could convince himself that buying a racehorse is a sound investment. Whether you spend a few thousand dollars or a million, the chances are your animal will never earn out his purchase price, and the tax laws are no longer kind to investors. The odds against you as an owner are not much better than those you face when you buy a lottery ticket. You might as well hope to kill a goose in flight by shooting arrows at it blindfolded. The horse experts talk bloodlines to you and conformation and soundness, and you put your money up and you've bought nothing. "There's only two things wrong with your horse," I heard a trainer tell the owner of an expensive maiden three-year-old in the paddock at Hollywood Park one day. "He has no speed and he can't run long." So kiss your money goodbye and don't chase it.

That particular horse is still around as I write these words and he has yet to win. He will probably never win, but the owner will almost certainly keep trying with him, at least for another few months or so, as his dollars flow merrily down the drain at the rate of about two thousand a month. And why? Because the fool has fallen in love. "You fall in love in your mind, in your imagination,"

Brendan Boyd, an ex-groom, wrote in a wonderful picture book called *Racing Days* a few years ago. "It happens when you're not looking. The Thoroughbred stirs everything without trying to, with its stillness, its inscrutability."

They stun your senses with their beauty. Artists have always responded to it. On the table in my living room is a sculpted reproduction of one of the horses' heads salvaged from the ruined Acropolis in Athens by Thomas Bruce, seventh Earl of Elgin, and now on permanent exhibition in the British Museum in London. Not a day passes that I don't look at that artifact in wonder. On the wall of my bedroom is an ancient Chinese drawing on parchment of a dancing horse, up on its hind legs in a vivid, impressionistic display of *élan vital*. By my front door are two small pictures, delicately woven in colored threads by a Victorian craftsman, of racehorses beginning and finishing a race. I have other equine pictures, other statuary, all of it testifying to the aesthetic pleasure of simply being around and connected, if only by the single small commitment of a two-dollar parimutuel ticket, to this spectacle of grace under pressure. Why not fall in love? Longing and loss are intrinsic to the process and the outcome, but so what? What's any better? In fact, what else is there?

Over the years I've invested from time to time in the dream, never with great success. After Parlay Time and a hiatus of several years to recuperate from that experience, I once again found myself part-owner with several friends of a filly named Sari's Tobin. She turned out to be the best horse I ever owned, but it was a brief affair. We claimed her for thirty-five thousand dollars out of a race at Hollywood Park one late spring afternoon, moved her up against allowance horses and watched her win for us her next time out. She popped a couple of more times, at Del Mar and then at Santa Anita, but she couldn't run very often because she had bad feet. They were too flat, our trainer told us, and so prone to bruising and infections. Eight months after we bought her, we sold her as a broodmare, too soon for me to fall deeply in love. She left behind some good memories and a fat bank account, two and a half times what we had invested in her.

We took our profit and bought another filly, a handsome, sturdily built dark bay named Supper. She was a morning glory. She worked like a zephyr in the early hours, but blew herself out of contention in the afternoons. Her speed always had her up there among the leaders at the head of the stretch, sometimes actually in front, but when the real running started she would spit out the bit. She reminded me of flowers wilting in the sun, a soul too delicate for competition. Not even the Wizard of Oz could have put heart into her. My wife took to calling her the Last Supper. I sold my interest in her, salvaging only a third of what Sari's Tobin had won for us. Most of her other owners chose to linger, hoping that somehow she would get the message, that by some miracle she'd find her courage and her steel. She never did. By the time she disappeared from view, over a year later, she had buried her connections under a small mountain of losing races.

I considered myself lucky and allowed nearly a decade to pass before once again buying into the dream. One day at Del Mar, during the summer of 1988, I became friends with a trainer named Brian Mayberry, a strongly built, affable-looking third-generation horseman who had begun his career in the Northeast and in Florida before moving west. He and his wife, Jean, who also came from a long line of horse people, trained a lot of good stock, mostly for a rich businessman who built shopping malls all over the country. Brian and Jean bought cagily and relatively modestly at sales in Kentucky and Maryland and Florida, as well as California, trusting in conformation and condition and attitude more than in pure bloodlines. Their horses won and won early, and they remained sound. Their shedrow was full of talented young animals, none of them of classic quality, but highly competitive, and they won more than their share of purses, large and small.

I trusted the Mayberrys, perhaps because they were both well-read. Trainers are not an intellectual and articulate bunch. They spend seven days a week, from dawn till sunset, around horses and the other people whose lives are bound to them. They know little about the outside world, only enough to distrust it profoundly, and they mostly vote fundamentalist Republican. They think the

ACLU is a Commie conspiracy, that homosexuals ought to be locked up in camps and that the Bill of Rights was written by Karl Marx. They're also good old boys who like to party and drink and tell jokes, and it's often fun to be around them, if you can overcome their distaste for reporters and writers in general, whom they regard as untrustworthy liberals bent on subverting traditional American values. Outside of their tiny area of expertise, they are totally unequipped for life in the modern world. With the possible exception of Wayne Lukas and a relative handful of others, I can't imagine them functioning successfully in any other profession. They are throwbacks to the long-vanished era of the American frontier, where men did what they pleased, the women stayed home and kept their mouths shut in public, and only the strongest flourished.

The Mayberrys had read books. They had even read one or two of mine. I hung around their shedrow at Del Mar that summer and liked everything I found out about them. These were people who cared about their animals, dogs and cats as well as horses, and whose employees looked cheerful and had been with them for a long time. They were generous and had helped some ex-riders and other racetrackers down on their luck to survive. They had two grown daughters, aptly named April and Summer, who had smiles that could light up a tack room and who also loved animals. They had friends at every level of the game, even among their owners.

That last fact impressed me more than any other. The relationship between owners and trainers of racehorses is one of the strangest and most frustrating, to both sides, in all of sports. Owners are generally people, mostly men, who have either been born into big money or made it in a big way. They are landed gentry or tycoons of one sort or another, men who wield power in their circles and who are used to making decisions, giving orders and being obeyed.

In the arcane world of the Thoroughbred, however, they find themselves helpless, almost completely at the mercy of citizens who would not ordinarily be invited to grace their dinner tables. No matter how bright and efficient an owner may be, no matter how much paper expertise he's managed to acquire through study and the same sort of application that has brought him success in his entrepreneurial endeavors, he finds himself in racing entirely dependent on his trainer.

It takes a lifetime of being around horses to be able to succeed at the racetrack. I've stood beside the Mayberrys at the rail in the early morning hours, watching them supervise the workouts and outings of their animals, and they never misidentify one of them. Often, Brian can't remember the name of the horse I ask him about, but he knows which one it is—"the gray one" or "the bay filly" or "that new two-year-old." He knows and I don't, and that's the key to the whole relationship between the two categories of people, trainers and owners, who dominate the sport.

No top trainer will put up with a meddling or dictatorial owner. It doesn't matter in the least to him that it isn't his money that's at risk or his property that he's taking care of. His basic attitude toward the average owner is one of benign contempt, which he will often disguise with good-natured banter; he doesn't want to lose an important client, so a certain amount of *schmoozing* is required of him, including a show at least of allowing the owner to feel that he's being consulted about the management and future of his champion. The reality is, however, that the trainer makes most of the decisions, not only about methods, medication and fitness, but also about where and when to run. "There's nothing more dangerous at a racetrack than an owner with a *Condition Book* in his hand" is another well-known racetrack maxim. It is not at all unusual for even a well-heeled investor to be told to move his horses out of a trainer's shedrow if he becomes too insistent and too bothersome in his demands.

The other side of this coin is the frustration intelligent, knowledgeable owners feel when their trainers ignore their suggestions. Some owners these days know a lot about the game, especially since the introduction of speed figures and a wealth of other information now readily available to the average horseplayer. Trainers know only their own horses. They rarely watch any races other than the ones their animals compete in, and few of them do any serious handicapping. The result is that they often enter their charges in races they can't win. They are also an unimaginative bunch, reluctant to experiment and take chances. Some horses, for instance, will run well in one sort of race and poorly in another. Trainers don't see this as readily as any good handicapper, who spends at least a couple of hours a day poring over past-performance stats, charts, speed figures, and studying videotapes. (I'd back any good handicapper, including myself, against any trainer I know, except possibly Bobby Frankel, in a head-to-head betting contest through a whole race meet.) Locked into their nineteenth-century mentality, and entirely ignorant of the computer age, trainers still regard their owners mostly as wealthy boobs whose ignorance of the sport is total.

The smarter owners, confronted by this Chinese wall of impassivity, do not confront their trainers. After all, they can't make the horse, as the saying goes. They needle, they cajole, they request, they nag a bit, they joke, and eventually, if they're lucky, their hired hand will consent to try something new. If man's earliest civilizations had been populated entirely by horse trainers, the wheel would never have been invented.

In the spring of 1989, I put together a small group of intrepid plungers and asked the Mayberrys to find us a horse. It took them nearly eight months, but eventually they came up with a good-looking yearling filly in Florida with the right connections and at the right price, thirty thousand dollars. Her name was Ultra Sass. She was the Kentucky-bred daughter of an undistinguished but hard-knocking mare named Graceful Retreat, who had won a handful of races, mostly at distances of a mile or more. Her sire was Sassafras, who had once won the Arc de Triomphe, France's most prestigious race, and gone on to become a successful, if not outstanding stallion. So we paid our money and sat back to wait for the spring, when our filly, who would then be two and already in light training, would be shipped west to join the Mayberry string at Santa Anita.

Ultra Sass arrived in mid-April of 1990 and I drove to the track to see her. No sooner had she been led out of her stall, so that I could have a good look at her, than I fell totally and completely in love. She was listed as a dark bay or brown color, but to my layman's eye her coat looked nearly black, gleaming with health and power. She seemed gentle and friendly, with a noble head and a soft eye, but also with just enough of an edge in her temperament to remind us that she was a racehorse. When I first saw her gallop on the track early one morning, she looked like a champion, immensely strong, eager to run, a classic portrait of power and grace. And her fast morning works confirmed this initial impression. She was hard to ride, I was informed by the Mayberrys, because she was so strong and so eager to run that she threatened to pull her rider out of the saddle in her efforts to take off. I could see a rainbow forming in the distance.

She ran her first race for us on July 15 at Hollywood Park and showed absolutely nothing. She broke poorly from the inside post, obviously didn't like the dirt being kicked up into her face, and fell steadily back to finish among the trailers, thirteen and a half lengths behind the winner. One of Mayberry's other owners, who happened to be at the track that day, commiserated with me. "She's a nice-looking filly," he said. "Too bad she can't run worth a shit."

One race doesn't make a career. In her second start, at Del Mar in August, Ultra Sass again broke poorly from the inside, but this time she rushed up along the rail into contention before fading back to third at the finish, beaten by about six lengths. Sassy, as I now called her, had picked up a piece of the purse, about three thousand dollars, and we were in the black for the month. I tried not to worry too much about the fact that the winner of the race, an expensive Kentucky-bred filly named Brazen, had pretty much coasted home, widening her margin of victory by several lengths in the charge down the lane.

Sassy ran again on September 6, against an easier field, and this time the outcome was never in doubt. "Ultra Sass dueled for the early lead," the chartmaker for the *Racing Form* wrote about the race, "drew clear after a half and maintained a clear advantage through the final sixteenth under a brisk hand ride." I could now make out the colors of the rainbow.

Three weeks later, on September 26, we vanned Ultra Sass to the fair meet at Pomona to run in the Black Swan Stakes for a pot of just over forty thousand dollars. She drew a favorable inside post position for the distance, a mile and a sixteenth around the tight turns of the Fairplex bullring, and we hoped for the best. The favorite in the race was Brazen, the filly that had beaten us so convincingly six weeks earlier.

Sassy broke alertly out of the gate and, to our surprise, made the lead around the first of the three turns. Her rider, Julio Garcia, nursed her along in front, letting her run just fast enough to withstand a couple of minor challenges. The real test would come, I knew, when Brazen made her move.

As the field started around the final turn for home, Brazen swept up alongside and the two fillies moved together as one. Halfway around the curve, however, I knew it was all over. Brazen was in an all-out drive, with her rider pumping and whipping, whereas Garcia was sitting chilly, asking Sassy for more but not demanding her full effort.

Suddenly, Brazen was done and began to drop back. Sassy turned into the stretch a length in front, and now Garcia asked for whatever she had left, as a late-running longshot named Nat's Lea took after her. Nat's Lea ranged up alongside, about a neck back, with less than a sixteenth to go, but there she stayed. Ultra Sass dug in and held her off, winning by a neck and paying $9.40 for every two-dollar ticket.

I can remember only a few other times in my life when I have been as excited and happy. I have a picture showing twenty-three of us, not including horse and rider, in the winner's circle that afternoon, all looking as if we've just done something really important, like being awarded a Nobel Prize or being acclaimed for having put an end to poverty. I don't know where such euphoria comes from; I only know the feeling was genuine, an incredible rush of glory to the head.

There aren't many such moments, in racing or in life. We had no way of knowing it at the time, but Ultra Sass was never again to achieve as much. The usual minor setbacks that overtake most racehorses now began to afflict her, mainly in the form of a painful mouth. It turned out that she had a wolf tooth, a vestigial cuspid from some prehistoric stage of evolution, pressing at the point where the bit sat. It had to be pulled, but there were also other problems calling for additional expensive dentistry, and it was nearly seven weeks before she ran again, finishing a badly beaten tenth in a sprint at Hollywood Park. Needless to say, I had never before heard a word about wolf teeth. One of the constants of racing is that horses will always find some new way to injure themselves and to lose.

Perhaps Sassy's speed and strength were drained out of her by this wolf tooth in much the same way that Samson's prowess wilted with the loss of his long locks. I know this can't be so, but how else to account for it? She has run fifteen times since then and has never approximated her old form. She hasn't exactly let us down, because she has won twice more since then and picked up pieces of other purses here and there, but she has evolved now into what most racehorses become, a mediocre competitor in the low claiming ranks. She has more than paid her way, however, having earned about eighty thousand dollars, so I have no right to complain. If not Paris, I'll always have Pomona.

As I sit here, writing these words, Ultra Sass will be running again in a few days, this time at Santa Anita against horses she'd have horrified a year ago. Every morning she comes out on the track, either to work or to gallop, looking every bit as awesome and powerful as when I first saw her. She still looks to me like one of heaven's small miracles, and there is no reason to stop caring for her.

Soon now we will lose her. Some other owner, some other trainer will take her from us. My wife and I don't talk about it. All we can hope for is that she will go to people who will treat her kindly, with the minimum of reverence her grace and beauty should require of us. Nobody ever said this was an easy game or promised any of us a happy ending. The rainbow remains out of reach, temporarily invisible.

There are days when I think every horse is the wrong horse.